American Politics and the Constitution

American Politics and the Constitution

Thomas G. Walker
Emory University

Duxbury Press
North Scituate, Massachusetts

Library of Congress Cataloging in Publication Data

Walker, Thomas G
    American politics and the Constitution.

    Includes index.
      1. United States—Constitutional law. I. Title.
KF4550.W34   320.9'73   77–16337
ISBN 0–87872–161–4

Duxbury Press
A Division of Wadsworth Publishing Company, Inc.

American Politics and the Constitution was edited and prepared for composition by Bowden Anderson. Interior design was provided by Richard Spencer and the cover was designed by Nancy Gardner.

L.C. Cat. Card No.: 77–16337
ISBN 0–87872–161–4

Printed in the United States of America
1 2 3 4 5 6 7 8 9 – 82 81 80 79 78

Contents

Part Two The Constitution and Political Participation   72

Chapter Four Public Opinion and the Expression of Political Views   74

Chapter Five Elections and Voting Rights   92

Chapter Six Political Parties and Interest Groups   110

Preface

Commenting in 1848 on American political life, Alexis de Tocqueville noted: "There is hardly a political question in the United States which does not sooner or later turn into a judicial one." Tocqueville's assessment is perhaps even more valid today than when he was writing more than a century ago. The judiciary has always been important in American politics, largely because it has been entrusted with the responsibility of interpreting the nation's fundamental law, the United States Constitution. In recent decades the importance of the Constitution and the judiciary's articulation of its principles have become more pronounced than ever. Today court rulings and constitutional interpretations affect every governmental function and a wide variety of private activities. In order to understand contemporary American politics, it is necessary to understand the American Constitution; and to understand the Constitution it is necessary to understand the American political process. The two cannot be separated.

The purpose of this short volume is to illuminate the interaction between American politics and the Constitution. It is specifically designed for those interested in a better understanding of the American governmental system. For this reason the book is organized not according to traditional legal topics and concerns, but according to the way in which the governmental system functions. Issues of particular interest to the constitutional lawyer have been given secondary treatment to those constitutional questions that have special relevance to the political process. Wherever possible, technical legal language has been avoided in favor of a vocabulary more familiar to a student of the social sciences. Each chapter begins with a short case study intended to introduce the subject of the chapter as well as to demonstrate that court decisions often involve interesting human conflicts with political ramifications.

The book is divided into three parts. It is organized according to the flow of the typical introductory course in American politics so that it may be used in conjunction with standard American government texts. Part one deals with the basic political environment and culture of the United States. It is written to help the student understand the relevance of the Constitution to the way in which the political system is structured and operates. Part two concentrates on political participation in the United States. Chapters are included on such topics as public opinion, voting, elections, political parties, and interest groups. For each of these subjects the focus is on how the Constitution affects the rights of American citizens participating in the democratic process. Part three discusses the governmental institutions of the United States. Emphasis is placed on the powers and limitations of the legislative, executive, and judicial branches. Each stage of the governmental process is discussed with the purpose of showing how the Constitution affects American politics and how, in turn, politics influences the Constitution.

The Constitutional Convention that met in Philadelphia in 1787 drafted the document that forms the legal base for the nation's guiding governmental principles, the structure of its political institutions, the basic rights of its citizens, and the powers of the nation's governmental agencies. It has been left to the nation's courts, and particularly the Supreme Court, to interpret the meaning of the Constitution and to apply it in conflicts over the legitimacy of governmental actions. The rulings of the Supreme Court have given meaning and vitality to the Constitution and have shaped the contours of our democratic institutions and processes. Individuals interested in grasping a more thorough understanding of American government must comprehend the interaction between law and politics. The following pages view the Constitution as both a legal and a political document. By examining the Constitution's relevance to the various stages of the political process, this book attempts to provide a means of better understanding how Americans govern themselves.

Thomas G. Walker

Part 1

The Constitution and Politics

The Constitutional Foundation of
American Politics

Principles of American Government

The Rights of Americans

The Constitutional Foundation of
American Politics

Chapter one

The Constitution, Courts, and Politics:
Marbury v. *Madison*

On February 24, 1803, Chief Justice John Marshall, flanked by Justices
Bushrod Washington and Samuel Chase, delivered the United States Supreme Court's decision in the case of *Marbury* v. *Madison*.[1] Outwardly, the
case appeared insignificant. The legal issue was whether William Marbury, a
disappointed aspirant for a position as justice of the peace in the District of
Columbia, could properly bring an action for a writ of mandamus on original
jurisdiction to the Supreme Court as stipulated in section 13 of the Judiciary
Act of 1789. The procedural technicalities, however, could not hide the real
significance of the litigation. Not only did this dispute constitute a fierce
battle between the dominant political forces of that time, but future generations have rated Chief Justice Marshall's opinion in this case the most significant decision ever rendered by the American judiciary.

The roots of this legal dispute dated back to the November elections of
1800. In that year Thomas Jefferson's Democratic-Republican party had
scored an overwhelming victory. Not only had Jefferson ousted the incumbent Federalist, John Adams, but the Jeffersonians also had gained control
of Congress. The Federalists, and particularly their leader, President Adams,
were embittered over the election defeat not only for personal reasons, but
also because they feared that the nation could not survive the "radical"
Jefferson.

The Federalists were not quite ready to leave office by graciously handing over the reins of power to Jefferson. Between the November 1800 elections

4

and the official transfer of power scheduled for March 1801, the Federalists quickly moved to dilute the impact of Jefferson's victory. While the presidency and Congress were lost, the Federalists moved to take firm control of the government's third branch, the judiciary. Adams and the Federalist Congress made three bold moves. First, a statute was passed reducing the number of seats on the Supreme Court from six to five, effective upon the next resignation from the Court. The effect of this law was to deprive President-Elect Jefferson of his first Supreme Court appointment. Second, Congress created sixteen new circuit court judgeships, to which Adams would nominate judges before he left office. And third, Congress enacted legislation allowing Adams to create and fill as many District of Columbia justice of the peace positions as he saw fit. Predictably, President Adams nominated Federalists to fill each of the new circuit judgeships and created forty-two justice of the peace positions which were to be occupied by members of his Federalist party. In addition, Adams had the good fortune of being able to receive the resignation of an ill Chief Justice Oliver Ellsworth and to replace him with his trusted secretary of state, John Marshall.

To fill judicial vacancies, three official actions were necessary. First, the president had to nominate individuals for each position. Second, the Senate was required to confirm each nomination. And third, official commissions signed by the president and affixed with the Great Seal of the United States had to be delivered to the nominee by the secretary of state. The first two requirements were easily met by the outgoing Federalists, but the paperwork required by the third step proved bothersome. Adams spent his last day in office, March 3, 1801, completing the commissions. He then sent the commissions to Secretary of State John Marshall (who doubled for a time as both secretary of state and chief justice) for delivery. While it is not clear what happened to each of the commissions, it is certain that Marshall, never a zealous administrator, failed to complete all of the deliveries before Jefferson's inauguration the next morning.

Once in office, the Jeffersonians were enraged to find the extent to which the Federalists had "packed" the courts. Two retaliatory actions were taken. First, Jefferson ordered his acting secretary of state, Levi Lincoln, and later his permanent secretary, James Madison, not to execute the undelivered commissions. Second, the Jeffersonians in Congress repealed the act that had created the sixteen new circuit judgeships.

At this point William Marbury and three others, who had received nominations as justices of the peace but to whom the required commissions had not been delivered, took legal action. They felt that they were entitled to the judicial positions in spite of the fact that the official procedures had not been completed. They elected to ask the judiciary for a writ of mandamus (a court order compelling a public official to carry out his assigned responsibilities) commanding Secretary of State Madison to deliver the commissions. According to the provisions of section 13 of the Judiciary Act of 1789, Marbury and the others could file their suit with the Supreme Court on original jurisdiction (that is, bypassing the lower courts and progressing immediately and directly to the Supreme Court for a hearing).

Marbury's suit against Secretary of State Madison became the focal point of the political clash between the newly empowered Jeffersonians and the old guard Federalists. The two central figures in the contest were Thomas Jefferson himself and the then highest-ranking Federalist officeholder, John Marshall. The two were not strangers. Both came from the state of Virginia and were, in fact, distant cousins. Yet their political hostility was acute, and the battle over Marbury's legal action was but a single round in their long-running battle.

The Jeffersonians saw the suit as a power struggle between the Federalist judiciary and the Democratic-Republican legislature and executive. A decision in favor of Marbury would, they felt, establish a precedent allowing the judiciary to meddle in executive affairs and would legitimize the distasteful Federalist "court-packing" strategy. Marshall was motivated not only by his distrust of Jefferson and loyalty to the Federalist cause, but also by his determination to assert the independence of the judiciary. To allow the Jeffersonians to prevail in this instance would establish the principle that the judiciary was weak and ineffectual relative to Congress and the president.

Marshall, however, was in a weak position. The Supreme Court had little prestige. Although the institution was slightly more than a decade old, Marshall was already the fourth person to serve as chief justice. A seat on the Court had little prestige, and it was not uncommon for the justices to leave the Court for state political office or for diplomatic assignments. During some years the Court did not sit at all, and the attendance of the justices was minimal. Even in the important *Marbury* case only three of the justices cared to participate. Furthermore, public opinion was decidedly against the Court. The Jeffersonians had been swept into office by large electoral margins, and the Court represented the last vestige of the rejected Federalist cause. Marshall, therefore, was without institutional power or public support. Moreover, he feared for his own position. Congress had made it quite clear that if Marshall ruled in favor of Marbury he could expect immediate impeachment.

Marshall, with his keen sense of politics, found the perfect solution to his dilemma. His February 24, 1803 decision in the case of *Marbury* v. *Madison* satisfied his own sense of justice, allowed him to remain true to his partisan loyalties, permitted the Jeffersonians to claim a partial victory, and yet established the independent power of the judiciary. Marshall accomplished this by ruling that Marbury and his fellow litigants were entitled to their commissions, but that the Supreme Court was powerless to order delivery of the commissions. The second portion of the decision is the more significant and deserves special attention.

Marshall, supported by his fellow justices, concluded that the Supreme Court was powerless to issue the requested writ of mandamus because the suit itself was improperly filed. Section 13 of the Judiciary Act of 1789 gave the Court the power to hear cases involving petitions for a writ of mandamus on original jurisdiction. However, article III of the U.S. Constitution stipulated that the Supreme Court was to hear only cases appealed from the lower courts, except when a suit involved foreign ambassadors or when a state was party to legal action. Since Marbury's suit did not come to the Court on appeal and did not involve an ambassador or a state as litigants, the Supreme Court, according to article III of the Constitution, had no jurisdiction over it. Obviously, a basic conflict existed. An act of Congress stated that the Supreme Court possessed jurisdiction over such mandamus cases, but the Constitution denied the Court such jurisdiction. Marshall resolved this conflict by concluding that as the Constitution is the "supreme law of the land"[2] and that federal judges swear to uphold the Constitution,[3] the Court is obliged to follow the Constitution and not the congressional statute. By so ruling, the Court struck down section 13 of the 1789 Judiciary Act on the grounds that it violated the Constitution.

In effect, Marshall told Marbury that his point was well taken but that the Court had no jurisdiction to hear the issue. Marshall was instructing Marbury to take his suit to the lower federal courts and then later to appeal it to the Supreme Court if necessary. Marshall, of course, knew full well that the term of office for Marbury's prized position as justice of the peace would expire before the suit ever returned to the Court on appeal.

Marshall's ruling accomplished several important objectives. First, it essentially held that Marbury was unjustly deprived of his judgeship, even though the Court did not order Madison to deliver the commissions. Second, by indicating that Marbury's legal action had merit, Marshall refused to capitulate to Jeffersonian pressure, thus asserting the independence of the judiciary. Third, by not compelling Madison to deliver the commission, Marshall permitted the Jeffersonians to claim a partial victory and, therefore, drop any plans to impeach Marshall or to take severe actions against the Court. Fourth, and most important, the decision established the power of judicial review—that is, the authority of the courts to examine actions of the other branches of government and to declare null and void those actions that violate the Constitution. While the Court was not to strike down another piece of congressional legislation until the passage of some fifty years, the mere establishment of that authority placed the judiciary on an equal basis with the other two branches of government and set the American court system apart from those of other nations.

Following the Court's ruling in this case, Marshall continued as chief justice for more than thirty years, establishing a record of unsurpassed judicial excellence. Jefferson, of course, was reelected in 1804 and became one of our most respected presidents. James Madison later followed Jefferson in the White House. And William Marbury became a bank president and died in 1835, the same year the nation lost the services of John Marshall.

Constitutional Government and the United States

Marbury v. *Madison* illustrates the fact that the United States is a "constitutional government." By this term we mean that the basic governmental structure, the powers of government, and the limitations on governmental authority are stipulated in the nation's fundamental law. In America, that fundamental law is the United States Constitution, a written document ratified in 1788. It is that document that serves as the final authority with respect to legitimate governmental actions. The Constitution is the supreme law of the land and takes precedence over all other state or federal laws and governmental policies. Any governmental actions contrary to this basic law, as the Marshall Court found section 13 of the Judiciary Act of 1789 to be, must give way to the dominance of the Constitution itself.

That our Constitution is the ultimate source of legal authority has been accepted almost without exception throughout the nation's history. Even when Marshall declared the 1789 act null and void there was no significant adverse public reaction. The logic that mere statutes must give way to constitutional provisions met general approval in spite of the fact that the power of judicial review was never formally granted to the judiciary. In America, therefore, politics and government are inextricably tied to the Constitution. Any governmental law, policy, regulation, or program must be capable of meeting the test of constitutionality if challenged in court. The American citizenry generally places great stock in our constitutional system and expects public officials to act within the bounds set by that Constitution.

Marbury's suit before the Supreme Court also highlights the importance of the judiciary to our constitutional scheme of government. While the primary function of the courts is to decide legal cases and controversies, including such matters as the disposition of criminal charges, negligence actions, contract violations, and divorce suits, the judiciary has special significance owing to its position as the final arbiter of the law. Even though the United States Constitution is a relatively specific and clearly drawn document, it is silent on many matters and ambiguous on others. Furthermore, it is an eighteenth-century body of law employed to govern a twentieth-century political machinery. The meaning of the Constitution and how it is to be applied to the unanticipated conditions of twentieth-century American society are primarily matters for the judiciary to decide. What the Constitution means is largely what the courts interpret it to mean. This is as true today as it was when the Marshall-dominated Supreme Court first exercised the power of judicial review.

Politics and the Constitution

A final lesson of *Marbury* v. *Madison* is the interaction between politics and the Constitution. Indeed, the entire litigation was clearly more political than legal. Marshall's exercise of judicial review was dictated much more by the political dilemma in which he found himself than by any application of clearly reasoned legal philosophy. Jefferson and Marshall were political foes who dominated the proceedings. The litigants, William Marbury and James Madison, were but pawns in the larger political struggle. Chief Justice Marshall was forced into the situation by his own administrative failures as secretary of state. His fellow justices were blatant Federalist partisans. Marbury's attorney, Charles Lee, was a former Federalist attorney general and had a political score of his own to settle because the Jeffersonians in Congress had abolished the circuit court judgeship for which he had been nominated. Congress attempted to bully the Court by using impeachment threats. All of these political maneuverings were over a relatively insignificant justice of the peace nominee. But the incident represented a battle over political control of the courts. Politics affected how the Court interpreted the Constitution, and that interpretation affected future politics.

In order to understand American politics, it is necessary to understand the American Constitution; and to understand the Constitution it is necessary to understand politics. The two cannot be separated. The basic purpose of this volume is to illuminate the interaction between American politics and the Constitution. To do so, we will examine each of the basic stages of the American political process and explore the influences of the Constitution in shaping the way in which Americans conduct their political affairs.

The Nation's First Constitution:
The Articles of Confederation

The Constitution that was the subject of Marshall's interpretation in the *Marbury* case was actually the nation's second attempt to develop a fundamental document to structure the powers and authority of government. The first constitution of the United States, known as the Articles of Confederation, was a complete failure; and yet it was an important failure, because it taught the new nation many lessons that were incorporated into our present Constitution.

In June of 1776, the Continental Congress of the United States took two important actions. First, it appointed a committee to draft what became the Declaration of Independence. Second, it designated a group of delegates to make recommendations for the formation of a national government to rule after independence was achieved. This second committee, under the direction of John Dickinson, included representatives from each of the thirteen colonies. It labored for several months before it finally reported its recommendations to the Congress.

The committee's task was not an easy one. The thirteen colonies had been acting as independent states. While they shared a common heritage and certainly a common desire to be free of English rule, there was no tradition of unity among the colonies. In addition, three basic conflicts plagued the committee's deliberations. First, the large states and the small states were divided on several issues, the most important being the apportionment of representation in the national legislature. Second, proponents of a strong national government opposed those who advocated states' rights, particularly on questions involving powers of taxation and economic regulation. And third, there was conflict over what to do about the western territories.

After seventeen months of committee action and congressional deliberations, the Articles of Confederation were adopted by the Continental Congress in November of 1777. However, the new national government did not immediately take effect. Under provisions adopted by the Congress, the ratification of all thirteen states was necessary. Opposition to the document centered among the smaller states, particularly Maryland, New Jersey, and Delaware. These states were not satisfied with the resolution of the western lands question. By 1779, twelve states had agreed to the Articles, with only Maryland continuing its opposition. Finally, in 1781, after winning certain concessions from her sister states, Maryland completed the ratification process. It had been five years from independence to the creation of the nation's first constitution and formal national government. During that period the Second Continental Congress acted as an ad hoc governing body, but with ratification Congress disbanded and the new government began operation.

Government under the Articles was predicated on the principle of state supremacy. The national government was quite weak. Each state retained basic governing powers and joined the national government only in loose federation. The central government resembled a league of states much more than it did a well-integrated governmental system. All of the important powers of government remained with the separate states.

The structure of the government under the Articles was relatively simple. The only agency of consequence was the legislature, known as the Congress. Congress was a unicameral body, having only a single house. Each state was entitled to be represented by a delegation varying in size from two to seven representatives, depending on the state's population. However, each state had only one vote. Therefore, each delegation would have to decide among its own members how the state's vote was to be cast. This rather strange representational system was the result of a compromise between the large and small states. To insure against excessive power gravitating into the hands of specific individuals, the Articles provided that no representative could serve more than three consecutive years. This was never to become a major problem, however, because congressional service was not regarded as a prestigious activity, and usually fewer than a third of the delegates were present for congressional business. Congress was empowered to appoint ministers to carry out what few administrative duties were necessary, but there was no executive branch of any substance whatever. Nor was there any developed system of national courts. What little power was given to the national government was exercised by Congress alone.

The powers granted to Congress under the Articles included only those over which the individual states were thought to be incompetent. For example, Congress was empowered to conduct war, administer the nation's foreign policy, fix the size of the military, coin and borrow money, enter into treaties, regulate Indian affairs, and maintain a postal service. These areas of governance were considered national in scope, and consequently a single national policy was thought preferable to thirteen independent policies. However, Congress was even hindered in exercising these few powers because the consent of nine states was required before Congress could take action, and all thirteen states had to approve any modifications in the Articles. Given the divisions among the states at that time, the approval of nine states for any action of substance was rare, and the required unanimity for amendment was never obtained.

Failures of the Articles: Taxation and Regulation of Commerce

The most important factor in the failure of the Articles government was that it lacked two essential governmental powers. First, Congress could not tax. It could request funds from the states, but was not empowered to collect or enforce such assessments. Second, Congress was not granted the authority to regulate commerce. Without these two essential powers, Congress was unable to cope with the nation's two most pressing problems: the national debt and a lagging economy.

Following the Revolution, the United States was some 40 million dollars in debt. Congress passed revenue quotas for the various states to contribute to the reduction of indebtedness, but the response was minimal. In all, Congress attempted to raise 15.5 million dollars, but succeeded in gathering only about 2.5 million dollars from the states.

Congress's inability to regulate interstate commerce meant that there was no central authority to guide the nation's economic growth. The economy following the war was in an unsettled condition, aggravated by a European economic boycott that England had instigated against the new nation. Since the states could not look to Congress for economic leadership, many took it upon themselves to take action, totally disregarding the central government. States began coining their own money, raising state military forces, regulating Indian affairs, and erecting state trade barriers. Congress was powerless, and any attempt to give the national government increased authority failed to attract support from the required number of states.

The end result of the indebtedness and commerce problems was an economic depression. The states were in economic situations similar to that of the national government. They too were heavily in debt, and attempts to raise revenue through increased property taxes and tariffs aggravated the problems facing the country by further burdening the commercial process. Most severely affected were the small farmers, who were having difficulty trading their products and who were increasingly unable to keep pace with the growing property tax burdens placed on them by the various states. Joining the farmers were groups of Revolutionary War soldiers who had never been fully paid for their services. It was political opposition from the small farmers and the disgruntled veterans which provided the final blow to the Articles government.

The most radical discontent was found in the New England region, where organized groups began demanding relief from the state legislatures. The most significant action took place in Massachusetts in 1786 when Daniel Shays, a Revolutionary War captain, organized a group of dissatisfied farmers and war veterans into a military force. When their demands for reforms in the areas of taxation, mortgages, and commerce were not met, Shays and his men organized for a march on the Massachusetts state capitol. Although the state militia was sufficiently strong to quash the revolt, Shays' Rebellion was to have great historical impact. The rebellion itself served as the psychological turning point. It became obvious to the political and economic elite that government under the Articles of Confederation was not working successfully. The open rebellion in Massachusetts was evidence that a stronger, more effective government was necessary to deal with the conditions of the times. Particularly fearful were the large property owners, who were disturbed by the prospects of the lower economic orders rising up and perhaps violently upsetting the nation's economic and social hierarchy.

Finally, in February of 1787, the Congress passed a resolution calling for a convention to reevaluate the state of the national government and to recommend modifications in the Articles to make it a more effective governing force. The intent of the resolution was only to promote suggestions for revising the Articles, not to discard the document altogether. The call for a new convention received the general approval of the states. The legislatures of twelve states quickly authorized delegations to attend the convention. Only Rhode Island, the new nation's smallest state, refused to attend, fearing that any moves toward a stronger central government would be at the expense of the interests of the smaller states.

The Lessons of the Articles

The new convention, which was to draft the constitution under which the United States is now governed, signaled the end of government under the Articles. Although the old government remained officially in power until the new Constitution was ratified in 1788, it further decreased its viability and effectiveness during its final months of life. However, the Articles of Confederation provided an extremely significant experience for the United States. While the nation's first Constitution in the final analysis was a failure, experiences under it offered an important set of lessons to the country's leaders. The present Constitution was written in large part as a direct reaction to the weaknesses found under the Articles. If nothing else, the Articles of Confederation teach that if government is to be successful, it must be capable of responding to the needs of the times. The Articles fell largely because of lack of power to cope with the new country's two most pressing problems: a heavy indebtedness and a poor economy. Unable to handle these major problems, it is not surprising that the states turned away from the central government even in areas of less significance. Lacking authority to manage under the conditions of the 1780s, it is certain that a government structured under the Articles of Confederation would be hopelessly unable to cope with conditions facing contemporary America.

Drafting the United States Constitution

Fifty-five delegates representing twelve states convened in Philadelphia's State House in May of 1787. During the next four months they deliberated and finally agreed upon a document that was to become the United States Constitution. The assembled group tended to represent the propertied and professional classes, who were particularly concerned with the ramifications of incidents such as Shays' Rebellion. While Revolutionary leaders such as Jefferson, Paine, and Henry were not present, the wartime generation was ably represented by the likes of Washington and Franklin. Others, such as Madison and Hamilton, were members of an American political generation whose leadership years were still ahead of them. The delegates were a well-educated group with considerable experience in commerce and public affairs.

From the very outset it was apparent that the convention was going to exceed the instructions of Congress and propose more than a mere revision of the Articles. To most the existing government seemed beyond repair. The majority of the delegates concluded that the national government was to be given new powers, but there was substantial disagreement as to how much new authority to grant to the central government and what kinds of limitations to place on the exercise of that power.

The delegates divided along several dimensions, but two were especially significant. First was the long-standing division between the small states and the large states. The smaller states were particularly concerned that a new central government would be dominated by the larger states, who would manipulate the central government against their best interests. Hence, the smaller states were intensely interested in the question of representation and in preserving the concept of state supremacy. The larger states, of course, preferred to develop a national government in which their large populations would transfer into substantial control over governmental policy making. The second major division was more philosophical, focusing on the question of democracy. A wide variety of opinion was represented on this issue, ranging from sympathies for an elitist government to advocacy of relatively widespread participation by the people. In its final form the document drafted by the Convention was the result of numerous compromises. The adopted version was not pronounced perfect by any of the delegates. Each, if so able, would have made changes of varying degree. But to a large majority the Constitution was a document that could be accepted. It was the product of delicate political balancing which in many ways permitted each of the diverse factions to claim a victory.

The Structure of the National Government

The greatest evidence of the compromise nature of the Constitution can be seen in the structure of the national legislature. There was no serious disagreement over the need for an effective legislative branch, but there was widespread distrust of executive power because of the excesses suffered under the English crown. A strong legislature was thought necessary as a check against the growth of executive dominance. There was a good deal of disagreement, however, over the structure of the new Congress. First, the delegates divided over whether the new Congress should be unicameral, as was the Articles legislature, or bicameral. Ultimately the bicameral proponents were successful, not so much by the merits of their case, but because bicameralism facilitated reaching a compromise on the second major controversy facing the Convention, the problem of representation. The large states, of course, wanted representation in Congress to be based on population. The smaller states desired to have each of the former colonies represented equally in the new legislature. The bicameral nature of the Congress allowed for effective compromise by permitting the upper house, the Senate, to have representation based on statehood, with each state having two senators, and the lower chamber, the House of Representatives, to have representation apportioned among the states on the basis of population.

A third legislative compromise occurred over slavery. The southern states argued that slaves should be counted as people for purposes of calculating the number of representatives a state would be granted in the House. The northern states rejected this notion. Finally, the Convention delegates compromised by agreeing that slaves should be counted as three-fifths persons for representation and taxation purposes.

A fourth clash over the legislature concerned the issue of selection. Proponents of democracy argued that members of Congress should be directly elected by the people, whereas those fearful of democracy thought selection by an elite group would produce superior results. Once again the bicameral nature of Congress facilitated compromise. Members of the House of Representatives were to be elected by the people directly. The authority for the selection of senators, however, was given to the state legislatures.[4]

Finally, there was disagreement over the length of the term of office for members of the new legislature. Some delegates preferred very short terms, fearing that longevity in office would encourage excessive power and corruption; others preferred long terms of office; Hamilton even argued for life tenure for the upper house. The compromise process again dominated; the Convention settled for two-year terms for members of the House and six-year terms for senators. No restrictions were placed on the number of terms that could be served. Deliberations over the proposed national legislature, then, were dominated by practical compromise solutions to the political problems facing the Convention.

Article I of the drafted Constitution contained a fairly detailed description of the powers of Congress. Foremost among these powers were the authority to levy taxes and the power to regulate interstate commerce. The delegates had learned their lesson well from their experiences under the Articles of Confederation and moved swiftly to grant the central government the two major powers it desperately needed to be effective. In addition to these revenue and economic powers, Congress was given authority over some of the government's most significant activities: the power to declare war, to appropriate funds, to impeach federal officials, to regulate the monetary system, to manage a postal system, and to regulate the military. The Senate was granted power to approve major executive appointments and to ratify treaties.

Many of the issues confronting the discussions over the structure of the legislature reoccurred in deliberations over the executive branch. There was relatively quick agreement over the creation of a single president, although there was some sentiment for developing a plural executive. However, the delegates were seriously divided over the selection and tenure questions. Once again proponents of democracy preferred to have popular selection of the president, whereas those reluctant to support mass participation favored an elite group making the selection. The final compromise called for a two-step process whereby the people would elect officials (called electors) who would in turn select the president. Hence, the Convention combined both democracy and elite selection systems. On the issue of tenure of office, those fearful of executive power abuses supported very short terms for president, while others leaned toward life tenure. At the conclusion of the deliberations on this question, the drafted Constitution allowed for four-year terms for the chief executive with no limitation on the number of terms an individual could serve in that post.[5]

The presidency was given limited powers by the framers. The most significant among these were the powers of the president as commander in chief of the military forces, the veto power, the power to nominate judicial and administrative personnel, and the authority to execute the laws. Yet each of these powers was offset by a specific congressional power designed to keep the executive in check. For example, the commander in chief power was muted by the congressional war power and military regulation authority; the veto power, by the legislative power to override vetos; the nomination power, by the Senate's authority to reject appointments; and the administrative power, by the congressional power to legislate. Nonetheless, the creation of a national executive was a substantial improvement over the Articles government, which lacked any form of independent executive authority.

The new Constitution stipulated the creation of a national judiciary. This, too, was an action directly related to the weaknesses of the Confederation period. Under the Articles there was no national court system. The judicial power was left to the courts of the various states. However, even the establishment of the federal judiciary was the result of compromise. The Convention could have allowed the state courts to continue their exclusive exercise of judicial functions; or, at the other extreme, it could have recommended a national judiciary that would supersede the court systems of the various states. Instead, the Convention took the middle course, establishing a federal judiciary to handle matters of federal law and allowing the state courts to remain and exercise jurisdiction over matters of state concern.

The States and the National Government

Of particular significance at the Constitutional Convention was the issue of the relationship between the national government and the various states. Under the Articles the relationship was clear: the national government was dependent upon the states, which remained sovereign. The smaller states preferred this relationship and submitted proposals that would have allowed the nation's chief executive to be removed by majority vote of the various state governors. Proposals of this variety failed to attract sufficient support for adoption. At the other extreme were delegates such as Hamilton, who proposed that the states be reduced to mere administrative units of the national government. The Convention adhered to its course of moderation. The final document spells out a federal system. The union of the states was much stronger than under the Articles, and yet the states retained many of the powers they had historically exercised. The Constitution stipulates grants of authority to the national government and directs that the remaining powers of government are to be held by the states. While the dividing line between state and federal spheres of authority is often cloudy, the Constitution establishes a meaningful role for the federal government without seriously jeopardizing the viability of the states.

The Convention concluded its business on September 17, 1787, after four months of deliberations. The drafting of the final document incorporating all of the various decisions and compromises was largely the work of Gouverneur Morris of Pennsylvania. The final draft received the signatures of thirty-nine of the delegates present at the final session. However, the new government was not to take effect immediately. The important stage of ratification by the states remained as the final obstacle to the implementation of the nation's new Constitution.

Ratification and the Federalist Papers

Even the ratification process bore the mark of the Articles of Confederation period. The unanimity requirement for ratification had blocked the inception of the Articles government for four years because of Maryland's refusal to approve the document. The delegates to the Constitutional Convention did not wish to repeat this mistake. After all, unanimity was out of the question owing to Rhode Island's stubborn refusal even to participate in the Convention. And substantial opposition to the new government appeared likely in New York and North Carolina. Therefore, the Convention stipulated that the new government would go into effect upon ratification by nine states.

The battle over ratification provided the nation with a rich debate over the nature of government and the meaning of the Constitution. The supporters of the proposed Constitution, known as the Federalists, stressed the need for a stronger national government than existed under the Articles. The confederation form of government was simply too weak and ineffective to secure and protect the rights of the citizenry. The proposed document, they argued, would be a sound and successful alternative. The Federalist Papers, written by Hamilton, Madison, and John Jay in support of the Constitution during the New York ratification struggle, remains the best record of the intentions of those who drafted the Constitution. The opposing position was articulated by a group referred to as the Anti-Federalists, who were led by men such as Patrick Henry and Richard Henry Lee. The opponents of ratification appealed to the lower economic classes, for the new document was perceived by many as the creation of the nation's economic elite. The Anti-Federalists stressed the lack of a Bill of Rights and their fear that the central government would become excessively powerful to the detriment of the best interests of the people and their state governments.

Within one year of the conclusion of the Constitutional Convention eleven states had ratified the document. In several states the Constitution had overwhelming support. But in the crucial states of Massachusetts, Virginia, and New York the votes in the state ratification conventions were extremely close. It is likely that the pledge of the Federalists to adopt a Bill of Rights in return for approval of the document was the key to gathering sufficient ratification votes in several states. Only North Carolina and Rhode Island failed to accept the Constitution during that first year, with ratification finally occurring in these states in November 1789 and May 1790, respectively.

Upon the required ratification by nine states the United States Constitution became the nation's fundamental law. The first elections were scheduled for January of 1789. Washington was selected by the presidential electors as the first chief executive and was inaugurated in April 1789. Congressional elections took place, and the first legislature, dominated by the Federalists, began taking those actions necessary for the full implementation of the new Constitution. It had been thirteen years since the nation had declared its independence from England, but after a shaky beginning, what was to become one of history's most stable republics was finally underway. Almost two hundred years later the document drafted by the Philadelphia Convention continues to be the fundamental law of the United States and the world's oldest written constitution.

The Supreme Court and the Constitution

Perhaps the most interesting inconsistency in the American political system lies in the fact that we grant the power to interpret the Constitution to our least democratic branch of government. It is to the judges that we entrust the responsibility of settling conflicts and disputes over the meaning of our fundamental law. Because of its position at the pinnacle of the judicial hierarchy, the Supreme Court becomes the final arbiter in questions of constitutional law. Given the power of judicial review, the Supreme Court is in a unique position to determine the meaning of the Constitution and to strike down governmental actions it decides are inconsistent with the document. The role of the Supreme Court in American society is quite different from the position of the judiciary in most nations. The Court becomes not only a legal tribunal committed to resolving traditional legal questions; it also becomes a political tribunal because of its obligation to hear fundamental issues of political power and authority. The lower federal courts share in this responsibility, but it is left to the Supreme Court to be the final voice in such matters. Because of the essential part played by the Supreme Court in the interpretation and application of the Constitution, the focus of this volume will be on the ways in which the Constitution has been given force and substance through the decisions of the nation's highest tribunal. This, of course, is not to say that the Court has always performed in an active and prudent fashion. To the contrary, certain periods of judicial history have been marked by the general abdication of the Court from its fundamental responsibilities. However, the Supreme Court has had a demonstrable impact on the American Constitution by its failures to act as well as when it has responded in an active and positive manner.

While the role of the Court as a major participant in the constitutional process is often traced back to the *Marbury* v. *Madison* decision, there is clear evidence that several of the Constitution's Framers intended such a place for the judiciary. Although the records of the Convention debates do not reveal widespread support for an exceptionally active and powerful judiciary, the Federalist Papers indicates that the proposed Constitution's supporters put great stock in a strong and independent judicial system. This attitude is cogently presented in Federalist Paper number 78, written by Alexander Hamilton. Hamilton explains that the judiciary is inherently the weakest of the three branches of government, but that the Constitution's commitment to an independent court system gives the judiciary a prominent role in the separation of powers scheme of government. He argues that occupants of the federal bench, serving for terms of good behavior, provide an excellent barrier to the possible encroachments and oppressions of the representative branches of government. To the writers of the Federalist Papers, a strong and independent judiciary was the surest way to guarantee steady, upright, and impartial administration of the laws. What is also important about Hamilton's essay on the proposed Constitution is his argument that the judiciary retains the power to strike down governmental actions found to be contrary to the Constitution. The logic employed by Hamilton to conclude that the Constitution must be supreme over other governmental actions and that the judiciary is the appropriate body to exercise the review power is remarkably similar to Chief Justice Marshall's opinion in *Marbury* v. *Madison*, drafted fifteen years later.

The Supreme Court's Power and the Public

The degree to which the Supreme Court has been active in interpreting the Constitution and imposing its judgments on the political branches has varied dramatically during the history of the country. At certain points in its development, especially during its first thirteen years and throughout the period immediately following the Civil War, the Court was quite passive. It generally retreated from conflict with the political branches and was most reluctant to assert its power. At such times the Supreme Court could be described as almost dormant. However, at other times the nation's highest tribunal has been forceful, zealous, and active. During Chief Justice Marshall's tenure the Court assumed such a posture, as it did under Chief Justice Earl Warren's pathbreaking years in the 1950s and 1960s. Over the long history of the Court, however, we find a general increase in judicial activity and power. The twentieth-century role of the Supreme Court has been much more activist in character than in earlier years. Furthermore, the nation's reliance on the judiciary as an active participant in the country's policy-making process has increased substantially during this century. We now look to the courts to answer questions that in earlier periods were not thought to have judicial resolutions.

While the Supreme Court is not directly tied to the citizenry in the same way as the legislative and executive branches, it is no doubt influenced by public opinion and attitudes. Judges are susceptible to the same national trends and moods as are other citizens. Furthermore, the Court will not often stray too far from dominant public beliefs for fear of losing popular support and provoking resistance to its rulings. It should also be kept in mind that federal judges are appointed by popularly selected presidents and confirmed by directly elected senators. For this reason the attitudes of the individuals selected for judicial service are usually in accord with the political views of the electorate. It has often been argued that the Supreme Court follows the election returns. That the Court is usually in step with the rest of the nation is largely attributable to the fact that judges are selected by politically responsive officials and respond to the same environmental, political, and social conditions as do other citizens.

However, the Supreme Court is not directly tied to the people. Once appointed to a position on the federal bench, a judge need not undergo reelection or popular review. He is free to assume his own decision-making course. For this reason, the judiciary does not always directly respond to the mood of the nation. At times the Court takes the lead, pursuing policies more advanced than the nation is eager to support. Such was the case when the Warren Court issued its monumental racial discrimination decisions. At other times the Court appears to drift with the general flow of public opinion, as it did when it upheld antisubversive activities legislation during the Cold War years of the 1950s. During still other periods the Court strikes out on a reactionary course, bitterly opposing popularly supported governmental changes. The most obvious illustration of this occurred when the Court, under Charles Evans Hughes, struck down numerous New Deal legislative programs sponsored by Franklin Roosevelt to lift the nation out of the Great Depression. The role of the Court, then, varies from progressive leadership to reactionary opposition.

Regardless of which posture the Court assumes, however, it has a major impact on the interpretation of the Constitution and the manner in which politics is practiced. Whether the Court is leading the nation into new areas of endeavor or is blocking popularly supported change, the fact remains that the decisions of the Court are influential. When the Supreme Court appears to go out of its way to rule on issues of social significance, it affects the nation's political and social conditions. However, its impact may be almost as great, although not as dramatic, when it refuses to rule on a major issue. For example, when the Supreme Court sidestepped the issue of the constitutionality of the Vietnam War, it had the practical effect of affirming the war effort, although a definitive legal decision was never issued.

Limitations on the Court's Power

The High Court has the final word on matters of constitutional and legal interpretation, but its power is not absolute. In the first place, Congress retains the authority to change the law if the Court's interpretation is not to the legislature's liking. Similarly, the Congress and the states have the power to propose and ratify amendments to the Constitution, which can have the effect of reversing Supreme Court rulings. Also, Supreme Court decisions are not automatically imposed on the American people. The Court has no enforcement powers of its own. Instead, it relies on voluntary compliance of the people and relevant public officials. If such voluntary conformity to the Court's rulings is not forthcoming, the judiciary must look to the executive branch to enforce compliance. For this reason, what the Court commands is not always perfectly followed in the various communities and neighborhoods across the nation. However, in the long run the rulings of the Supreme Court have been remarkably successful in attracting general compliance and support from the people.

It has often been said that the United States is a nation of Constitution worshipers. There is a good deal of truth in this statement, but the favorable attitudes of the American people toward the Constitution did not occur spontaneously with the birth of the country in 1788. They were the product of a political ideology, heritage, and culture that developed over the years. Our strong national support of the Constitution and the generally high regard the American people have for the Supreme Court are largely twentieth-century phenomena. These feelings are very real and are held fervently by many Americans. This general support for the Constitution and the Supreme Court is one of the contributing factors to the remarkable stability the American republic has enjoyed over the years.

Summary

The Constitution of the United States cannot be fully understood without understanding the nation's politics. The very birth of the Constitution gives testimony to the interlocking nature of this country's law and political struggles. The drafting of the provisions of the Constitution, which provided the framework for the way the government has operated over the last two centuries, was guided by political forces. Each compromise made in Philadelphia in 1787 was a careful balancing of political interests: North against South, small states against large states, aristocrats against democrats, and states'-rights advocates against supporters of strong national government. The Constitution is both a political and a legal document. It came into being and took its final shape in direct response to the failures of its predecessor, the Articles of Confederation, to deal with the political realities of the times and to secure social and personal rights. Once the new government was in operation, the linkage between politics and the Constitution did not disappear, but politics molded the Constitution and the Constitution helped shape politics. The case of Marbury's lost commission and the subsequent political struggle between Marshall and Jefferson provide ample evidence for the close relationship between political and legal affairs. In subsequent chapters we will see additional examples of this important interaction.

Notes

1. 1 Cranch 137 (1803).
2. U.S. Constitution, article VI, section 2.
3. U.S. Constitution, article VI, section 3.
4. Popular election of U.S. senators did not occur until ratification of the Seventeenth Amendment.
5. Limiting the president to no more than two full terms of office did not occur until ratification of the Twenty-Second Amendment in 1951.

Further Reading

Bancroft, George. *The History of the Formation of the Constitution of the United States of America.* 2 vols. New York: Appleton, 1882.

Beard, Charles A. *An Economic Interpretation of the Constitution of the United States.* New York: Free Press, 1935.

Brown, Robert E. *Reinterpretation of the Formation of the American Constitution.* Boston: Boston University Press, 1963.

Dewey, Donald O. *Marshall versus Jefferson: The Political Background of Marbury v. Madison.* New York: Knopf, 1970.

Garraty, John A. (ed.). *Quarrels That Have Shaped the Constitution.* New York: Harper and Row, 1966.

Hamilton, Alexander; Madison, James; and Jay, John. *The Federalist Papers.* Garden City, New York: Anchor Books, 1966.

Jensen, Merrill. *Articles of Confederation.* Madison: University of Wisconsin Press, 1940.

Konefsky, S. J. *John Marshall and Alexander Hamilton: Architects of the American Constitution.* New York: Macmillan, 1964.

Levy, Leonard W. (ed.). *Essays on the Making of the Constitution.* New York: Oxford University Press, 1969.

Lewis, John D. (ed.). *Anti-Federalists versus Federalists: Selected Documents.* San Francisco: Chandler Publishing Company, 1967.

Main, Jackson Turner. *The Sovereign States, 1775–1783.* New York: New Viewpoints, 1973.

Warren, Charles. *The Supreme Court in United States History.* 2 vols. Boston: Little, Brown, 1947.

Principles of American Government

Chapter two

Basic Features of the Federal Union:
McCulloch v. *Maryland*

The ratification of the Constitution gave the United States government its basic framework. The document was general enough to be applied in a wide range of situations and yet was specific enough to detail the limitations on governmental power. The Constitution, however, was nothing more than a written agreement. It was not self-executing and did not answer all of the questions that the new nation was going to ask. Written principles must be given shape and substance in actual practice. In spite of the fact that all the states had finally ratified the Constitution, there was far from full agreement as to what that document meant.

It did not take the nation long to undergo its first major conflict over the interpretation of the Constitution. This incident occurred during the first administration of George Washington. Washington had appointed Alexander Hamilton the nation's first secretary of the treasury. As such, Hamilton had responsibility for developing the nation's economic policies and dealing with the government's large indebtedness. One of the key elements in Hamilton's plan for economic recovery was the creation of a national bank. The bank was intended to aid the government in executing its economic programs. Hamilton's proposal was controversial. It received the general backing of the Federalist-controlled Congress, but the Democratic-Republican party of Jefferson was violently opposed. To the Jeffersonians the authority to charter banks was a power reserved to the states and was not to be exercised by the central government. Over the opposition's arguments the Congress passed Hamilton's legislation.

Before the national bank bill became law, however, it had to undergo presidential scrutiny. Washington was undecided as to the validity of the bill. He asked Secretary of the Treasury Hamilton and Secretary of State Jefferson to advise him on the question of the bank's constitutionality. Jefferson argued that the national government was given only those powers explicitly mentioned in the Constitution, and nowhere in that document was the power to charter banks mentioned. Therefore, according to Jefferson's constitutional philosophy, the power to create banks was to be left to the states. Hamilton, on the other hand, claimed that the power to charter a national bank was part of the general fiscal authority given to the Congress under article I of the Constitution. Congress was empowered to coin and borrow money, levy taxes, pay debts, and regulate commerce. Having a national bank, according to Hamilton, was a necessary means to carry out these explicitly granted powers. Washington ultimately was convinced by Hamilton's logic. He signed the bill and the bank was established in 1791.

The constitutionality of the first national bank was never seriously challenged in court. When the Jeffersonians came to power in 1801, the bank was retained, but it finally went out of existence in 1811. However, in the years immediately following the dissolution of the bank the nation's economy weakened. The national treasury was low on funds, the monetary system was in disarray, and a weak fiscal program was unable to improve the nation's conditions. Support began to build for the reinstitution of the national bank. Surprisingly, this support came largely from Jefferson's old political party (now known as the Republicans) which over the years had become more and more responsive to the needs of business and commerce. Therefore, in 1816, during the final years of President Madison's tenure, a second national bank was created.

The second national bank became even more unpopular than its predecessor. A major factor prompting this lack of support was the bank's great size. The bank commanded capital in excess of $35 million, making it the largest corporation in the country. Its home office was in Philadelphia, but it had major branches in eighteen cities located in every region of the nation. A second reason for public criticism of the bank involved the interests that controlled it. The federal government had direct control over only one-fifth of the bank's shares and directors. The remaining control was retained by private investors. Most of this private control was in the hands of large monied interests who had previously supported the Federalist party. In addition, many bank shares were owned by foreign investors. A final factor contributing to the dissatisfaction with the bank was the way in which it was managed. The bank was never a model of efficiency and openness. In fact, scandal frequently occurred. Corruption was evident. Public trust was never established.

Given the problems that beset the central bank, active opposition was predictable. It came mainly from the southern and western regions of the country, where fear of mammoth corporations, monied interests, and foreigners was particularly acute. The states saw the national bank as a threat to their own sovereignty as well as a danger to state-chartered banking institutions. Eight states passed legislation designed to curb the activities of the national bank.

The state of Maryland was one of the eight that moved against the national bank. The strategy Maryland chose was to place a tax on the operations of the bank. The Maryland statute held that all banks not chartered by the state itself could not issue bank notes unless they were printed on special paper which the state taxed at a very high rate. In lieu of this tax, the bank could pay an annual fee of $15,000 to the state. The penalty for issuing a bank note without paying the tax was $100 for each offense. The target of Maryland's legislative action was the national bank's branch in Baltimore, one of the more prosperous and active of the system's offices.

The response of the Baltimore branch of the national bank was a policy of noncompliance. The bank continued operations in its normal manner without paying the state-imposed tax. Only days after the tax law went into effect the state brought legal action against James W. McCulloch, cashier of the Baltimore branch. This suit culminated in one of the most significant Supreme Court decisions, involving the nature of the American union and the powers of the federal government.

On February 22, 1819, the Supreme Court began proceedings in the case of *McCulloch* v. *Maryland*.[1] The attorneys appearing before the Court constituted some of the finest legal talent in the nation. Representing the bank were Attorney General William Wirt, Daniel Webster, and William Pinkney. For the state were attorneys Joseph Hopkinson, Luther Martin, and Walter Jones. The oral arguments lasted a total of nine days, quite an extraordinary period in comparison to the one hour of oral argument granted to Supreme Court litigants today.

Maryland based its case on the argument that the national bank was unconstitutional. This position was for the most part an articulation of the basic Jeffersonian philosophy that the national government could exercise only those powers explicitly granted to it under the Constitution. Maryland found no such grant of power to create a national bank. Therefore, attorneys for the state contended, the act of Congress establishing the bank was unconstitutional. It violated the Tenth Amendment, which stipulated: "The powers not delegated to the United States by the Constitution . . . are reserved to the States. . . ." The power to charter corporations, including the authority to create banking institutions, was a state and not a federal power.

McCulloch's attorneys challenged the Maryland contention. Ample authority to create the national bank could be found, they argued, in article I, section 8 of the Constitution, which granted Congress the power "to make all Laws which shall be necessary and proper for carrying into Execution the foregoing Powers. . . ." According to their arguments before the Court, the national bank was a "necessary and proper" means of executing national authority to regulate the monetary system, control interstate commerce, and levy taxes.

In addition to the contention that the bank was constitutionally valid, lawyers for the bank charged that the state tax was an unconstitutional action. If the federal union was to be maintained, surely the states could not be allowed to nullify through restrictive legislation every federal action with which they did not agree. By permitting this variety of state action, the central government would ultimately be crippled. Maryland argued that this charge was without merit. The states retained their sovereign powers, including the power to tax corporations. Simply because the corporation in this instance was the child of the federal government did not mean that the state lost its authority to levy taxes upon it.

The Supreme Court's decision was delivered just three days after the close of oral arguments. True to his Hamiltonian philosophy, Chief Justice Marshall strongly supported the validity of the bank and struck down the Maryland tax as unconstitutional. While Marshall's position was not surprising, the response of the remaining members of the Court was. The decision was unanimous, despite the fact that in 1819 only two Federalist justices remained on the Court. Five of the Court's number were appointees of Jefferson and Madison and thought to be loyal to Jeffersonian orthodoxy. They nonetheless supported the bank's validity, largely in response to William Pinkney's persuasive reasoning in his three days of oral argument.

Marshall's opinion for the Court constitutes a logically presented, strongly worded case in favor of the power of the national government. As to the question of the authority of Congress to create the bank, Marshall gave constitutional legitimacy to the position taken by Hamilton years earlier during the debate over the validity of the first national bank. This had become known as the "implied powers" doctrine. Essentially, this position held that the Necessary and Proper Clause implied certain powers that were not explicitly granted to the federal government. Certainly the men who drafted the Constitution could not reasonably be expected to detail every possible action that the government might legitimately take. Instead, the Framers listed the specific ends that Congress could pursue and then granted Congress the authority to take the measures "necessary and proper" to execute those ends. Marshall's own words indicate well the meaning of the implied power doctrine: "Let the end be legitimate, let it be within the scope of the Constitution, and all means which are appropriate, which are plainly adapted to that end, which are not prohibited, but consistent with the letter and spirit of the Constitution, are constitutional. . . ." While the Court was unable to find any reference to the power to create a banking corporation, the Constitution was replete with references to the fiscal powers of the federal government. The ends Congress was pursuing included the powers to lay and collect taxes, to borrow money, to regulate commerce, to declare and conduct war, and to raise and support armies. The national bank, concluded the Court, was a convenient, useful, and essential instrument in executing these constitutionally valid powers. Therefore, the creation of the national bank was valid under the Necessary and Proper Clause of article I.

After establishing the validity of the bank's creation by Congress, the Court turned to the tax imposed by the state of Maryland. The state in its arguments had asserted its sovereignty. The power to tax obviously resided with the states; no one challenged the authority of Maryland's general taxation powers. But Maryland argued that since there was no specific constitutional prohibition to taxing operations such as the issuing of bank notes by the national bank, the state was free to levy taxes at its own discretion. This states' rights contention was rejected by the Court. Marshall's opinion striking down the Maryland tax statute rests solidly on what he termed the "great principle" found in article VI, section 2. According to Marshall: "The Constitution and laws made in pursuance therefor are supreme; that they control the Constitution and laws of the respective States, and cannot be controlled by them." To allow the state to tax the operations of the federal government would be to allow the state to destroy the activities of the national government. If the Court permitted the state to tax the national bank, Marshall feared that the various states would begin to place harsh taxes on the mail, the mint, the issuing of patents, the federal court system, and any other activity of the central government which did not happen to meet the approval of a particular state. This was not what was intended by those who drafted the Constitution. The Framers would not have granted powers to the national government and at the same time allowed the states to block the execution of those powers through the authority of the state to tax. Through this process of logic Marshall's opinion reaches three important conclusions. First, the power of the federal government to create implies the power to preserve. Second, the power to destroy by means of the state taxing authority is incompatible with the power to create and preserve. And third, when the state's power to destroy through taxation clashes with the central government's power to create, the Supremacy Clause of article VI commands that the actions of the federal government prevail over those of the states. Based upon this reasoning, the Court declared the Maryland tax unconstitutional.

The Court's decision in *McCulloch* v. *Maryland* resolved the nation's first major constitutional controversy after the passage of almost thirty years and four different presidential tenures. Marshall's opinion, written in but three short days, remains as one of the most outstanding contributions to our understanding of the Constitution.

Federalism

The Supreme Court's decision in the *McCulloch* case helped solidify the federal union. Maryland's cause was championed by states' rights advocates, who saw the federal union in a much different light than did John Marshall. Following the *McCulloch* decision there was no turning back. The tide was in favor of a strong national government and against the states' rights forces. While the supremacy of the national government was severely tested during several periods of the nation's history (most notably during the Civil War), Marshall's articulation of the dominance of the federal government remains a basic principle of our republic.

Powers of the States and the National Government

McCulloch v. *Maryland* is one example of the Supreme Court acting as an umpire in disputes over the distribution of powers between the central government and the states. Questions regarding this power distribution have constantly plagued the judiciary. No period of American history has been without important litigation seeking to resolve disputes over our federal system. The reason questions of federalism are so persistent is that our system of governmental powers stands halfway between confederation and unitary forms of power distribution. Under a confederation the basic powers reside with the states, and little independent authority is given to the central government. The Articles of Confederation are an example of government organized in this fashion. Under the Articles the central government operated at the pleasure of the states. Under a unitary system the central government possesses all of the essential powers of government. If the United States had such a system, our various states would either be abolished or be retained only as administrative units of the national government. Instead of selecting either of these options, the Framers of the Constitution charted a middle course, delegating certain powers to the national government and reserving others for the states. Theoretically there is a sphere of authority in which the central government's interests are paramount and another sphere of activity in which the states are to be dominant. In practice the distribution of powers often gives birth to complex questions. There is a great deal of overlapping authority between the central government and the states. There are instances in which the valid exercise of power by one level of government infringes upon the sphere of authority generally reserved for the other. Given this blending of powers and authority it is not at all surprising that the judiciary has often had to resolve disputes between the national government and the various states.

Throughout all of the stress placed on the federal union, the basic nature of the nation has remained the same. Legal controversies, political struggles, and even rebellion have failed to alter the fundamental fabric of the federal system. The uniting of the various states is clearly considered a permanent relationship. Once a state enters the Union, she agrees to a perpetual union with her sister states. Constitutionally there is no acceptable means to rescind the bonds between a state and the federal union. This principle was established both on the battlefields of the Civil War as well as in the courtroom.

In 1869, the Supreme Court was called upon to settle a dispute that required a response to the question of the permanence of the Union. At stake was some $10 million in United States bonds which were in the hands of the state of Texas and then later transferred to private parties during the Civil War. After the war the state of Texas sought to recover the bonds, but met stiff resistance from the current bondholders on the grounds that since she had seceded from the Union, Texas was no longer a state and therefore no longer had the standing to sue in the Supreme Court. Before the Court could adjudicate the substantive merits of the rightful possessor of the bonds question, it first had to rule on whether Texas's withdrawal from the Union during the war was valid and if she could legitimately renounce and forfeit her statehood. The Court's decision in *Texas* v. *White*[2] was a strong and unequivocal determination that no state once in the Union could renounce that relationship. In the words of Chief Justice Salmon Chase: "The Constitution in all of its provisions, looks to an indestructible Union, composed of indestructible states." There was no place for reconsideration or revocation of the decision to enter the Union. The states were to be perpetually united.

The Supremacy Clause

Another basic tenet of the federal relationship is the doctrine of national supremacy. This, too, is a principle that the judiciary has consistently enforced. We have already seen the importance placed upon national supremacy by Chief Justice Marshall. Both the *Marbury* and *McCulloch* cases relied heavily on article VI, section 2 of the Constitution, which has become known as the Supremacy Clause. The Supremacy Clause provides a valuable means for deciding conflicts between the state and national governments. That particular provision states:

> This Constitution, and the Laws of the United States which shall be made in Pursuance thereof; and all Treaties made, or which shall be made, under the Authority of the United States, shall be the supreme Law of the Land; and the Judges in every State shall be bound thereby, any Thing in the Constitution or Laws of any State to the Contrary notwithstanding.

In the case of conflict between an action of the national government and a law or policy of a state, the courts will first examine the constitutionality of the federal action. If the federal government's action is not prohibited by the Constitution, then the national government's interest is dominant over that of the state and the state policy must give way. Therefore, the actions of any state must always be in accord with the Constitution and treaties as well as with constitutionally valid federal laws. When state measures are repugnant to the Constitution, treaties, or laws of the national government, they may be declared null and void. While the Supremacy Clause certainly does not strip the states of their sovereignty, it does give preference to the interests of the national government in cases of conflict.

The Distribution of Governmental Powers

The Constitution itself attempts to draw lines of demarcation between the authority of the federal government and the authority of the states as clearly as practicably possible. The result is a distribution of specific governmental powers into three classifications: powers granted or prohibited to the federal government, powers granted or prohibited to the state governments, and powers that may be exercised by both state and federal governments.

The Constitution is very explicit about the basic authority of the federal government.[3] To the central government the Framers gave the most important political powers. First, the national government is given exclusive authority over the nation's foreign relations. This broad grant of responsibility includes such specific powers as the authority to declare and wage war, raise and support armies, provide for the national defense, make treaties, and authorize ambassadors. Second, the national government is granted exclusive powers over the country's fiscal policy. This authority is comprised of the specific powers to coin and borrow money, regulate the monetary policy, collect duties, and regulate interstate and foreign commerce. Third, the national government was given exclusive authority over certain specialized areas of regulation which were designed to promote the general welfare.

These specialized grants include the power to manage a postal service, to issue copyrights and patents, to regulate bankruptcies, and to manage nationally owned lands and territories.

In return for these exclusive powers the Constitution demands that the federal government restrain itself from engaging in certain activities. One such restraint is the Tenth Amendment, which requires that any action taken by the federal government must be related to one of the powers specifically granted to it or reasonably inferred from a specific grant. Hence, we often say that the federal government is a government of delegated powers, that the national government can only exercise those powers explicitly granted to it or reasonably inferred. A second restraint focuses on the Bill of Rights. The first eight amendments to the Constitution protect individuals from various kinds of governmental actions. Therefore, the federal government cannot abridge the freedom of expression, of religion, or of fair criminal procedures. In addition, there are specific prohibitions against passing ex post facto laws, imposing legislative punishments, and granting titles of nobility.

Since the primary purpose of the federal Constitution was the creation of the national government, there is no systematic expression of the powers that the states possess. The general theory is that the states retained all of the powers which they exercised prior to the ratification of the Constitution except those which the Constitution specifically prohibits. Often the term "police powers" is used to describe the authority of the states. The police powers refer to the general prerogative of the state to regulate for the health, safety, morals, and general welfare of its citizens. Therefore, while the powers of the federal government are specifically granted or reasonably inferred, the powers of the state are all those not specifically denied. The Tenth Amendment reinforces this general grant of power by stipulating that the "powers not delegated to the United States by the Constitution, or prohibited by it to the States, are reserved to the States respectively, or to the people." State powers are, therefore, very broad and defined only in terms of limitations rather than specific grants of authority.

The powers of the states are limited in two ways. First, there are those actions that the Constitution specifically prohibits the states from committing. Section 10 of article I speaks to this particular matter. States are explicitly prohibited from entering into treaties or alliances with foreign governments, coining money, and issuing bills of credit or letters of marque. Furthermore, the states, without congressional approval, cannot constitutionally lay duties on exports or imports, enter into agreements with other states, maintain an army or navy, or engage in war. These prohibitions are for the most part designed to protect from state encroachment those powers that the national government is to exercise exclusively. A second type of limitation of state power are those prohibitions the state governments share with the national government. Like the federal government, the states cannot impose legislative punishments, pass ex post facto laws, or issue titles of nobility. Nor can the states violate those civil liberties guaranteed in the Bill of Rights and subsequent amendments to the Constitution.

Finally, there are concurrent powers. These are powers given to the national government, but not prohibited to the states. Therefore, both state and federal governments can exercise such rights. The most important of these concurrent powers are the authority to tax and the right to regulate commerce. Of course, the central government may exercise these powers nationally, whereas the state governments may only tax or regulate commerce within their own boundaries. The two levels of government may exercise these powers unimpeded until a conflict between the two arises. If the actions of the state and federal governments collide, of course, under the Supremacy Clause the state must give way to the national government. For example, the state is free to regulate local commerce, but if that regulation impedes the execution of a congressional regulation of interstate commerce, then the state legislation must be nullified.

Obligations of the National Government and the States

In addition to these grants of power to the federal and state governments, the Constitution includes various pledges and promises designed to facilitate the functioning of the federal system. These guarantees generally fall into two classes: the national government makes certain pledges to the states; and the states agree to behave in particular ways with respect to their sister states.

If the states were to surrender a substantial portion of their sovereignty to the central government, they were entitled in return to receive certain protections from the federal government. At least five such protections are evident in the language of the Constitution. First, the federal government guarantees to every state in the Union a "republican form of government."[4] While this provision would appear to be potentially important, allowing the national government to supervise the states to insure that "republican" principles are followed, this has not been the case. The Supreme Court has consistently refused to give meaningful interpretation to the republican form of government guarantee, declaring that the question of whether or not a state government is a "republican" one is political and can best be answered by Congress or the executive branch. Unless a particular state would go so far as to initiate a state monarchy or dictatorship, it is doubtful whether the federal government would ever take significant action based on the republican form of government guarantee. Second, the federal government promises to protect the various states from invasion and upon request of state authorities to provide military assistance to quell domestic violence.[5] When the states agreed to forfeit their powers to maintain military forces, they felt it necessary to have some guarantee of security. Hence, they demanded that the federal government pledge military assistance in time of emergency. This provision has been invoked several times, primarily in the form of federal military assistance to stop rioting or violence stemming from civil unrest. Third, the federal government agreed not to regulate commerce in such a manner as to give preference to the ports of one state over the ports of another.[6] Having abandoned their powers to regulate interstate commerce by imposing duties and other protectionist measures, the states demanded that they be protected against the federal government regulating in such a manner as to cripple the commerce of a given state or the states of a particular region. Fourth, the Constitution guarantees the integrity of the various states.[7] Congress may not join two or more states into a single state nor may it create a new state from a portion of an existing one without the relevant state's permission. Finally, the Constitution guarantees that the various states will be forever equally represented in the Senate.[8] This provision, of course, was insisted upon by the smaller states, who wanted to be treated as equals with the larger states. Through these five specific provisions, the Constitution guarantees the status of the states and protects them from certain potentially damaging actions by the federal government.

The final relationship dealt with in the Constitution's attempt to outline the nature of the federal union focuses on the interactions among the various states. If the union was to be a viable one, certain provisions were necessary to insure that the states would treat each other with a degree of respect. The first provision inserted into the document with these objectives in mind is the Full Faith and Credit Clause.[9] This particular section requires that each state give full faith and credit to the acts, records, and judicial proceedings of every other state. If the states were to be unified into a single nation, a mutual recognition of administrative and judicial actions was essential. The Full Faith and Credit Clause dictates, for example, that if a person is legally married in one state, the marriage must be recognized by each of the other forty-nine states. A second provision regulating the relationships among the states guarantees that the citizens of each state are entitled to the privileges and immunities of citizens in the several states.[10] The intent of this provision was to reduce the instances of a state treating citizens of other states in a discriminatory manner. A state, for example, may not pass a statute denying citizens of other states the right to obtain a business license, to have access to the courts, or to travel freely within its boundaries. Nor may a state tax its own residents at one rate and nonresidents at a higher rate. Third, the Constitution addressed the question of interstate flight of fugitives. Conflicts had occasionally arisen between states over persons charged with, or convicted of, criminal actions who would seek refuge in another state to escape punishment. In order to govern future instances of such situations, the Constitution stipulated that "a Person charged in any State with Treason, Felony, or other Crime, who shall flee from Justice, and be found in another State, shall on Demand of the executive Authority of the State from which he fled, be delivered up, to be removed to the State having jurisdiction of the Crime."[11] While the Supreme Court has ruled that this provision imposes more of a moral than a legal obligation on the state apprehending an interstate fugitive, this provision has led to a substantial reduction in the number of disputes among the states. Extradition of criminals now occurs in a rather routine fashion. In each of these three sections of the Constitution the Framers attempted to foresee potential disputes and to make provisions governing them. In this manner the stresses involved in the unification of the states into a single nation were reduced and the probability of interstate comity increased.

Federalism is an important constitutional principle because it structures political authority and responsibility. The division of powers between state and national governments has prompted periodic legal disputes throughout our nation's development. Generally the national government has predominated over the interests of state governments. This has precipitated a gradual increase in the responsibilities of the federal government and a corresponding reduction in relative authority of the states, although recent programs such as federal revenue sharing have prompted renewed interest in state and local governments. We will be discussing additional aspects of federalism in subsequent sections of this book, but for now it is important only to keep in mind the basic constitutional provisions that divide the federal and state spheres of authority.

Separation of Powers

The Framers of the Constitution were uniformly distrustful of concentrations of political power. One advantage of federalism was the establishment of a division of power between the various states and the federal government. In this way excessive power could not gravitate to the central government or to any of the state capitols. This philosophy was also applied when those who drafted the Constitution distributed powers among the various agencies of the national government. One way to reduce the incidences of political abuse was to create three branches of government with relatively equal powers. Each branch would perform a check and balance function. If one agency violated the boundaries of its authority, it would be called back into proper perspective by the other two branches. This theory is known as "separation of powers." Montesquieu and Locke, the most influential political philosophers at the time the Constitution was drafted, both had advocated the separation of powers principle, and their writings had a good deal of impact on the positions taken at the Constitutional Convention.

The Three Branches of Government

The Constitution recognizes three basic agencies of the national government: the legislature, the executive, and the judiciary. The powers and responsibilities of each branch are outlined in the first three articles. To each branch is given a specific sphere of authority: Congress is given the legislative power, the president is entrusted with the executive power, and the federal courts are to exercise the judicial power.[12] Dividing these essential powers among three branches guaranteed that governmental authority could not become concentrated in the hands of one person or one agency; therefore, abuses of power would become less likely.

In addition to distributing powers among the three, each branch was also linked to a different constituency and selected by different means. The president was to be chosen by a group of political elites called the electoral college; the legislature was chosen by the people directly (in the case of the House of Representatives) or the state legislatures (with respect to the Senate); and the judges were chosen by presidential selection and Senate confirmation. By distributing the selection powers in this way, no one constituency or selection authority could control the entire government. The three branches were also granted differing terms of office. The judges for all practical purposes were granted life tenure, the legislators either two or six years depending upon in which house of Congress they served, and the president a four-year term with possible reelection. By staggering these terms of office the Framers of the Constitution prohibited the entire government from radically changing in response to momentary fads of public opinion.

Custom and constitutional amendment have modified the applications of these original concepts of separation of powers. The electoral college as an independent selector of the president has withered away. Unlimited reelection of a president was prohibited in 1951 with the ratification of the Twenty-Second Amendment. The selection of senators by the state legislatures was abolished with the passage of the Seventeenth Amendment in 1913. The president has become increasingly active in the process of legislating, and many would argue that the judiciary has grown beyond the bounds of simply interpreting the law. Nonetheless, the separation of powers doctrine remains engrained in our constitutional fabric.

The System of Checks and Balances

The men who constructed our Constitution went one step beyond merely outlining a sphere of independent authority for each of the three branches. They also developed a checking system by allowing specific intrusions of one branch into the affairs of the others. For example, the president is given a degree of authority over the legislature by the powers to recommend legislation and the power to veto bills passed by the legislature. The president has a degree of control over the judiciary by having the power to appoint individuals to the bench. The legislature influences the president by controlling the government's appropriations, by its constitutional authority to declare war and raise military forces, and by its power to approve presidential appointments and to authorize the creation of executive agencies. The legislature controls the judiciary to the extent that Congress approves judicial nominees, creates the lower courts, and passes rules of appellate jurisdiction. The judiciary enters the legislative and executive arenas by interpreting the meaning of the laws and regulations passed by Congress and the various executive agencies, as well as determining when either the legislature or the executive branch has gone beyond constitutional limitations. Hence, each branch checks the actions of the others by means of these specifically granted powers.

The principle of separation of powers as written into the Constitution, therefore, accomplishes two basic objectives. First, it parcels out basic governmental functions to each of the three branches so that their powers are relatively equal. And second, it allows each branch to have a certain amount of authority over the affairs of the other branches. This separation of powers, a checks and balances system, was designed to discourage excessive concentration of power. Over the years the balance of power has shifted from one branch to another, with the executive being the overall beneficiary. However, the separation of powers theory has not radically changed. How this principle applies to the specific branches of government will be discussed in greater depth in chapters 7, 8, and 9, when we shall examine the constitutional status of Congress, the presidency, and the courts.

The Constitution and Change

The United States is currently governed under a document that was drafted and ratified during the eighteenth century. It should be obvious to all that the conditions of the world and the nature of the United States as a country are different today than they were at the time the Framers of the Constitution met in Philadelphia to agree on a governmental structure that would be responsive to conditions existing at that time. Had the Constitution been excessively rigid and inflexible, it would not have survived the test of almost two centuries of experience. To the Framers' credit, however, the document was constructed in such a fashion as to allow for reasonable change, and therefore it has been a viable governing document throughout the years. Moderate change has been sufficient to keep the Constitution current, and rarely has there been any serious thought of replacing it.

The Constitution undergoes change in three ways. First, the document itself provides for a formal amendment process whereby the constitutional provisions can be altered. Second, the interpretation of the Constitution by the courts can change the meaning of the Constitution as applied. And third, the interpretations of the Constitution may gradually change over the years through the development of custom and practice. Each of these avenues to constitutional change merits brief discussion.

Amendment of the Constitution: Proposal and Ratification

Delegates at the Constitutional Convention were aware of the necessity to allow for amendment of the proposed document. After all, one of the reasons for the fall of the government under the Articles of Confederation was that the amendment process was so difficult that for all practical purposes constitutional change was impossible. And, in fact, the Articles were never seriously amended, because it required the unanimous approval of the states to make any alteration whatsoever. In the final analysis the Articles had to be discarded totally rather than undergo a reasonable amount of change by amendment.

The delegates at the Constitutional Convention called for an amendment process that would have rigorous requirements, but not so rigorous as to make amendment highly unlikely. As carefully spelled out in article V, the amendment process requires two separate stages: proposal and ratification.

There are two ways in which a constitutional amendment may be proposed. First, a change in the document may be initiated through a two-thirds vote of both houses of Congress. Such actions by Congress are not subject to the presidential veto power. Proposing amendments under this alternative is the sole responsibility of the legislature. A second alternative is that two-thirds of the state legislatures may petition Congress to call a constitutional convention for the purpose of proposing amendments. To date, all amendments to the Constitution have been proposed by Congress. The constitutional convention route has been ignored not only because it is a less efficient process but also because there is the fear that once formed, a constitutional convention might well act similar to the 1787 convention and propose radical changes in the government.

Regardless of whether an amendment is proposed by Congress or by a constitutional convention, it does not become part of the Constitution until it is ratified by three-fourths of the states. This ratification process also may take two forms. First, ratification by the states may be accomplished by the vote of the various state legislatures; second, the ratification decision may be the responsibility of special state constitutional conventions. Whether the state legislatures are used or state conventions are relied upon is a matter to be determined by the Congress. Historically, Congress has favored action by the state legislatures. Only one amendment (the Twenty-First, which repealed prohibition) has been ratified by state conventions. The Supreme Court has upheld the authority of Congress to place time limits on the ratification process. It is common for Congress to stipulate, once an amendment is proposed, that ratification must take place within a period of seven years, or the proposed amendment dies.

Literally thousands of constitutional amendments have been suggested by state legislatures or by the initiation of congressional action. Only thirty-two have been officially proposed. Of this number, twenty-six have been formally ratified, five have failed to pass the ratification process, and one is currently in the midst of consideration by the state legislatures (the Equal Rights Amendment, which will die unless ratified by March 1979).[13] By all counts this is sparing use of the amendment power. Of the twenty-six formal amendments, ten were adopted immediately after the nation came into existence. Excluding these first ten, we have amended the Constitution less than once per decade, and during certain periods the nation has gone without a constitutional amendment for more than forty years. This indeed speaks well for the original document.

The Judiciary and Constitutional Change

Constitutional change can also occur through judicial interpretation. We have already seen an example of this in chapter 1, in the case of *Marbury* v. *Madison*. The result of the Court's decision in the *Marbury* case was the formal recognition of the judiciary's most powerful weapon, the authority to declare legislation and other governmental actions unconstitutional. The document itself did not mention the power of judicial review. It was not a power specifically granted to the federal courts. Yet through judicial interpretation of the Constitution, a major power was added to one of the branches of government.

Many constitutional changes by judicial interpretation do not occur as abruptly as did the creation of judicial review. The Constitution quite often evolves very slowly so that change occurs only after decades of incremental interpretations. The increasing role of the federal government relative to the powers of the states did not occur by constitutional amendment, nor did it occur with a single court decision. Rather, the constitutional balance of power between state and nation evolved over long years of both litigation and practice.

Many times the courts have been obliged to modernize the Constitution by judicial interpretation because of changes in society and technology. Commonplace matters of today were often not anticipated by the Framers, and therefore, the judges are required to apply the Constitution to circumstances in which the intent of the Framers is impossible to determine. For example, the men who met in Philadelphia to draft the Constitution and those in the first Congress who improved the document with a Bill of Rights could not have anticipated the development of television and radio. Therefore, when contemporary judges interpret the First Amendment's guarantees of freedom of the press, they must include the broadcast media, although these forms of the press were not included in the original wording of the amendment. Similarly, the development of modern electronic surveillance techniques has prompted judges to revise interpretations of the Fourth Amendment guarantees against unreasonable searches and seizures. Periodic modification in judicial interpretations of the Constitution is obviously necessary if that document is to remain relevant to contemporary society.

Custom and Practice

A final way the Constitution changes is through custom and practice. If the government engages in a certain activity that may be of marginal constitutionality without prompting a court challenge, then as the months pass the activity becomes more and more acceptable. American law is very precedent conscious. In the absence of explicit provisions to the contrary, a governmental action with a long history will be assumed to be constitutionally valid.

Earlier in this chapter we discussed the case of *McCulloch* v. *Maryland*. The national bank controversy is a good example of the importance of custom and practice. Obviously, the bank was of questionable validity by the constitutional standards of the day, but the first national bank was passed by Congress and approved by the president. It existed without constitutional challenge for several years. Much later when the second national bank was attacked in court, one of the major strengths of the probank forces was the fact that an earlier version of the bank had been allowed to operate without serious challenge. The first national bank provided a precedent for the second. By practice the federal government had established a new area of activity. And the Supreme Court's ruling upholding the validity of the national bank reinforced this action as a constitutionally proper one. Custom and practice do not always establish that an activity is constitutionally valid. The long decades of official racial segregation of public facilities, for example, did not stop the Supreme Court in 1954 from declaring such practices in violation of the Constitution. Nonetheless, firmly established customs and traditions can affect the way the courts interpret and apply basic constitutional principles. And in so doing, custom and practice can gradually change the meaning of the document.

The United States Constitution is not static. It is flexible enough to allow for the give and take of historical forces. Through amendment, interpretation, and experience the Constitution constantly, if gradually, evolves. And that evolution is one of the most important reasons for its longevity.

Summary

The United States Constitution establishes the fundamental principles of governmental power and authority. It is distinctive in its commitment to a balancing of powers. Every major article of the document deals in some way with dividing governmental authority and distributing power to differing levels and branches of government. It first distributes certain powers to the national government and leaves the remaining authority to be exercised by the states. The most important powers are granted to the national government, and in case of conflict between state and federal governments the Constitution stipulates the superiority of the national interests. Power is also divided between the legislative, executive, and judicial branches. Each is given a particular sphere of governmental action in which it is to be superior. And yet each branch is given a certain degree of authority over the other branches. Both the theory of federalism and that of separation of powers accentuate the belief of the Framers that to reduce abuses of power, authority must be divided. The best way to check the use of power is to create equal and offsetting powers. To date the original formula developed by the Philadelphia Convention has been an unqualified success. While the balance of power may have shifted from one branch or level of government to another, no one agency of government has ever dominated the entire political process. Excesses and abuses have been relatively infrequent. Processes of constitutional change have been sufficiently effective to maintain the viability of the Constitution through periods of intense stress and change. The Constitution has survived largely because, unlike its predecessor, the Articles of Confederation, it has been capable of responding to the needs of the times.

Notes

1. 4 Wheat. 316 (1819).
2. Wall. 700 (1869).
3. Article I, section 8.
4. Article IV, section 4.
5. Article IV, section 4.
6. Article I, section 9.
7. Article IV, section 3.
8. Article V.
9. Article IV, section 1.
10. Article IV, section 2.
11. Article IV, section 2.
12. Article I, section 1; article II, section 1; article III, section 1.
13. In late 1977 Justice Department representatives issued an opinion that Congress possessed the power to extend the ratification time limit for the Equal Rights Amendment.

Further Reading

Baker, Leonard. *John Marshall: A Life in Law*. New York: Macmillan Publishing Company, 1974.

Burns, James MacGregor. *The Deadlock of Democracy*. Englewood Cliffs, N.J.: Prentice-Hall, 1964.

Elazar, Daniel J. *American Federalism: A View from the States*. New York: Thomas Y. Crowell, 2nd ed., 1972.

Farrand, Max. *The Framing of the Constitution of the United States*. New Haven: Yale University Press, 1963.

Garraty, John A. (ed.). *Quarrels That Have Shaped the Constitution*. New York: Harper and Row, 1966.

Gunther, Gerald (ed.). *John Marshall's Defense of McCulloch v. Maryland*. Stanford: Stanford University Press, 1969.

Gwyn, W. B. *The Meaning of the Separation of Powers*. New Orleans: Tulane University Press, 1965.

McDonald, Forrest. *E Pluribus Unum*. Boston: Houghton Mifflin, 1965.

McLaughlin, Andrew C. *The Foundations of American Constitutionalism*. Gloucester, Mass.: Peter Smith, 1972.

Orfield, Lester B. *The Amending of the Federal Constitution*. Ann Arbor: University of Michigan Press, 1942.

Riker, William H. *Federalism: Origin, Operation, Significance*. Boston: Little, Brown, 1964.

Vile, M. J. C. *Constitutionalism and the Separation of Powers*. London: Oxford University Press, 1967.

The Rights of Americans

Chapter three

Personal Rights and Governmental
Authority: *Francis* v. *Resweber*

On January 13, 1947, the United States Supreme Court handed down a decision interpreting the constitutional rights of convicted murderer Willie Francis. The case arose from a bizarre set of circumstances. The opinion of the Court, written by Justice Stanley Reed, noted: "So far as we are aware, this case is without precedent in any court." Coupled with the unusual facts of the case were the complicated constitutional issues it presented. The Court was badly divided, finally resolving the important questions by a five-to-four vote. Today, more than three decades after that decision, many students of the Court remain unconvinced that justice was done.

The events that gave birth to the Supreme Court litigation began in November of 1944. In that month a white pharmacist from a small town in St. Martin Parish, Louisiana was shot to death. Several of the victim's articles were missing, including a wallet, a watch, and a small amount of cash. The local sheriff, E. L. Resweber, began an immediate investigation. Evidence was scanty and for several months no arrests were made. Finally, Sheriff Resweber was notified by Texas authorities that a fifteen-year-old black youth had been picked up on a routine matter and had in his possession the wallet of the victim. After questioning, Texas authorities obtained a written confession from the suspect, Willie Francis, admitting that he had committed both the murder and the robbery. The confession was later repeated orally to Louisiana law-enforcement officers upon the suspect's return to the state. After a routine trial, Willie Francis was found guilty of the crimes charged, and the court sentenced him to be executed.

At noon on May 3, 1946, Willie Francis was led from his cell by Sheriff Resweber and other corrections officials to the state's electric chair. Sheriff Resweber asked Francis if he had any final words, but the convicted murderer remained silent. He was then strapped into the chair and the execution hood was placed over his head. The order was given to the electrocutioner to throw the switch. The appropriate mechanisms were placed into action and at the same time one of the officials softly said: "Goodbye, Willie."

Exactly what happened at that point was later disputed. What is clear, however, is that the farewell uttered by the official was premature. There was a mechanical failure and Willie Francis did not die. State authorities later argued that the electric chair did not function at all, that Francis received no demonstrable shock. Affidavits from several witnesses, however, supported the conclusion that Francis did receive a considerable electric charge. One official witness stated: "I saw the electrocutioner turn on the switch and I saw his lips puff out and swell, his body tensed and stretched. I heard the one in charge yell to the man outside for more juice when he saw that Willie Francis was not dying and the one on the outside yelled back he was giving him all he had." The official chaplain who witnessed the event stated: "Willie Francis' lips puffed out and his body squirmed and tensed and he jumped so that the chair rocked on the floor. Then the condemned man said: 'Take it off. Let me breathe.' Then the switch was turned off." While there was some division of opinion regarding the intensity of the shock received by Francis, the fact remained that because of some unanticipated mechanical failure, the accused did not die.

Authorities attempted to adjust the electric chair so as to enforce the sentence against Francis. But an immediate second execution attempt was stopped by the governor, who issued a reprieve. However, a second execution was scheduled for May 10, 1946, one week following the original attempt. By this time the plight of Willie Francis had gained the attention of the public. A Louisiana attorney, Bertrand de Blanc, began legal proceedings against a second execution attempt. He was joined in this legal battle by Attorney J. Skelly Wright, who was later to become a prominent federal judge. Attorneys for Francis were able to have the second execution attempt postponed pending the determination of the legal issues involved. Francis's case was heard by the state pardons board, the governor, and the Louisiana Supreme Court. In each instance the officials refused to set aside the execution order. Finally, the attorneys took the appeal to the United States Supreme Court.

In behalf of Willie Francis, de Blanc and Wright submitted four basic arguments. First, they argued that the second execution attempt would be in violation of the Fourteenth Amendment's command that no state "shall deprive any person of life, liberty or property without due process of law." Fundamental fairness would be ignored by requiring a person to undergo such a serious experience a second time. Placing Francis in the electric chair a second time would offend the conscience of civilized man. Second, subjecting Francis to another execution attempt, they argued, would violate the Constitution's Fifth Amendment protection that no "person be subject for the same offense to be twice put in jeopardy of life or limb." To expose Francis again to the electric chair would violate this provision against double jeopardy. Third, attorneys for the accused contended that a second execution session would be repugnant in light of the Eighth Amendment, which prohibits the infliction of "cruel and unusual punishments." To place Francis in the electric chair again would be to subject him to death by installments. It would require him to undergo once again the psychological torment required by waiting for the execution day to come. Certainly, they argued, a second electrocution would be both cruel and unusual, given what Willie Francis had already undergone. Finally, a violation of the Constitution's Fourteenth Amendment Equal Protection Clause was alleged. That provision holds that no state shall "deny to any person within its jurisdiction the equal protection of the laws." Since no other person convicted of murder was required to undergo two execution attempts, Francis would be denied equal treatment if he were required to submit to two death sessions.

The Supreme Court's answer to claims made on Francis's behalf can be found in the decision formally entitled, *The State of Louisiana* ex rel. *Francis* v. *Resweber*.[1] On each of the questions submitted, a majority of the Court ruled in favor of the state authorities, a ruling that allowed the Louisiana corrections officials to conduct a second execution attempt. While obviously sympathizing with the plight of Willie Francis, the Court's majority held that upon a strict application of the constitutional principles involved, the arguments of Francis's attorneys were not valid. The Court found that the mechanical failure occurred completely by accident. There was no intent on the part of the state authorities to parcel out Francis's death sentence by installments. Given the fact that the officials attempted to execute Francis in a careful and humane manner, concepts of fairness had been followed. As to the claim of double jeopardy, the Court held that the arguments of Francis's attorneys were beyond the bounds of the intentions of those who drafted that amendment. The primary purpose of the double jeopardy provision was to prohibit the government from placing a person *on trial* for the same crime more than once. It was not designed to prohibit the carrying out of a legitimate sentence that was not executed because of an unintended failure of a mechanical device. The Court's previous decisions made it clear that the double jeopardy provision applied to situations other than that faced by Francis; and the Court explained that it was not going to expand its interpretation of the Fifth Amendment in this case. Similarly, the Court rejected the cruel and unusual punishment argument. Since American courts had previously upheld the validity of the death penalty, the Supreme Court found no cause to prohibit the execution of this convicted murderer. In the words of Justice Reed: "Even the fact that the petitioner has already been subjected to a current of electricity does not make his subsequent execution any more cruel in the constitutional sense than any other execution." Finally, the Court refused to accept Francis's equal protection claim. Again, the justices put great emphasis on the fact that the mechanical failure was unintentional. Denial of equal protection of the laws assumes that the state has purposefully discriminated against someone. But according to the Court's interpretation in this case: "We have no right to assume that Louisiana singled out Francis for a treatment other than that which would generally be applied." Hence, the Supreme Court ruled that a second execution attempt was not prohibited by the federal Constitution. Willie Francis had brought his constitutional claims to Court and had lost.

The members of the Supreme Court were not without their misgivings about the decision. One of the members of the majority, Justice Felix Frankfurter, wrote a special concurring opinion justifying his vote in the Francis case. He stated that he was personally opposed to the death penalty and would never have allowed a second execution attempt if his personal views were controlling the case. However, Frankfurter explained that as a Supreme Court judge he must rule not according to his personal beliefs, but according to the meaning of the Constitution. And, by Frankfurter's analysis, not a single provision in the document prohibited the state of Louisiana from imposing a second execution attempt.

The four dissenting justices felt that the constitutional rights of Willie Francis would be violated by a second execution attempt. Foremost among their reasons was the cruel and unusual punishment contention. Speaking for the dissenters, Justice Harold Burton said: "Taking human life by unnecessarily cruel means shocks the most fundamental instincts of civilized man. It should not be possible under the constitutional procedure of a self-governing people." The Court's minority concluded that any death sentence that was not both instantaneous and relatively painless violated the Constitution's prohibition against cruel and unusual punishment. In the case of Willie Francis, death by installments did not meet these requirements.

Following the decision of the Supreme Court, the state of Louisiana scheduled a date for the execution of Willie Francis. Attorneys remained active in his behalf, exploring every possible means of legally blocking the execution. However, one day before the scheduled electrocution, Willie Francis told his attorneys to cease their efforts, that he was ready to die. On May 9, 1947, Francis was led from his cell to the place of the execution. He was placed in the same electric chair that had failed previously. He was strapped into place and the hood was placed over his head. At the command of the official in charge the switch was thrown. On this occasion there was no mechanical failure. Willie Francis died.

In previous chapters we have dealt with the Supreme Court as an umpire of disputes involving political power. We have seen how the Court has had to decide questions of the distribution of power between the central government and the states. Similarly, we have viewed the role of the Court as an arbiter of the proper spheres of responsibility for the three branches of government. The case of Willie Francis illustrates still another role of the Court. The Supreme Court must interpret those sections of the Constitution that deal with personal liberties. The judiciary is the ultimate authority in deciding when government has violated those basic human freedoms guaranteed by the Constitution. In cases involving the civil liberties of Americans the Court is almost always faced with a choice between freedom and order. On one side the government argues that restrictions on freedom are necessary to maintain national security, keep order in the streets, penalize criminal violators, or for a host of other reasons. The opposing side claims that government should not be empowered to deny human liberties. The Supreme Court must draw the line; it must decide the point at which freedom must end and governmental regulation may begin. In this chapter we will discuss those freedoms that are recognized under our Constitution and how the Supreme Court has interpreted these rights.

The Bill of Rights and the Incorporation Doctrine

One of the more compelling arguments advanced by the Anti-Federalists during the debates over the ratification of the Constitution was that the proposed document had no protections for individual liberties. So damaging was this defect that the proponents of the Constitution promised to amend the document to include a Bill of Rights if it should be ratified. The Constitution was ultimately accepted by the states, and the Federalists honored their pledge by proposing a Bill of Rights during the First Congress. These guarantees were accepted by the states, and the Constitution was amended to include protections of basic liberties. The Bill of Rights is comprised of the first eight amendments to the Constitution, each of which guarantees basic freedoms against governmental abuse. In addition to the original Bill of Rights, the Constitution has been subsequently amended several times to include new protections. Most notable are the Thirteenth and Fourteenth amendments, which extended protections to black Americans, and the Fifteenth, Nine-teenth, Twenty-Fourth, and Twenty-Sixth Amendments, which protect the right to vote.

The Bill of Rights and the States

The first eight amendments had but one purpose: to prohibit the federal government from infringing upon the rights of the people. Many feared that the new government would be sufficiently powerful to abuse individual citizens; the Bill of Rights was intended to restrict such excesses. It is important to remember that the Bill of Rights was not originally intended to restrict the state governments at all. The sole target was the federal government. Hence, the First Amendment begins: "*Congress* shall make no law. . . ." The amendment says nothing about the states. Each of the states had their own form of a Bill of Rights, and so it was thought to be unnecessary to include the states in the wording of the federal Constitution.

The theory that the Bill of Rights applied only to the national government and not to the states was officially approved by the Supreme Court in 1833 in the case of *Barron* v. *Baltimore*.[2] The case involved one John Barron, who operated a wharf in Baltimore harbor. The wharf enjoyed an excellent business because it was situated in deep water and could accommodate very large ships. However, in the course of paving and repairing several of its streets, the city of Baltimore found it necessary to alter the course of several streams. A consequence of this alteration was the depositing of a large amount of soil, sand, and gravel in the vicinity of Barron's wharf. Soon these deposits filled the inlet and Barron's operation became no longer situated in deep water. In fact, the larger ships could no longer navigate into the wharf, making Barron's once lucrative business almost worthless. Obviously upset, Barron sued the city, claiming that it had violated the Fifth Amendment to the Constitution, which holds that private property shall not be taken for public use without just compensation. Barron argued that the city had taken his deep port for the public purpose of improving roads, but had failed to give him just compensation.

When the case was appealed to the Supreme Court, the city emerged as the victor. The Court's opinion, announced by Chief Justice Marshall, held that Barron could not claim any violation of the Fifth Amendment because that amendment, along with the other provisions of the Bill of Rights, were designed to restrict the federal government and not the state or local governments. Since Barron's property had not been taken for a public purpose by the national government, he therefore had no claim.

The rationale in *Barron* v. *Baltimore* meant that the federal government was restricted by the provisions of the Bill of Rights, but that the states were free to develop their own protections of individual rights. And this is in fact what had happened. Each state had its system for protecting human liberties from encroachment by state government. In some states the protections were equal to, or even more comprehensive, than the federal Bill of Rights. But in other states fewer rights were recognized than the U.S. Constitution protected. This meant, for example, that while the federal government had to observe the First Amendment guarantee of freedom of the press, the states did not have to observe such liberties unless their specific state guarantees included such a right.

The Due Process Clause and Incorporation

The constitutional status of the Bill of Rights changed with the passage of the Fourteenth Amendment in 1868. That amendment included what has become known as the Due Process Clause. It holds that "nor shall any State deprive any person of life, liberty, or property without due process of law." Several constitutional scholars argued that the impact of the Due Process Clause was to make the Bill of Rights applicable to the states as well as to the federal government. The theory held that the Due Process Clause was "shorthand" for the Bill of Rights. This position became known as the incorporation doctrine because it argued that the Due Process Clause incorporated the Bill of Rights. Proponents of the incorporation doctrine contended that the Due Process Clause should be interpreted to read: "nor shall any State deprive any person of life, liberty, or property without observing the Bill of Rights."

In several cases brought to the Supreme Court over the years the litigants attempted to convince the Court to accept the incorporation doctrine. The Court never did. However, what the Court finally accepted was a modified version of the incorporation doctrine which has become known as "selective incorporation." The best statement of this position can be found in the Court's decision in the 1937 decision of *Palko* v. *Connecticut*.[3] In that decision, while rejecting complete incorporation, the Court held that the Due Process Clause should be interpreted as protecting all "fundamental liberties" from state infringement. That conclusion, of course, begs the question "Which rights are fundamental rights?" The Court gives a partial answer to this question by defining fundamental rights as those without which liberty and justice could not survive. The Court noted that certain provisions of the Bill of Rights obviously qualify as fundamental rights. Among these are the freedoms of speech, press, and religion. But the Court failed to review the entire Bill of Rights and designate which rights are fundamental and which are not. The Court's policy, as announced in the *Palko* decision, would be to decide whether or not a right is fundamental on a case-by-case, right-by-right basis. Hence, when a case was appealed to the Supreme Court requiring the Court to answer, for example, the question of whether states had to observe the right to a jury trial, the Court would then determine whether the jury trial provision was a fundamental right. Therefore, the Court would incorporate some provisions of the Bill of Rights and not incorporate others, depending upon whether or not the right was deemed fundamental.

Following the *Palko* decision, a long line of cases sought to convince the Court that a particular provision of the Bill of Rights was fundamental and, therefore, had to be observed by the states under the Due Process Clause of the Fourteenth Amendment. This selective incorporation approach continues today. Over the past four decades the Court has considered at one time or another almost every provision of the Bill of Rights. At the present time nearly every provision has been declared to be fundamental. Only the Second Amendment's right to bear arms, the Third Amendment's protection against quartering soldiers, the Fifth Amendment's guarantee of a grand jury hearing, the Seventh Amendment's right to a jury trial in civil cases, and the Eighth Amendment's prohibition against excessive bail and fines have not been incorporated. With these exceptions in mind, we may now say that the Bill of Rights applies not only to the federal government directly, but also to the states via the Due Process Clause of the Fourteenth Amendment. The incorporation process is extremely important because it has expanded the protections that Americans enjoy. The Bill of Rights cannot be violated by the federal government, nor can it be abused by the states.

Freedom of Religion

The first freedom mentioned in the Bill of Rights is religious liberty. The First Amendment's opening words lend solid and unambiguous support for religious toleration: "Congress shall make no law respecting an establishment of religion, or prohibiting the free exercise thereof." Thus, the First Amendment actually guarantees two aspects of religious freedom. First, the amendment prohibits the establishment of religion; and second, it protects the right to practice religion. While these twin pillars of religious liberty are often intertwined, they can be distinguished, and it will be to our benefit to discuss them separately.

The Establishment Clause

There has always been a good deal of controversy over the meaning of the Establishment Clause. Most would agree that at a very minimum the Constitution prohibits religious establishment as it existed in England at the time the First Amendment was ratified. That is, the government cannot, under the meaning of the First Amendment, create or promote an official church. There can be no state religion. But beyond the prohibition against the establishment of a state religion, the amendment is not so clear. Does the Establishment Clause mean that the government must only remain neutral when it comes to religion? Or does it dictate that a high wall of separation be erected between government and the church? While Supreme Court rulings have not been totally consistent on the question of religious establishment, they generally favor the position that there must be a rather rigid barrier between church and state.

The Supreme Court first confronted a religious establishment case in 1899 in *Bradfield* v. *Roberts*.[4] This suit challenged the appropriation of $30,000 in federal funds for the construction of a new wing on a Washington, D.C. hospital. The new wing was to be used to care for indigent patients. The suit was filed because the recipient, Provident Hospital, was owned and operated by Roman Catholic nuns. Therefore, it was charged that Congress was appropriating money to a church in violation of the Establishment Clause. The Supreme Court unanimously rejected this attack. In doing so it developed what has become known as the "secular purpose test." This doctrine holds that if government aid has as its primary intent a secular purpose, then it is of no consequence that the money is administered by a religious group. If, however, the aid has religion as the primary purpose, then the First Amendment is violated. Just because the hospital was operated by Catholic nuns did not make the hospital "religious."

Beginning in the 1940s, the Supreme Court was forced to hear several cases involving aid to educational institutions with religious affiliations. Several states passed statutes allowing financial support for religious schools. This support was granted because states found it more economical to give partial support to religious schools rather than have the religious schools fail requiring the public schools to absorb the students, and because state legislatures came under political pressure from large religious groups, usually Catholics, to provide some form of assistance. The first challenge to state aid for religious schools occurred in *Everson* v. *Board of Education*,[5] decided in 1947. This suit challenged the constitutionality of a New Jersey plan that allowed parents of students attending private and religious schools to be compensated for bus transportation to the schools. The Supreme Court allowed this type of assistance under what has become known as the "child benefit theory." This doctrine holds that as long as the aid is given directly to the children or to their parents (rather than to the religious school itself) and is primarily for the benefit of the child (rather than for the benefit of the school), then the Establishment Clause is not violated. Under this theory the Court has also allowed nonreligious textbooks and other instructional aids to be given to students attending religious schools.[6]

Governments, therefore, may give aid to those attending religious schools. The assistance must be for secular purposes. A state, for example, may give parochial school students biology or mathematics texts, but could not give them religious books. The assistance must be for the primary benefit of the students. The state, however, must not become excessively entangled with the religious institution in disbursing the funds.[7] Finally, it should be noted that the Court has applied these conditions somewhat differentially. For example, the Court will be less strict in the application of these rules if the aid is going to religious colleges and universities than if it is going to elementary and secondary schools. The reason for this is that younger children are more impressionable to religious teachings than are young adult students.[8] Hence, the Court is more vigilant in dealing with aid to primary education. Also, the Court has treated federal aid much differently than state aid. In its long history, the Supreme Court has never ruled against the federal government in a major Establishment Clause case, whereas the Court has frequently struck down state aid programs.

Another interesting and controversial issue in the area of religious establishment is the question of the validity of prayer in public schools. During the 1960s the Court received several appeals in which citizens challenged the practice of praying in the classroom. In one, *Engle* v. *Vitale*,[9] educational authorities in New York had devised a nondenominational prayer and encouraged it to be said in all classrooms at the beginning of each school day.[10] In another, *Abington School District* v. *Schempp*,[11] citizens challenged a Pennsylvania requirement that ten verses of the Bible be read without comment each day in the public schools. And in still another case, *Murray* v. *Curlett*,[12] the Court was faced with the issue of reading the Lord's Prayer in the classrooms of Maryland. In each instance the Court responded by striking down the religious practices. The Court's rationale was that government must be prohibited from establishing religion. This means that government cannot be in the business of composing prayers, encouraging prayer in public classrooms, or requiring such religious expression. To have government active in the practice of prayer is wholly inconsistent with the First Amendment's Establishment Clause. The Court received harsh criticism for its decisions in these cases, but an objective appraisal of the history and meaning of the Establishment Clause leads one to the conclusion that the Court in the constitutional sense ruled quite correctly. The Court was not, as some charged, outlawing prayer. What the Court simply ruled was that the Establishment Clause would not permit the government to engage in religious worship. If freedom of religion is to thrive, it needs to be free from any government interference and regulation.

The Free Exercise Clause

The second provision of the First Amendment dealing with religious liberty is known as the Free Exercise Clause. It is stated in very direct language that Congress shall make no law prohibiting the free exercise of religion. This language is misleading, however. The Free Exercise Clause has never been interpreted to protect all forms of religious worship. In practice our freedom to exercise religion is not as absolute as a simple reading of the First Amendment would have us believe.

There is little controversy over the practice of conventional religious worship. Government in the United States has never engaged in blatant regulation of matters of religious conscience or standard forms of religious services. But occasionally the courts have been faced with the question of validity of the regulation of unconventional forms of religious worship. As early as 1879, for example, the Supreme Court was required to rule on the validity of a congressional statute making polygamy a crime.[13] This statute was enforced against members of the Mormon faith, who at that time practiced polygamy. Here the Court was challenged with a basic dilemma. Could a person on the basis of religious freedom be exempt from an otherwise valid criminal statute? The Court concluded that religion could not be used as a shield against criminal prosecution. In so ruling, the Supreme Court held that in spite of religious practices, government could validly regulate certain social evils such as polygamy. This holding has been followed over the decades and has caused courts to rule that a person, in the name of religious freedom, cannot violate narcotics laws, laws against murder or infliction of pain, laws requiring compulsory medical procedures, or laws that prohibit certain dangerous practices, such as the handling of poisonous snakes.

While it has ruled that government may regulate social evils even if connected with religion, the Court has also handed down a number of restrictions on government activity. For example, government cannot attempt to define religion,[14] nor can it deny government benefits because of a person's religious affiliation.[15] The government is not constitutionally permitted to restrict orderly religious gatherings,[16] nor can it tax purely religious activities.[17]

The First Amendment protects religious liberty. It generally declares religious establishment and government restrictions on religious worship to be invalid. And while the courts have allowed certain departures from the absolute language of the First Amendment, the Constitution has worked reasonably well at protecting religious liberty from governmental abuse. The Framers wanted the First Amendment to insure that government would neither advance nor hinder religious practices. It has generally accomplished that goal.

Freedom of Expression

Perhaps the most valued of all civil liberties is the freedom of expression. In the United States citizens can generally speak their minds without fear of governmental reprisal. The freedom of expression guarantees of the Constitution are found in the First Amendment. Expression is a general term composed of the specifically guaranteed rights of speech, press, assembly, and petition. The words of the First Amendment give blanket protection to these freedoms: "Congress shall make no law . . . abridging the freedom of speech, or of the press; or the right of the people peaceably to assemble, and to petition the Government for a redress of grievances." However, like other provisions of the Constitution, the absolute language written by the Framers has not been applied so absolutely. We will reserve the bulk of our discussion of the freedom of expression for chapters 4 through 6 when we examine the process by which citizens express their views to the government, but it is important at this point to review briefly some of the basic concepts involved in the right to freedom of expression.

Freedom of Speech and Press

The cornerstone of the right to expression lies in the right to freedom of speech. Those who wrote the First Amendment desired a clear statement of intent that under the new government open discussion of public issues would be allowed. Under such a system the free marketplace of ideas would thrive. A rich exchange of views on governmental policies and procedures would make the nation strong. But it is also important to keep in mind that the First Amendment's freedom of speech provision was never intended to cover all forms of utterances in all circumstances and surroundings. We have always allowed certain restrictions on speech. Justice Holmes was fond of noting that the First Amendment does not give one the right to yell "Fire" in a crowded theater. Similarly, one cannot begin an oration in a public courtroom, incite riots, issue death threats over the telephone, or give away military secrets to the enemy. Courts have consistently ruled that government can restrict oral articulations of these varieties without running afoul of the First Amendment. Freedom of speech does not give one license to say anything and everything without governmental interference. But as a guarantee that a free public debate on governmental issues will be permitted, the First Amendment has been vigorously enforced by the courts.

The freedom of press clause of the First Amendment was designed with the same basic purposes in mind as the speech provision. By insuring that the press is free from governmental controls, the people are given a means of disseminating their views and receiving news about public concerns. The press was considered an important check on governmental actions, for it is through the press that political abuses are often exposed. The press provides a means by which the free flow of ideas is able to enjoy mass circulation. But like the freedom of speech, press liberties are not absolute. Court interpretations have held that certain press activities are beyond the protections of the First Amendment. For example, government can place restrictions on irresponsible journalism that manifests itself in libel. Government can regulate the publication of obscenities. In reporting and discussing public affairs, however, the press is well protected against governmental controls.

Freedom of Assembly and Petition

The freedom of assembly normally receives less attention than it deserves. The right to assemble peacefully is one of the more important protections of political expression. Assembly protects two very important means of political participation. First, it allows individuals to join with others to demonstrate their views publicly. The mass demonstrations against the war in Vietnam and against the Selective Service system during the late 1960s had a great impact on the course of governmental policy. Similarly, the many and varied demonstrations in support of civil rights for black Americans increased the speed with which the bonds of racial segregation were torn down. It is crucial to remember that the words of the First Amendment protect only peaceful assembly. Public demonstrations that involve violence, a breakdown in order, trespass, or an interruption of legitimate governmental activity can be regulated. Second, the right to peaceful assembly implies the right to freedom of association. Therefore, Americans are free to join with others into groups of all kinds, including political parties and interest groups which are essential to the functioning of our republic.

The right to petition the government for redress of grievances is the final specific liberty which constitutes the freedom of expression. If government is to be responsive to the will of the people, citizens must be entitled to bring their demands and needs to the attention of the government. The right to petition adds little substance to what is already included in the freedoms of speech, press, and assembly. The very fact that it is specifically protected under the First Amendment, however, gives stature to the principle of citizen input to governmental processes.

Without the freedom of expression provisions of the First Amendment the American political system would be much different than it is today. The liberty to engage in discussions of public affairs and express those opinions individually or collectively, by speech or in the press, forms the foundation for our contemporary democratic institutions.

The Rights of the Criminally Accused

There is evidence in the Bill of Rights that the Framers placed a great deal of importance on the way in which criminally accused persons would be treated. The colonists were well aware of the often cruel and unfair criminal prosecutions that occurred in Europe. Consequently, they elevated procedural safeguards to constitutionally protected status with the ratification of Amendments Four through Eight. Each of these additions to the Constitution discusses the manner in which an accused individual must be processed through the criminal justice system. These procedural protections were designed to make criminal trials as fair and impartial as possible. In the words of the Fifth Amendment, "due process of law" must be observed whenever the government takes action against a person because of alleged violations of criminal law.

Illegal Search and Seizure and the Exclusionary Rule

The Fourth Amendment was written to prohibit governmental excesses when conducting searches and seizures. It guarantees that individuals will be "secure in their persons, houses, papers, and effects, against unreasonable searches and seizures." The key word in this amendment is the term "unreasonable." When law enforcement officials are challenged for conducting an illegal search and seizure, the courts must decide whether, under the circumstances of the case, the search was reasonable. Several justifications for police searches meet the reasonableness requirement. First, a law-enforcement official may search a person or place if he possesses a validly issued search warrant. Search warrants can only be issued by a judge and only if there is "probable cause" to conduct a search. In addition, warrants must be specific about the person or place to be searched and the things to be seized. Second, a police officer may search immediately upon making a valid arrest. If the arrest is a lawful one, then law-enforcement personnel may search the arrested suspect and anything under his immediate control.[18] Third, police may search in order to insure their own safety. If there is probable cause to believe that a suspect might be concealing a dangerous weapon or in some other way putting the life or limb of the officer in jeopardy, then a search for the weapon is valid. Fourth, police may search and seize in the case of evidence that is about to be destroyed.[19] And finally, police can search upon obtaining voluntarily granted permission from a person having authority over the place or things to be searched.[20] Each of these five justifications for a search and seizure normally provides proof that the search is a reasonable one. The Fourth Amendment was not designed to prohibit needed search and seizure operations by law enforcement personnel, but only to keep such activities within the scope of reasonableness. Since 1971, the United States Supreme Court has handed down several rulings that have expanded the authority of police to search and seize.[21]

The Fourth Amendment is generally enforced through what has become known as "the exclusionary rule."[22] This rule holds that if police illegally obtain evidence of a crime, the evidence cannot be admitted in court or used against the accused. The theory behind the exclusionary rule is that if police know illegally obtained evidence cannot be admitted in court, they will not be so likely to violate Fourth Amendment guidelines.

Self-Incrimination and Involuntary Confession: Escobedo and Miranda

The Fifth Amendment contains a number of criminal justice provisions. The most important of these is the privilege against self-incrimination. In the words of the Constitution: "No person . . . shall be compelled in any criminal case to be a witness against himself." For a violation of this provision to occur two events must happen. First, there must be some form of compulsion; and second, the accused must incriminate himself. Generally, the self-incrimination provision means that an accused individual need not take the witness stand during his trial. The prosecuting attorney is, therefore, prohibited from calling the defendant as a witness and under pain of perjury asking him if he in fact committed the crime. Nor is the prosecutor able to make reference to the fact that a person exercised his constitutional right not to testify. The self-incrimination provision also outlaws involuntary confessions. It prohibits any coercion or physical abuse by law-enforcement personnel to force a suspect to confess. Confessions must be voluntarily and freely given if they are to be used as evidence against a person at his trial.

In the 1960s, the Supreme Court handed down two rulings designed to discourage involuntarily obtained confessions. The first of these, issued in the case of *Escobedo* v. *Illinois*,[23] held that at all critical stages of the criminal process beginning with arrest the accused must have access to legal counsel. With an attorney present, police are much less likely to convince a suspect to make incriminating statements. Second, in *Miranda* v. *Arizona*,[24] the Court ruled that upon arrest criminal defendants must be informed of their constitutional rights to remain silent, to have the assistance of counsel, and to have a lawyer provided for them if they are indigents; and they must be told that any statements they make may be used as evidence against them in a court of law. These decisions prompted a great deal of criticism from the law-enforcement agencies as well as the public, but contrary to the fears of many, there has been no noticeable decrease in law-enforcement because of them.

Fair Trials and the Right to Counsel

The Fifth Amendment also guarantees that no person can be put on trial more than once for the same offense. This provision was designed to prohibit the practice of prosecutors repeatedly trying an individual until at long last a conviction is obtained. Such prosecutorial harassment had been a practice in certain European countries. As applied to our criminal justice system, this guarantee means that once a person is found by a court to be not guilty of an offense, he may never be tried again for that same crime. The prosecutor has but one opportunity to convict a person of a specific offense. If an acquittal occurs, the prosecutor is given no second chance. The protection against double jeopardy, of course, does not bar the defendant from requesting a retrial when he feels that his first court hearing was improperly conducted. Nor do double jeopardy rights prohibit the government from retrying a defendant when the jury is unable to agree on a verdict after the first trial. The purpose of this constitutional protection is only to prevent the government from harassing an individual who has already been acquitted of criminal accusations by subjecting him to subsequent trials on the same charges.

The Sixth Amendment contains a host of criminal rights. It first guarantees the criminally accused a speedy and public trial. This provision prevents the government from arresting a person and then holding him in jail for extensive periods of time without conducting an impartial trial. It furthermore guarantees that the trial is conducted in public where it can be placed under citizen scrutiny. This amendment seeks to outlaw the secret Star Chamber trials so detested by the people during certain periods of English history.

During the trial itself the Sixth Amendment protects the objectivity of the proceedings by granting that the accused will have ample notice of the charges. This allows the defendant to come to trial having had sufficient time to prepare a defense against the charges preferred against him. The prosecution is obligated to produce the witnesses who have brought evidence or accusations against the defendant; and the defendant is entitled to cross-examine those witnesses. Furthermore, the defendant has been granted the constitutional right to produce evidence in his own behalf and has the right to request that the government compel witnesses favorable to the defense to testify at the trial. The decision as to the guilt or innocence of the defendant relative to the official criminal charges against him is to be decided by an impartial jury. This has been interpreted by the courts to mean that each defendant is entitled to be tried by a jury that generally represents a cross-section of the community. No official discrimination may be employed in the jury selection process which would systematically exclude members of any racial, ethnic, economic, or sexual classification. Furthermore, the defendant has the right to be tried by persons who are not biased in their attitudes regarding his possible guilt.

Perhaps the most important of the Sixth Amendment rights is the right to counsel. Until 1938 this provision of the Sixth Amendment was interpreted to mean that if the individual desired to hire the services of an attorney he was entitled to have that lawyer present during the various stages of the criminal process. However, in the case of *Johnson* v. *Zerbst*,[25] the Supreme Court ruled that the right to counsel meant much more than bestowing upon the economically secure the right to the assistance of a lawyer. The Court held that indigent persons who did not have the funds to purchase the services of an attorney were entitled to have the government provide counsel for them. To do otherwise would be to perpetuate one standard of justice for the rich and a much lower standard of justice for the poor. The 1938 decision was restricted to prosecutions in federal courts only. It was not until 1963, in the famous case of *Gideon* v. *Wainwright*,[26] that the Supreme Court extended the *Johnson* v. *Zerbst* rationale to prosecutions in state courts. Today the right to have an attorney for advice and preparation of a defense against criminal charges begins with the arrest stage and continues throughout every critical stage in the process. Attorneys may be present at all pretrial stages (excluding grand jury hearings) that are important to the process, at the trial itself, and even to the appeals stage and certain postconviction relief hearings. If the charged person is without the economic resources to retain an attorney, then the government must provide one for him.

The Cruel and Unusual Punishment Clause and the Death Penalty

The final amendment dealing specifically with criminal due process rights is the Eighth. In this amendment the Framers restricted the kinds of criminal punishments which the government could impose on persons charged with or convicted of crimes. The Eighth Amendment stipulates: "Excessive bail shall not be required, nor excessive fines imposed, nor cruel and unusual punishments inflicted." In recent years the most significant aspect of the Eighth Amendment has been its ban on cruel and unusual punishments. Originally this provision was intended to prohibit such punishments as the rack, the stocks, crucifixion, dismemberment, and other types of penalties which inflict great pain and suffering. For the most part the various jurisdictions in the United States have not attempted to impose such penalties. Consequently, the Supreme Court has rarely found any violations of this section of the Eighth Amendment. Even in the case of Willie Francis and a second electrocution attempt the Supreme Court did not find any violation of this provision. There has, however, been a long history of attempts to have the courts declare capital punishment unconstitutional. The Supreme Court has seriously addressed this issue twice during the past decade. Under current interpretations of the Constitution, capital punishment for murder is not in violation of the cruel and unusual punishment provision unless it is applied in an arbitrary or discriminatory manner.[27] It is doubtful that the Supreme Court has heard its last death penalty case. Opponents of capital punishment undoubtedly will attempt new legal challenges to using execution as a criminal penalty.

During the 1960s, the liberal Supreme Court, led by Chief Justice Earl Warren, extended the expanded various criminal due process rights to those charged with crimes. Never had the criminally accused been granted so many procedural safeguards. To many citizens the Supreme Court had gone too far in protecting the rights of the criminally accused. In 1968, President Nixon campaigned on a pledge to appoint persons to the Court who were not so sympathetic to the plight of persons charged with violations of criminal law. True to his word, Nixon appointed four justices to the Court who could be described as favoring a "law and order" position. These new appointments were enough to change the balance of power on the Court, and today, under Chief Justice Warren Burger, the Supreme Court is much more conservative and less willing to expand procedural safeguards for those on trial for criminal offenses.

The Right to Privacy

As we noted in chapter 2 the meaning of the Constitution is constantly changing by interpretation and by changes in custom and tradition. In the area of civil liberties we often find rights evolving through court decisions. Such is the case with the right to privacy. One can read the Constitution of the United States and all of its amendments and never see the word privacy. Nowhere is it specifically protected. At the same time most people would agree that in a free society individuals should be protected against unwarranted intrusions by governments into private lives. Because of this general agreement that the right to privacy needs to be recognized, it has evolved through several decisions of the United States Supreme Court. And today the right to privacy is one of the most vigorous liberties enjoyed by Americans.

The Supreme Court did not officially recognize a right to privacy until 1965 in *Griswold* v. *Connecticut*.[28] Before that time the Court had found other constitutional or statutory provisions to discourage blatant government infringements into the private lives of citizens, but had balked at officially recognizing the right. The *Griswold* case challenged the constitutionality of a Connecticut statute that made it unlawful to use birth control devices or to give out information or instruction in their use. Estelle Griswold, a director of the state Planned Parenthood League, had been convicted of giving out birth control information in violation of the law. She challenged the statute as an unconstitutional infringement on the fundamental right of privacy in marriage. A majority of the Court favored striking down the statute, but this was difficult to do, since a right to privacy was not officially mentioned in the Constitution. The result was a seven-to-two vote in favor of Ms. Griswold, but the majority was unable to agree on a specific rationale for the decision. Justice Douglas argued that the right to privacy was formed out of several other constitutional rights, including the right against unreasonable searches and seizures, the right against quartering soldiers, and the right against self-incrimination. Justice Goldberg said that the right to privacy should be interpreted as being protected by the Ninth Amendment, which states: "The enumeration in the Constitution, of certain rights, shall not be construed to deny or disparage others retained by the people." Justice Harlan argued that the right to privacy was part of the general protection against violations of "due process of law." But regardless of their various reasons for upholding it, the majority collectively agreed that the right to privacy was protected by the Constitution. In dissent, Justice Hugo Black argued that the Court had no business creating a new constitutional right that was not included in the Constitution. If the people desired constitutional protection for the right to privacy, Black contended, they should amend the Constitution to that effect. If such an amendment were to be ratified, Black noted, he would vigorously uphold it, but until that time he was unable to recognize a constitutional right that could nowhere be found in the words of the Constitution.

All of the repercussions of the *Griswold* case have yet to be felt. By recognizing the right to privacy the Supreme Court opened up a broad area for litigation. Already the Court has followed up the privacy decision by striking down a Georgia law that made it a criminal offense to possess obscene materials even if those materials were for private, personal use only[29] and by ruling that bans against distributing birth control devices or information to unmarried persons violated the privacy rights protected by the Constitution.[30] Most significant, the Court has ruled that the right to privacy prohibits the state from disallowing abortions during the first six months of pregnancy.[31] The decision on whether to bear or beget a child is a private personal choice that cannot be restricted by the state. The lower federal courts as well as the state courts have already been faced with numerous cases that challenge laws against homosexual relationships between consenting adults on the grounds that such laws are contrary to the constitutionally protected right to privacy. Similarly, privacy rights have been alleged to protect individuals who possess illegal drugs for private personal use, engage in prostitution, gamble, or are participants in a great number of various kinds of activities that are often classified as "victimless crimes." How far the right to privacy will be extended in the coming years in the face of pending lawsuits will be an interesting constitutional development to follow.

Discrimination

We often hear claims of unconstitutional discriminatory actions on the part of the government. These claims usually allege that the government is treating some group (usually racial, sexual, or economic) unfairly. The constitutional basis for such claims is found in the Equal Protection Clause of the Fourteenth Amendment, which, as we previously noted, holds that no state shall "deny to any person within its jurisdiction the equal protection of the laws." The purpose of the Equal Protection Clause was to eliminate state discrimination against black citizens. It was proposed and finally ratified in 1868 as part of the Reconstruction program following the Civil War. While the intention of the provision clearly was to grant equal stature under the law to former slaves, the wording of the amendment does not specifically restrict its application to any particular group. It is a general provision which applied to state discrimination against any person or group. Therefore, the Equal Protection Clause has been applied to racial discrimination as well as discrimination based upon sex, economic class, ethnic group, or other classificatory schemes considered irrational.

The Equal Protection Clause

For a violation of the Equal Protection Clause to occur, two requirements need to be met. First, there must be some form of "state action." The Equal Protection Clause was designed to stop public governmental discrimination. It was not intended to eliminate discriminatory actions by private persons. Therefore, before a successful case may be brought to Court alleging a Fourteenth Amendment violation, some form of action by the state government must be shown. This may be in the form of a state law or administrative regulation, action by state officials, or actions taken by state agencies. It is important to note that the Fourteenth Amendment only outlaws discrimination by state governments (or their subdivisions). It does not prohibit discrimination by the federal government. The courts, however, have compensated for this by interpreting the Fifth Amendment's Due Process Clause as prohibiting the federal government from discriminating on the basis of arbitrary criteria.[32] The second requirement is that some form of discrimination must be proven. It must be shown that unequal treatment was perpetuated by the government. If both elements are present, state action as well as discrimination, then a violation has occurred.

Obviously, not all forms of discrimination or unequal treatment are prohibited by the Fourteenth Amendment. States discriminate with almost every regulation and law passed. For example, the state may allow one person to practice medicine and yet deny this right to another. Such discrimination may be based on whether or not a person has met the required educational and testing standards. One person may be allowed to operate a factory on his land, and another may be denied such a right. The discrimination in this case may be based on the appropriate zoning regulations. No one has ever contended that the Fourteenth Amendment was designed to forbid reasonable discrimination. What the amendment was intended to do was to curtail "invidious" discrimination. The courts have interpreted the term "invidious" to mean discrimination without a rational basis.

Racial Discrimination

The longest history of litigation in this area has been based upon unequal treatment of racial minorities. At first the courts allowed a certain degree of discrimination based upon race in accordance with the separate but equal doctrine. This legal doctrine held that it was permissible under the meaning of the Equal Protection Clause to dictate segregated facilities based on race, as long as the facilities were in all other respects equal. The United States Supreme Court gave its approval to this doctrine in 1896 in the case of *Plessy* v. *Ferguson*.[33] Homer Plessy had challenged the constitutionality of a Louisiana statute that segregated railroad cars on the basis of race. The Supreme Court upheld the Louisiana statute on the ground that as long as the railroad cars were equal (similar accommodations, schedules, and routes) the requirements of the Equal Protection Clause were met. That constitutional provision did not dictate the mixing of the races, but only that they be treated equally.

The separate but equal doctrine was the approved interpretation of the Constitution until the year 1954, when an entirely new interpretation of the Fourteenth Amendment was proclaimed. Linda Carol Brown, an eight-year-old Kansas girl, had been denied the right to go to a public school just four blocks from her residence on the grounds that she was black. The schools of Topeka, Kansas were segregated on the basis of race, and in order to receive public education, she was required to attend a black school in another section of the city. Her father filed suit in her behalf challenging the constitutionality of the Kansas statute that required racial segregation of the public schools. The case was ultimately decided by the U.S. Supreme Court in the suit now known as *Brown* v. *Board of Education of Topeka, Kansas*.[34] In that case a unanimous Supreme Court, in an opinion written by the newly appointed Chief Justice Earl Warren, struck down the Kansas statute and with it the old separate but equal doctrine. Legal segregation of the public schools, the Court declared, was inherently unequal. To place students into special schools solely on the basis of racial classification was to assign them a badge of inferiority. From that date on, racial segregation of public schools was no longer permissible under the meaning of the Fourteenth Amendment's Equal Protection Clause.

The *Brown* decision initiated a long line of rulings handed down by the Supreme Court in the area of racial discrimination. The Court consistently held that it was a violation of the Fourteenth Amendment for any state to make or enforce laws that discriminated on the basis of race. Race, according to the Court, by its very nature was an arbitrary criterion upon which to classify individuals. The Court declared race a constitutionally "suspect class." Consistent with this position, the Court struck down laws that commanded segregation of parks, jails, and other public facilities. It ruled antimiscegenation laws unconstitutional as well as a long list of other state regulations that treated blacks and whites unequally or otherwise distributed governmental benefits or protections on the basis of race. It is abundantly clear that any program or policy of any state government which classifies according to race is constitutionally suspect.

While the principle that government-imposed discrimination based upon race is unconstitutional has been firmly established, the question of remedies remains clouded. How far must government go to erase present and future racial discrimination as well as remove the effects of past segregation? This question has been particularly troublesome in dealing with school desegregation. In order to remedy past discriminatory policies, federal courts have often ordered school districts to institute policies clearly designed to accomplish racial integration. These policies have included integration of teaching faculties, merging schools, modifying school attendance zones, and busing students to schools outside their residential areas.[35] There has been a good deal of public criticism of these policies, particularly those that call for students to attend schools outside their neighborhoods or in school districts other than their own. All of the constitutional questions involving implementation of desegregation orders have not been answered by the courts, and this area continues to be one of the more perplexing ones facing the judiciary.

Sex Discrimination

In recent years questions of sex discrimination have been increasingly brought before the American courts. In the absence of the ratification of the proposed Equal Rights Amendment,[36] claims of sex discrimination have been based on the Equal Protection Clause. The response of the Supreme Court to questions of official sex discrimination has been similar to its rulings on the race issue. The difference between the Court's decisions on race and sex discrimination has been a matter of degree. While the Court has said that any discrimination based upon race is presumed to be unconstitutional, its pronouncements on sex discrimination have not been so unequivocal. The position of the Court has been that any arbitrary discrimination based upon sexual classification is unconstitutional. This leaves the door open for the possibility that some forms of reasonable sex discrimination may be permissible. Nonetheless, the actual decisions of the Court have overwhelmingly been in favor of individuals who have claimed that their rights have been violated. For example, the Court has struck down laws that give preference to males in the managing of estates,[37] place a burden on female participation in jury service,[38] allow women to reach legal maturity at an earlier age than men,[39] impose different standards for receiving military benefits based upon sex,[40] and create arbitrary employment regulations for pregnant workers.[41] The area of sex discrimination law has been expanding rapidly. Not only is the Fourteenth Amendment's Equal Protection Clause involved, but there is the possibility that the Equal Rights Amendment may be ratified in the near future. Such an addition to the Constitution would undoubtedly precipitate an avalanche of litigation on questions of discrimination based upon sex.

Racial and sex discrimination have enjoyed the constitutional spotlight in recent years, but these specific forms of discrimination have not been the only ones the judiciary has been forced to consider. Problems involved with governmental discrimination based upon economic status, property ownership, residency, and legitimacy have also come before the Supreme Court. In each of these areas, the response of the Supreme Court has been similar. If the government can prove that the discrimination imposed is based upon a rational foundation, then the Court is likely to rule that the Fourteenth Amendment's Equal Protection Clause has not been violated. If, on the other hand, those persons challenging the discrimination can show that it is arbitrary or unreasonable, then the Court is likely to strike down the discriminatory policy.

Affirmative Discrimination

The most controversial current issue in the field of discrimination law is the question of affirmative discrimination. The theory of affirmative discrimination can be applied to almost any group of individuals who have been discriminated against in the past. Proponents of affirmative discrimination argue that the only way to rectify the negative consequences of past discrimination is to practice reverse discrimination for a period of time until the effects of past discrimination are eliminated. Under this interpretation of the Fourteenth Amendment, government would be required not only to stop discriminating but also to employ certain measures to insure that equality is brought about. If, for example, blacks have been underrepresented in state government jobs, the state might institute an employment policy that would bring the proportion of minority workers up to their approximate percentage of the general state population. Similarly, a state law school or medical school might pursue an admissions policy that would guarantee that a certain percentage of its students would be from designated minority groups. Policies such as these insure that minorities will not be discriminated against, but opponents argue that the natural consequence of such programs is to discriminate against majority students. It is quite possible, for example, that an otherwise qualified white male might be denied admission to a professional school not because of a lack of ability, but solely because the school has reserved a certain number of entrance positions for minority applicants, some of whom may be less qualified than the student who has been denied admission. This, according to opponents, should be declared unconstitutional on the grounds that discriminating against majorities is no less constitutionally invalid than discriminating against members of minority groups. The Supreme Court has yet to devise a satisfactory answer to the question of affirmative discrimination, but in the very near future it will have to address itself to this issue.

The Supreme Court and Civil Liberties

Today American society looks to the judiciary, and particularly the Supreme Court, for definitive answers on questions involving civil rights. Furthermore, we expect the courts to defend basic liberties and to provide remedies when those rights are violated. The tendency to rely on the federal judiciary in such matters, however, is a relatively recent phenomenon. While the

Supreme Court has been visibly active in civil rights over the last three decades, historically the courts have not been particularly vigorous in this area. The role of the Supreme Court as a defender of our liberties is largely a twentieth-century development. Prior to that time, the Court rarely handed down a ruling in cases presenting civil rights questions. When the Court did answer a civil liberties claim, it almost always pertained to federal encroachments on civil rights. The Court did not consider as part of its role the surveillance of possible state denials of civil rights. Instead, the High Court was more interested in property rights, contract obligations, governmental powers, and federal relationships. The question of civil liberties was largely left to the state governments.

During the last thirty years, however, the Supreme Court has been primarily a civil liberties court. Almost all of the important rulings issued by the nation's highest tribunal during this period have been related to governmental deprivations of basic constitutional rights. The Court has been particularly active in striking down state statutes and administrative actions that restrict protected liberties. When judged by historical standards, the last thirty years have truly constituted a civil liberties revolution. No area of basic rights has been left untouched.

The rapid pace of changes in civil liberties law that occurred under Earl Warren's leadership of the Supreme Court during the 1950s and 1960s, however, has slowed in recent years. This is largely attributable to President Richard Nixon's 1968 campaign pledge to appoint members of the Court who were less prone to assume an activist posture. The Nixon appointees have had a decided impact on the development of civil liberties law. While the Court is still enlarging the sphere of protected liberties, the growth rate has decreased. Furthermore, the Court has failed to go beyond the advances of the Warren Court in areas such as racial desegregation[42] and the rights of the criminally accused.[43] The contemporary Court is also less likely to impose strict supervision over the way in which the states deal with civil liberties questions.[44]

In addition, it should be remembered that the federal judiciary is not the only government agency that has been active in the protection of civil rights. Many of the basic rights now enforced have been the product of acts of Congress. Obvious examples are the Civil Rights Act of 1964 and the Voting Rights Act of 1965. Federal administrative regulations passed by such agencies as the Department of Health, Education and Welfare have reduced the number of remaining incidents of racial and sexual discrimination. The state governments have also been leaders in the development of civil liberties protections. Several states, for example, adopted equal rights laws or constitutional amendments far in advance of the Equal Rights Amendment actions taken by the federal government.

All this, of course, does not reduce the importance of the Supreme Court's role in the area of civil rights. The Court remains the final voice in the interpretation of American liberties. It alone may provide the last answer to questions of governmental deprivation of basic liberties. This very fact, along with the Court's contemporary interest in civil liberties questions, accounts for the tendency of Americans to look to the judiciary for leadership in matters relating to constitutional rights.

Summary

One of the most significant aspects of the United States Constitution is that it guarantees certain basic civil liberties. Americans have placed such a great importance on prohibiting government infringements on personal freedoms that we have reserved a place in our most fundamental law for the protection of those rights. These liberties fall into five basic categories: freedom of religion, freedom of expression, criminal due process, personal privacy, and freedom from unreasonable governmental discrimination. While the original intention of the Bill of Rights was to protect Americans from abuses by the federal government, interpretations of the Due Process Clause of the Fourteenth Amendment have extended these protections to abuses by state governments as well.

The judiciary has played an important role in the development of our constitutionally protected freedoms. As we have seen, the courts have been called upon to interpret the meaning of the Bill of Rights and other constitutional amendments involving personal liberties. The courts have often expanded the meaning of certain liberties and interpreted freedoms in light of contemporary conditions. At times, such as with respect to the right to privacy, the courts have even created new rights and given them constitutional status.

A free society cannot long endure without the protection of basic civil liberties. A republican form of government, if it is to be successful, demands a certain degree of informed participation by the citizenry. Citizens must be free to express their views openly and without fear of repression. They must be free to worship as they see fit. They must be confident that excessive governmental intrusion into their private matters will be curtailed. They must be assured that the prosecutorial arm of government will not move against them without observing fair procedures. And they must be assured that the government will not discriminate against them simply because of their membership in a specific racial, sexual, economic, or other group.

Notes

1. 329 U.S. 459 (1947).
2. 7 Pet. 243 (1833).
3. 302 U.S. 319 (1937).
4. 175 U.S. 291 (1899).
5. 330 U.S. 1 (1947).
6. Board of Education v. Allen, 392 U.S. 236 (1968).
7. Lemon v. Kurtzman, 403 U.S. 602 (1971).
8. Roemer v. Board of Public Works of Maryland, 426 U.S. 736 (1976).
9. 370 U.S. 421 (1962).
10. The New York prayer read: "Almighty God, we acknowledge our dependence upon Thee, and we beg Thy blessings upon us, our parents, our teachers and our country."
11. 374 U.S. 203 (1963).
12. Ibid.
13. Reynolds v. United States, 98 U.S. 145 (1879).
14. United States v. Ballard, 322 U.S. 78 (1944).
15. Sherbert v. Verner, 374 U.S. 398 (1963).
16. Douglas v. City of Jeanette, 319 U.S. 157 (1943).
17. Murdock v. Pennsylvania, 319 U.S. 105 (1943).
18. Vale v. Louisiana, 399 U.S. 30 (1970).
19. Cupp v. Murphy, 412 U.S. 291 (1973).
20. Bumper v. North Carolina, 391 U.S. 543 (1968).
21. See Adams v. Williams, 407 U.S. 143 (1972); United States v. Robinson, 414 U.S. 218 (1973).
22. Mapp v. Ohio, 367 U.S. 643 (1961).
23. 378 U.S. 478 (1964).
24. 384 U.S. 436 (1966).
25. 304 U.S. 458 (1938).
26. 372 U.S. 335 (1963).
27. Furman v. Georgia, 408 U.S. 238 (1972); Gregg v. Georgia, 428 U.S. 153 (1976).
28. 381 U.S. 479 (1965).
29. Stanley v. Georgia, 394 U.S. 557 (1969).
30. Eisenstadt v. Baird, 405 U.S. 438 (1972).
31. Roe v. Wade, 410 U.S. 113 (1973); Doe v. Bolton, 410 U.S. 179 (1973).
32. Bolling v. Sharpe, 347 U.S. 497 (1954).
33. Plessy v. Ferguson, 163 U.S. 537 (1896).
34. 347 U.S. 483 (1954).
35. Swann v. Charlotte Mecklenburg County Board of Education, 402 U.S. 1 (1971).
36. The proposed Twenty-Seventh Amendment states: "Equality of rights under the law shall not be denied or abridged by the United States or by any State on account of sex."
37. Reed v. Reed, 404 U.S. 71 (1971).
38. Taylor v. Louisiana, 419 U.S. 522 (1975).
39. Stanton v. Stanton, 421 U.S. 7 (1975).

40. Frontiero v. Richardson, 411 U.S. 677 (1973).
41. Cleveland Board of Education v. LaFleur, 414 U.S. 632 (1974).
42. Milliken v. Bradley, 418 U.S. 717 (1974).
43. Oregon v. Mathiason, 97 S. Ct. 711 (1977).
44. Younger v. Harris, 401 U.S. 37 (1971).

Further Reading

Abraham, Henry J. *Freedom and the Court*. New York: Oxford University Press, 3rd ed., 1977.

Casper, Jonathan D. *The Politics of Civil Liberties*. New York: Harper and Row, 1972.

Dionisopoulos, P. Allan, and Craig, R. Ducat. *The Right to Privacy*. St. Paul: West Publishing Company, 1976.

Dorsen, Norman. *Discrimination and Civil Rights*. Boston: Little, Brown, 1969.

Glazer, Nathan. *Affirmative Discrimination*. New York: Basic Books, 1975.

Graglia, Lino A. *Disaster by Decree*. Ithaca, N.Y.: Cornell University Press, 1976.

Meltsner, Michael. *Cruel and Unusual*. New York: Morrow, 1974.

Morgan, Richard. *The Supreme Court and Religion*. New York: Free Press, 1972.

Sigler, Jay A. *Double Jeopardy*. Ithaca, N.Y.: Cornell University Press, 1969.

Sorauf, Frank J. *The Wall of Separation*. Princeton, N.J.: Princeton University Press, 1976.

Tresolini, Rocco J. *These Liberties*. Philadelphia: J. B. Lippincott, 1968.

Way, H. Frank, Jr. *Liberty in the Balance*. New York: McGraw-Hill, 4th ed., 1976.

Part 2

The Constitution and Political Participation

Public Opinion and the
Expression of Political Views

Elections and Voting Rights

Political Parties and
Interest Groups

Public Opinion and the
Expression of Political Views

Chapter four

Expressing Political Attitudes:
Cohen v. *California*

On April 26, 1968, Paul Robert Cohen entered the Los Angeles County Court-house. As he walked down the courthouse corridor people may have stared at him or looked at him a bit strangely, but his trip down the hall was uneventful. Reaching the courtroom of his interest, Cohen entered the chamber, removed his jacket, and quietly sat down. He observed the proceedings for a period of time and then peacefully left the courtroom. Upon reentering the hallway Cohen was met by law-enforcement officers who placed him under arrest. He was charged with willfully and unlawfully and maliciously disturbing the peace by "engaging in tumultuous and offensive conduct." The arrest initiated more than three years of legal hearings which ultimately received the attention of the United States Supreme Court.

The reason for Cohen's arrest was not his demeanor in the courthouse, nor any spoken words, nor any reaction from others that he may have provoked. It was his jacket. In bold letters on the jacket were displayed two slogans voicing opposition to the United States war effort in Vietnam, accompanied by a large peace symbol. One of the slogans was a call to "Stop War." The other expressed hostile feelings toward the United States Selective Service System and included a word that most mature citizens would consider offensive and inappropriate for use in a public place. The particular word inscribed on the jacket technically denotes an act of unlawful carnal knowl-edge, but in American slang is often used to express intense feelings. The clear message emanating from the jacket was that Cohen had rather negative feelings about the possibility of being drafted.

According to information at his trial, Cohen, a nineteen-year-old department store employee, had attended a meeting of individuals opposed to the war on the night before his appearance at the courthouse. During that meeting one of the persons in attendance had written the words in question on Cohen's jacket. Although he did not participate in placing the words on the jacket, Cohen was fully aware that they had been inscribed. When questioned about why he had knowingly worn the jacket in the public courthouse, Cohen offered two reasons, one practical and the other principled. First, he noted that it was a chilly day and comfort required some form of outer garment. The jacket in question was the only one he owned of a weight appropriate for the day. Second, the jacket was worn to express his feelings about United States policy in Southeast Asia. The trial court did not find these reasons compelling and sentenced Cohen to thirty days in the Los Angeles County jail. With the support of the Southern California Civil Liberties Union, Cohen appealed his conviction on constitutional grounds. Attorneys in his behalf argued that the freedom of expression provisions of the First Amendment had been violated when the state of California ordered Cohen to go to jail for expressing his attitudes about the war. Four different appeals hearings were conducted within the California judicial system, ending with the state supreme court rejecting Cohen's petitions. The final appeal was to the United States Supreme Court.

When the appeal of Paul Robert Cohen was argued before the Supreme Court, the primary issue was whether or not California had unconstitutionally infringed on the freedom of expression. Attorneys for both sides clashed over several different points of constitutional interpretation. First, there was the question of whether the First Amendment was applicable in this case at all. California authorities argued that Cohen had not engaged in speech as protected by the First Amendment, but that his 1968 walk down the courthouse corridor was conduct. The state contended that since conduct and not speech was at issue, authorities had full power to take action against Cohen. Cohen's attorneys refused to accept this interpretation, arguing that "speech" in a constitutional sense covers more than mere spoken words. The First Amendment was designed to protect the freedom to express opinions and attitudes, especially those dealing with matters of public concern. Expressing political views can take many forms other than traditional forms of speech, including the method of communication chosen by Cohen.

Second, the parties clashed over the impact of Cohen's expression. Lawyers representing the antiwar youth argued that there was no justification for the state to take action since Cohen's expression did not cause a breakdown in public order or promote any other substantive evil that California had a right to stop. Short of such negative consequences, the state was not constitutionally permitted to restrict freedom of speech. California countered with the argument that the Constitution does not dictate that authorities must wait until an emergency situation occurs before taking action. The state argued that Cohen's jacket constituted an expression of "fighting words" which could cause an immediate provocation of disorder and a threat to the orderly conducting of business in a governmental building. So offensive was Cohen's message to many people that the state deemed it necessary to take action before violence actually erupted.

Third, the state claimed that it had proper authority to arrest Cohen on the grounds that his expression fell under the power of the state to regulate obscenity. Obscenity has always been considered outside the protections of the First Amendment, and the words Cohen used were obscene. To rule that Cohen's expression was constitutionally protected would mean that anyone could publicly display the grossest obscenities, which would ultimately lead to a breakdown in public order and morality. Cohen's lawyers countered by arguing that the incident was clearly outside the normal definitions of obscenity. While the word used might have sexual connotations in some contexts, it was not used by Cohen in such a way as to incite lustful or lascivious thoughts or actions on the part of others. Antiobscenity statutes are intended to curtail pandering to prurient interests. Cohen's expression was political speech, not expression designed to incite sexual depravities.

Finally, the litigants disagreed on the issue of the rights of the public who happened to be in the courthouse corridor at the time Cohen displayed his artistically adorned outer garment. The state claimed that it had the right to protect the interests of the unsuspecting public who found themselves faced with Cohen's offensive expression. A public courthouse in which both women and children are commonly found should be kept free of the type of conduct engaged in by Cohen. The public's right to privacy includes the freedom from having obscenities thrust upon them in a public building dedicated to the orderly processing of law. Cohen's representatives claimed that if the First Amendment is to have any meaning, it must protect political expression directed at persons who do not necessarily agree with the communicator's position. The First Amendment would be virtually meaningless if it only protected the right to express views to individuals already in agreement. American society was founded on the concept of the free marketplace of ideas. To enter public places in a free society is to take the risk of coming into contact with opinions divergent from one's own views. This is one price that must be paid for a free and open society.

Constitutional scholars waited with a great deal of interest while the Supreme Court deliberated on the *Cohen* case. The Court had just undergone a considerable change in personnel. Chief Justice Earl Warren had retired and been replaced by Richard Nixon's nominee, Warren Burger. Associate Justice Abe Fortas had resigned under criticism of his ethical conduct and had been replaced by another Nixon appointee, Justice Harry Blackmun. Both Burger and Blackmun were considered to be more conservative on civil liberty issues than the men they replaced. Many people thought these changes in personnel would tip the balance of power to the conservative wing of the Court. Cohen's appeal was one of the first tests of the "new" Court. Everyone knew that the vote would be close, but which side would be the victor was completely in doubt.

On June 7, 1971, as the Court was approaching its traditional summer recess, the decision on Cohen's appeal was announced. The majority opinion was written by Justice John Marshall Harlan. The Court could not have made a better choice in selecting a spokesman for its decision. Harlan was undoubtedly the Court's most dignified member. He possessed an aristocratic bearing and a noble manner that allowed him to treat Cohen's vulgarities with constitutional solemnity. His scholarly prose drew a stark contrast with Cohen's tawdry jacket. His sixteen years on the Court were marked with a learned conservatism that earned him the respect of constitutional scholars of both liberal and conservative persuasions.

Harlan announced that the Court, with four justices in dissent, reversed Cohen's conviction, finding the actions of the state of California unacceptable to the standards imposed by the First Amendment.[1] First, the Court held that Cohen's expression was protected under the freedom of speech provisions of the Constitution. Cohen was communicating his views on the government's war policy; there was no "conduct" beyond this pure act of communication of opinion. Second, the Court stressed the fact that there was no reaction by the people in the courthouse. No violence, no breakdown in order, no interruption of the orderly flow of governmental business. Nor was there any substantive threat to a breakdown in order. In the absence of an immediate and clear threat to public order, the state was not entitled to restrict the expression of political views. Third, the Court dismissed the obscenity issue. Obscenity regulation is the regulation of expression that is in some way erotic. In the words of Justice Harlan: "It cannot possibly be maintained that this vulgar allusion to the Selective Service System would conjure up such psychic stimulation in anyone likely to be confronted with Cohen's crudely defaced jacket." Finally, the Court did not find the rights of public privacy to have been violated by Cohen's expression. The First Amendment prohibits the state from restricting political expression that happens to be unwelcome to some persons. Cohen did not force his message on any person. He moved down the hallway in an orderly fashion. He did not act so as to bring attention to his jacket. Those members of the public who saw the message could easily remove its impact by a turn of the head.

After rejecting each of the arguments of the state of California in orderly progression, Harlan turned to what may well be the most compelling aspect of this case: the ultimate importance of the First Amendment as the foundation of a free society. Harlan's words express well the great significance the Court attaches to First Amendment protections:

> The constitutional right of free expression is powerful medicine in a society as diverse and populous as ours. It is designed and intended to remove governmental restraints from the arena of public discussion, putting the decision as to what views shall be voiced largely into the hands of each of us, in the hope that use of such freedom will ultimately produce a more capable citizenry and more perfect polity and in the belief that no other approach would comport with the premise of individual dignity and choice upon which our political system rests. . . . For, while the particular four-letter word being litigated here is perhaps more distasteful than most others of its genre, it is nevertheless often true that one's man vulgarity is another's lyric.

Justice Harlan was never to return to the Court following the summer recess of 1971. *Cohen* v. *California* was one of his last written opinions. In August of 1971 Harlan entered the hospital. Shortly thereafter came the announcement that poor health was forcing his resignation from the Court. Four months later, Justice John Marshall Harlan died, leaving the Court with a noticeable gap which was not to be easily filled.

Democratic governments are designed to respond to the will of the people, and public opinion comprises much of the fuel upon which such governments are run. Unless they are expressed, the attitudes of the citizenry are of no use to democratic governmental institutions. Private opinions must become public opinions. The First Amendment guarantees the integrity of the public opinion process. Not all opinion is well received. Much of it is unpopular opinion, which expresses views contrary to the will of the majority and those holding positions of political power. The First Amendment guarantees protection for the right to express opinion no matter how unpopular that opinion might be. Repression of political expression is directly prohibited. It is not at all an exaggeration to say that democracy in America will only work so long as the First Amendment is zealously enforced. Without a constitutional guarantee that citizens may speak freely, publish freely, associate freely, and freely petition the government for redress of grievances, our republican institutions would gradually erode. For this reason it is important to understand the meaning of the First Amendment with respect to the expression of political views. Without such an understanding, our comprehension of the way in which the American political process operates would be defective.

The *Cohen* case has introduced a number of difficult constitutional questions involving the First Amendment and the expression of political views. What is freedom of speech? When does speech become conduct? Does conduct that conveys a message deserve the same constitutional protection as pure speech? At what point may governments restrict the expression of opinion if it causes a possible breakdown in order? What limitations can be placed on the articulation of opinion? It is to these and other significant questions that we must now turn our attention.

Freedom of Expression and Violent Reactions

As we noted in chapter 3, protections of freedom of speech are not absolute. Certain forms of expression may be validly restricted by government. A traditional justification for infringing on free speech liberties is the responsibility of government to maintain public order. If the exercise of freedom of expression causes a breakdown in safety and order, it is obvious that society must make a choice. It must either tolerate the disturbance of normal order or it must accept restrictions on certain forms of speech. For the most part, American law has chosen the latter. If speech prompts violence, then speech can be curtailed.

The major stumbling block in the application of this principle involves a determination of the point at which authorities may begin to take action that infringes upon expression rights. Consider the example of a street corner speech. Assume that an individual climbs upon a soapbox on the sidewalk of a heavily populated area and begins to deliver an oration expressing his views against Catholics and Jews. Further assume that the speech is filled with hateful language and bitter charges against these two religious minorities. At what point in the delivery of such an address should police be allowed to terminate the exercise of freedom of expression? At the first use of derogatory language? When a crowd begins to form? When members of the crowd begin to taunt the speaker? When the crowd appears on the verge of violent reaction? When a member of the crowd picks up a rock? Or when the rock is thrown in the direction of the speaker? In other words, when can we say that the limits of freedom of expression have been reached and government may take action to insure order and safety? These are not easy questions. To err on the side of speech may mean that bodily harm occurs; but to err on the side of order may mean that freedom is dealt a severe blow.

The United States Supreme Court has not been at all consistent on this question. At times it has ruled that expression must be protected even in the face of rather serious rioting,[2] and at other times it has held that fairly moderate reactions by a crowd are sufficient reason to restrict freedom of speech.[3] In attempting to set a standard for determining a proper resolution of delicate issues such as these, the Court has often developed certain "tests," or judicial criteria, which may be applied to such cases. While the Court generally has been unsuccessful at agreeing upon permanently accepted standards, the "clear and present danger" test is one interesting attempt to develop a formula for the freedom versus order dilemma. The clear and present danger test was first articulated by Justice Oliver Wendell Holmes in 1919.[4] Holmes argued that in cases pitting the freedom of speech against the right of the government to insure order judges should ask "whether the words used are used in such circumstances and are of such a nature as to create a clear and present danger that they will bring about a substantive evil which government has the right to prevent." In applying this standard to the street corner speech, we would say that the police have the right to terminate the speech at the point at which there is a clear danger that violence will erupt and that the danger is immediate. Even this standard does not answer all questions. There can be obvious differences of opinion as to when the danger becomes both clear and present. Such differences must ultimately be resolved by the courts, who are entrusted with the responsibility of balancing the interests of expression and order.

Another standard used to delineate the limits of expression is known as the "fighting words" test. This standard originated in the case of *Chaplinsky* v. *New Hampshire*[5] in 1942. The litigation rose out of the proselytizing efforts of a Jehovah's Witness who was preaching on the streets of Rochester, New Hampshire. In the course of his preaching he made derogatory comments about various organized churches. The city marshal warned him to tone down his presentation. When he refused to do so, the crowd that had gathered became unruly. Police led Chaplinsky away from the scene in order to defuse the situation. Chaplinsky resisted the officials and screamed at a city marshal: "You are a God damned racketeer" and "a damned Fascist, and the whole government of Rochester are Fascists or agents of Fascists." For this outburst police placed Chaplinsky under arrest. After being convicted, Chaplinsky appealed, claiming his rights to freedom of expression had been violated. When the United States Supreme Court received the case, the justices upheld the conviction by unanimous vote and developed the "fighting words" standard. The Court said that certain expressions go beyond the limits of the First Amendment, expressions which by their very nature tend to incite violence.

Decisions such as these indicate that the limits of freedom of expression are determined by more than just the expression itself. Courts must also examine the impact of the expression. A person's freedom of speech rights are often determined by the reaction of those upon whose ears the expression falls. Government is given the responsibility to insure that relative order and safety exist on the streets. At times this obligation prompts officials to curtail expression. When this occurs it is the duty of the judiciary to determine whether the government has acted in an overzealous fashion, or whether the expression has transgressed the normal limits of constitutional protection.

Collective Expression

Up to this point we have focused on articulations by a single individual. In contemporary times law-enforcement officials are often faced with public opinion expressed by collections of individuals. This phenomenon was largely born during the civil rights demonstrations of the 1950s and 1960s and the antiwar protests that quickly followed. Collective expression of opinion deserves no less constitutional protection than individual speech. Law-enforcement officials, however, are often more cautious in dealing with mass demonstrations because of the greater potential of serious damage and injury should large groups become disruptive. As in many controversial areas of the law, the Supreme Court has not been able to reach complete agreement on the limits of collective expression, but the decisions handed down by the Court allow for relatively clear standards to be inferred. A comparison of two cases decided by the Court during the period of frequent civil rights demonstrations illustrates some of the criteria employed by the judiciary in drawing the line between expression and public order.

The first of these cases, *Edwards* v. *South Carolina*,[6] decided in 1963, centered on the arrest of 188 protesters who had marched to the South Carolina state capitol in 1961. The object of the march was to protest certain policies of racial discrimination. The group assembled in an orderly fashion in a section of the state capitol complex which was open to the public. Some thirty law-enforcement officers had gathered, anticipating possible violence. The demonstrators sang, gave speeches, and prayed. A crowd of about 250 spectators gathered. There was no substantial threat to public order, no interruption of government business, and no obstruction of traffic flow. Police, fearing that a clash might possibly occur between the demonstrators and the spectators, informed the protesters that they must conclude their activities and disperse within fifteen minutes. If they failed to do so, police officials indicated that arrests would be made. The response of the demonstrators was to continue their activities beyond the fifteen-minute deadline. Police then arrested the demonstrators for breach of peace. Upon their conviction in the lower courts, the demonstrators appealed, claiming that South Carolina authorities had infringed upon their rights to freedom of expression. The Supreme Court accepted their appeal and ruled that the convictions should be reversed. The Court's majority stressed the fact that the Constitution was designed to protect the rights of those who peacefully assemble in order to petition the government for redress of grievances. This is exactly what the protesters were doing. Since there was no violence, no disruption or obstruction, no trespass, and no clear and present danger that any of these events might occur, there was no justification for the action of the police. The protesters had a right to express their opinions at the seat of the state government.

The Court's position on collective expression can best be seen by comparing the *Edwards* decision with the Court's response to the case of *Adderley* v. *Florida*[7] in 1966. This case arose from but one incident during several days of protests by Florida A and M students against racial discrimination. Some two hundred students marched from the school's campus to the local jail, where several of their classmates were being held after being arrested for earlier protest activities. The students sang, clapped, and gave speeches in support of their incarcerated friends. The protesters blocked one of the entrances to the jail and interrupted the flow of vehicular traffic into the jail. After allowing the protest activities to continue for a period of time, sheriff's department employees informed the protesters that they must leave within ten minutes or they would be arrested for trespass. Most of the students obeyed this command and moved away from the area, but several students did not. Sheriff's department officials made good on their promise and proceeded to arrest thirty-two protesters who remained in spite of orders to leave the premises. They were convicted on trespass charges and immediately appealed. The Supreme Court upheld the convictions, citing several differences between the facts in this case and the protests in the *Edwards* decision. In the first place, the *Edwards* protests occurred on government property intended for public use. In *Adderley*, however, the place of protest was a jail, and jails are not places for traditional public gatherings. Second, in *Edwards* there was no blockage of any entryway, but in the *Adderley* case there was evidence that the door to the jail was at least partially blocked. Finally, the protesters in *Adderley* hindered the flow of traffic into the jail area, whereas the protesters in *Edwards* did not impede the flow of any traffic in or around the state capitol grounds.

The position articulated by the Court has been that collective expression clearly comes under the purview of First Amendment protections. Peaceful demonstrations remain outside the authority of the government to regulate. However, law-enforcement authorities may restrict demonstrations and even place individuals under arrest if the protests extend beyond certain established limits. Mass demonstrations must be peaceful, must occur in a location appropriate for such gatherings, and may not impede governmental or other legitimate public business. The protections extended to mass gatherings legitimize them as a major vehicle for the articulation of public opinion.

Symbolic Speech

As American society has become more complex, so too has the variety of ways that Americans express their political views. At the time of the drafting of the First Amendment, political opinions were articulated through speeches, newspaper reports, and pamphleteering. Hence, Amendment One protects "speech" and "press," the two conventional methods of expression. Today individuals often articulate their opinions by methods that go far beyond these traditional means. Many times these more novel forms of expression combine traditional speech and press with various forms of conduct. We can distinguish between "pure speech," which denotes traditional oral expression, and "symbolic speech," which includes various forms of action in the communication process. Since 1968, the Supreme Court has accepted several cases that have required it to resolve the constitutional status of symbolic expression.

On March 31, 1966, David Paul O'Brien and three companions climbed the steps of the South Boston Courthouse and proceeded to burn their Selective Service cards. They admitted that they were engaging in this activity in violation of federal law, but claimed that it was a means of expressing their views on the Vietnam War. Among the crowd assembled to watch the protest were a number of federal agents, who placed O'Brien and his associates under arrest for mutilation and destruction of draft cards. The protesters were convicted, and they appealed on the grounds that First Amendment protections should be extended to symbolic forms of speech such as the burning of a Selective Service card. The Supreme Court upheld the convictions, refusing to extend immunity from federal prosecutions to actions such as those committed by O'Brien.[8] The majority opinion written by Chief Justice Earl Warren held that whenever speech and nonspeech elements of a communicative act are intertwined, a sufficiently important governmental interest in regulating the nonspeech element can justify incidental limitations on

First Amendment freedoms. According to the Court's conclusions, the federal government has a legitimate interest in maintaining an efficient system of conscripting individuals into military service. One of the ways that such a system is conducted includes the draft card method of registration and identification. While the net impact of O'Brien's action may have been minimal, it was an action directed against the implementation of the constitutionally valid policy of the federal government to raise armies. Hence, the government's right to punish individuals for destroying Selective Service cards is well established. The Court did not go so far as to say that no forms of symbolic speech deserve First Amendment protection, but did affirm that the burning of draft cards is not beyond government regulation.

Another symbolic speech case came to the Court the year following the *O'Brien* ruling. High school and junior high school students in Des Moines, Iowa planned a peaceful protest of the government's war effort in Vietnam. The protest called for those opposed to the war to wear black armbands on a designated school day as a symbol of protest. No disruptive activities were planned, nor were normal school affairs to be the target of any protest activity. School officials, fearing that the wearing of armbands might provoke hostilities between the protesters and students with prowar feelings, ordered that the scheduled day of demonstration be canceled. Officials went so far as to promise that students who wore the black armbands would be suspended. Three students wore the symbols of protest and were subsequently suspended. They appealed to the United States Supreme Court, claiming that their actions were a form of symbolic speech that merited the protection of the First Amendment. In this instance the Court found in favor of the students.[9] Unlike the *O'Brien* case, the Court said that the wearing of armbands in no way impeded the legitimate execution of government programs. Since there was no substantive evidence that order might be jeopardized, the school officials had no right to suspend the students for peacefully expressing their views on a public issue.

The black armband case of *Tinker* v. *Des Moines* gave a good deal of encouragement to those who supported extending First Amendment protections to symbolic forms of expression. The next issue to come to the Court involved a much more difficult question of symbolic speech—flag desecration. In rapid succession the Court was forced to hear three cases involving symbolic speech which included disrespectful conduct directed at the American flag. In each case the Court was badly divided. First, in *Street* v. *New York*,[10] the Court, largely on a technicality, reversed the conviction of a New York bus driver who had burned a flag on a public street corner in order to protest the killing of civil rights activist James Meredith. The vote in that case was five to four, with the Court unable to arrive at a satisfactory answer to the question of whether or not the First Amendment protects symbolic speech in the form of showing disrespect for the flag.

It was not long, however, before the Court had a second chance to confront the issue. Stephen Radich, a New York art gallery proprietor, was convicted of being in violation of the state flag desecration statute in that he had publicly displayed the American flag in the form of an erect and protruding male sex organ. Radich claimed that this was a form of artistic expression protesting the Vietnam War. The Supreme Court, with Justice William Douglas not participating, was hopelessly split in a four-to-four deadlock and was, therefore, unable to resolve the thorny question of respect for the flag.[11] Finally, the Court decided the case of *Spence* v. *Washington*,[12] in which a college student had flown an American flag, adorned with a large peace symbol, upside down. He was convicted of violating state statutes prescribing the way the flag was to be flown and handled. He appealed on the grounds that his actions were a form of symbolic speech and deserved the protection of the First Amendment. Spence claimed he was protesting the government's Southeast Asian war policy. The Court was finally able to gather a majority of its members to resolve the issue, holding in a six-to-three vote that the communicative act of Harold Spence expressing his views on an issue of public policy was protected by the First Amendment. The Court, however, made it quite clear in its opinion that the facts in the case did not include any evidence of violence or a breakdown in public order.

The constitutional status of symbolic speech is still a bit unsettled. The termination of the war in Vietnam carried with it a reduction in the number of symbolic free speech protests, and consequently the Court has not recently been faced with major cases involving this issue. Nonetheless, we are able to extract certain principles from the Court's past decisions. First, it is fair to conclude that the Court will grant First Amendment protections to at least some forms of symbolic speech. The Court is not interpreting Amendment One to include only the traditional forms of expression, press, and pure speech. Second, the Court will not tolerate symbolic speech that impedes the execution of a legitimate governmental policy or program. And third, the symbolic speech, if it is to merit First Amendment protection, must be of a peaceful nature and must not incite a violent reaction on the part of others.

Public Opinion and the Mass Media

The public opinion process in the United States includes more than just citizens individually or in groups expressing themselves through speeches, demonstrations, petitions, and certain symbolic acts. It also includes activities by the mass media: newspapers, magazines, and the broadcasters. The mass media are important not only because they express opinion, but also because they provide the citizenry with most of its information about public affairs. The Framers realized the importance of the media by placing freedom of the press protections in the First Amendment. If American society is to remain one in which the people exercise a degree of control over the government, the press must remain open and free. The judiciary has generally been most supportive of the free press provision of the First Amendment, but once again we must note that Amendment One does not give members of the press absolute freedom in their activities. Certain restrictions have been tolerated by the courts.

Censorship and Gag Laws

Perhaps the most important freedom of the press principle embodied in our Constitution is that government is in no way permitted to censor the content of the press. Authorities cannot require that governmental approval be obtained by the press before publishing occurs. This standard was first set in the important decision of *Near* v. *Minnesota*[13] in 1931. The case involved a Minnesota "gag law" which allowed officials to shut down a newspaper that had printed scandalous, malicious, and defamatory material. The newspaper could resume its publishing activities only if it could convince the state judiciary that it would no longer print objectionable material. The Supreme Court struck down the Minnesota law, declaring that it was a classic example of prior censorship, which could not be permitted under First Amendment protections. This does not mean, however, that government cannot take action against a newspaper that in some way breaks a valid law. If, for example, a newspaper prints material that violates criminal libel laws, the responsible parties may be punished. But government cannot move to suppress the publication before it appears in print. This same principle of prior restraint was invoked by the Court in 1971 when the federal government sought to prohibit the *Washington Post* and the *New York Times* from publishing portions of the "Pentagon Papers," which were classified government documents detailing governmental decisions relevant to the Vietnam War policy. The Court held that government could not impose such censorship except in the case of the most extreme danger to national security.[14] The press must be free to print materials related to government activities if the spirit of the First Amendment is to be realized.

Libel Laws and Public Figures

One restriction on freedom of the press always considered permissible under the First Amendment is the prohibition against libel. Libel is written expression that falsely defames the reputation of a person. Libelous statements are those that place a person under ridicule, shame, disgrace, or contempt. Laws against engaging in libel are found in various forms in all of the American states. It is common to allow an individual who has been libeled to sue the parties responsible for damages. In spite of the fact that libel laws obviously curtail what the press may wish to publish, the Supreme Court has said that libel laws do not necessarily violate the First Amendment.[15] But the judiciary in recent years has granted a wide degree of latitude to the press in the publication of statements made about public officials and public figures.[16] In order to insure that the citizenry is given a full, free, and robust debate of public issues, the Court has set standards that make it difficult for public persons to win libel cases. The Court has held that overzealous application of libel laws to members of the press reporting on public officials would place a "chilling effect" on the reporting of the news. Reporters and publishers must be assured that if they make an honest mistake in reporting the news, they will not be leaving themselves in jeopardy of incurring large libel damage awards. Hence, the Court has held that public officials and public figures must prove two points before they are able to win a libel suit. First, they must prove that the statements made in the press were in fact falsehoods; and second, they must prove that the printed statements were made with reckless disregard for whether or not they were false. This has meant that the press is free from libel actions brought by public officials unless the press acts in an irresponsible manner, ignoring the standard rules of journalistic investigation and reporting.

Criminal Trials and Restraint of the Press

The Court has also allowed certain restrictions to be placed on the press in the reporting of criminal actions and trials. Here the Court has found itself in a position where two important rights need to be balanced. On one hand, a person charged with a crime is entitled to a fair and objective trial held in a court of law. The right to a fair trial can be jeopardized if the press engages in excessive reporting about the case before the trial begins. A criminal defendant must not be tried in the press. Potential jurors must not have their minds poisoned by press reports prior to the commencement of the trial. On the other hand, the press must be free to report the news, including news about criminal activity and the actions of the criminal courts. The Supreme Court has taken a middle course, allowing certain moderate restrictions on the press in reporting about criminal prosecutions. Trial judges have been given a great amount of power to restrict the activities of the press during a trial.[17] Members of the press can have their activities limited so they do not disrupt the fair and open procedures of a trial. Judges can ban the live broadcasting of trials, the use of cameras, typewriters, and other journalistic activities which might detract from the integrity of the hearing. Judges may also grant motions for changes of venue, which have the effect of moving a trial to another location where press coverage is not as extensive. In order to insulate jurors from prejudicial publicity, the courts can order the jury to be sequestered during the trial itself so that the court can control the types of information and communications to which the jurors are exposed. However, one power the criminal court judge does not have is the authority to impose news blackouts on press coverage of a trial.[18] The courts cannot order the press to refrain from reporting the news. This would constitute a form of prior restraint, which is not permissible under the First Amendment.

Government Regulation of the Media

Governments have occasionally attempted to impose regulations on the content of mass media communications. For the most part, these have been well-intended efforts to insure that the press cover matters of public concern in a fair and objective manner. With respect to the print media, the courts have been exceptionally intolerant of such regulations. An example of such restrictions on press content was the Florida "right of reply" statute, which required any newspaper that assailed the personal character or the official record of anyone running for public office to print, upon the demand of the candidate and without fee, any reply the candidate wished to make. The candidate's reply had to be printed in the newspaper in a conspicuous place, and the reply was to be of similar length and typesetting as the original charges. In 1972, when Pat Tornillo, a candidate for the Florida legislature, was denied the right to reply to charges made in the *Miami Herald*, the candidate sued the newspaper for damages. The damage suit permitted the judiciary to rule on the constitutionality of the Florida statute, which the newspaper claimed was offensive to the First Amendment. In 1974, a unanimous Supreme Court ruled in favor of the newspaper.[19] The Court struck down the Florida statute, finding it repugnant to constitutional guarantees of freedom of the press. The Court held that while a responsible press was a desirable goal, it could not be legislated. Any law that tells the press what to print is not consistent with the First Amendment.

The Court, however, has taken a much different position with respect to restrictions on the broadcast media. The federal government, through the Federal Communications Commission, has set down certain regulations regarding the content of radio and television broadcasts. Among these are rules that require that a certain portion of broadcast time be devoted to a discussion of public issues and that equal time be given to opposing sides on issues of public concern. Similarly, the commission has ruled that radio and tele-

vision stations that broadcast endorsements of political candidates or criticisms of candidates must give equal time to the opposing side. In 1969, the
Supreme Court was faced with an appeal from the Red Lion Broadcasting
Company challenging the validity of the FCC regulations.[20] Red Lion argued
that the FCC rules were direct violations of the First Amendment, that
government had no authority to dictate the content of broadcast journalism.
The Supreme Court unanimously rejected Red Lion's challenge and held in
favor of the government. The Court said that the broadcast media was different from other forms of the press in that it operated on the public airways.
There are only a restricted number of broadcast frequencies, and because of
this scarcity the government had to allocate the rights to use the available
frequencies. A radio or television station is granted a form of governmental
monopoly to operate on a given public frequency. In return for that monopoly, the station must subject itself to reasonable governmental regulation. The
rules passed by the FCC were promulgated to insure that the best interests
of the public are served. The fairness and equal time provisions provide for
equitable treatment of those who cannot broadcast on their own because of
the scarcity of available frequencies. In addition, the FCC regulations are
designed to insure that the public is given a fair reporting of public affairs
with all viewpoints represented. This contributed to the goal of free and
robust discussion of public issues. According to the Court, the First Amendment could not be used as a sanctuary for unlimited private censorship
operating in a medium not open to all.

Summary

The success of American democracy depends upon the articulation of public
opinion. Only through such public expression are governmental officials informed of the will of the people on various issues of public concern. The success of the civil rights movement of the early 1960s and the antiwar protests
of the same decade testify to the importance of the right of the people to
express their views to public officials.

    The First Amendment to the Constitution protects the right of the people
to convert their private opinions into public opinions. The freedoms of speech,
press, assembly, and petition cannot be abused or abridged by the government. This is especially important because the expression of views critical of
the government and of officials in power can be the subject of governmental
repression. The First Amendment is a powerful antidote to the danger of

governmental repression of citizen opinion. It has been protected by the judiciary over the decades to such an extent that it has remained a significant bulwark of American liberty.

As methods of expression have changed over the years, so too have court interpretations of the First Amendment. In the beginning the First Amendment was intended to protect only standard forms of expression such as speech and press. But the judiciary has extended Amendment One liberties to cover demonstrations, symbolic speech, and electronic media that did not exist at the time of the drafting of the Constitution. The courts have not allowed the censorship of expression, nor have they tolerated the punishment of those who engage in legitimate forms of expression. That First Amendment guarantees have remained viable throughout almost two centuries of experience attests well to the significance Americans place on the free communication of opinion.

Notes

1. Cohen v. California, 403 U.S. 15 (1971).
2. See, for example, Terminiello v. Chicago, 337 U.S. 1 (1949).
3. See, for example, Feiner v. New York, 340 U.S. 315 (1951).
4. See Schenck v. United States, 249 U.S. 47 (1919).
5. 315 U.S. 568 (1942).
6. 372 U.S. 229 (1963).
7. 385 U.S. 39 (1966).
8. United States v. O'Brien, 391 U.S. 367 (1968).
9. Tinker v. Des Moines, 393 U.S. 503 (1969).
10. 394 U.S. 576 (1969).
11. Radich v. New York, 401 U.S. 531 (1971).
12. 418 U.S. 405 (1974).
13. 283 U.S. 697 (1931).
14. New York Times v. United States; United States v. Washington Post, 403 U.S. 713 (1971).
15. See Beauharnais v. Illinois, 343 U.S. 250 (1952).
16. See, for example, New York Times v. Sullivan, 376 U.S. 254 (1964); Garrison v. Louisiana, 379 U.S. 64 (1964); Curtis Publications v. Butts, 388 U.S. 130 (1967); Gertz v. Robert Welch, Inc., 418 U.S. 323 (1974).
17. See, for example, Estes v. Texas, 381 U.S. 532 (1965); Sheppard v. Maxwell, 384 U.S. 333 (1966).
18. Nebraska Press Association v. Stuart, 427 U.S. 539 (1976).
19. Miami Herald Publishing Company v. Tornillo, 418 U.S. 241 (1974).

20. Red Lion Broadcasting Company v. Federal Communications Commission, 395 U.S. 367 (1969).

Further Reading

Berns, Walter. *Freedom, Virtue and the First Amendment*. Baton Rouge: Louisiana State University Press, 1957.

Chafee, Zechariah, Jr. *Free Speech in the United States*. Cambridge, Mass.: Harvard University Press, 1954.

Cord, Robert L. *Protest, Dissent and the Supreme Court*. Cambridge, Mass.: Winthrop Publishers, 1971.

Cortner, Richard C. *The Supreme Court and Civil Liberties Policy*. Palo Alto, Calif.: Mayfield Publishing Company, 1975.

Emerson, Thomas I. *The System of Freedom of Expression*. New York: Random House, 1970.

Emerson, Thomas I. *Toward a General Theory of the First Amendment*. New York: Random House, 1967.

Fortas, Abe. *Concerning Dissent and Civil Disobedience*. New York: New American Library, 1968.

Hudon, Edward G. *Freedom of Speech and Press in America*. Washington: Public Affairs Press, 1963.

Meiklejohn, Alexander. *Political Freedom*. New York: Oxford University Press, 1965.

Murphy, Paul L. *The Meaning of Freedom of Speech*. Westport, Conn.: Greenwood Press, 1973.

Shapiro, Martin. *Freedom of Speech*. Englewood Cliffs, N.J.: Prentice-Hall, 1966.

Summers, Marvin. *Free Speech and Political Protest*. Boston: D. C. Heath, 1967.

Elections and Voting Rights

Chapter five

Voting Rights and the Integrity of Elections: *Buckley* v. *Valeo*

The year 1974 placed enormous stress on the United States political system. This was the year that the Watergate scandal reached its greatest intensity, the first American president resigned in disgrace, and public confidence in the government plummeted to historic lows. At the root of these problems was a series of events during the 1972 presidential election campaign. Fraud, misuse of campaign funds, illegal campaign contributions, and unlawful campaign tactics appeared to have been common practices during that election year. In the investigations that followed, every day brought new disclosures of illegal or unethical activities.

By 1974 the pressure on Congress to enact legislation to clean up America's elections reached extremely high levels. Members of Congress began great efforts to construct new laws to insure the integrity of the American electoral system. These efforts were undoubtedly prompted by the sincere feelings on the part of many that positive action was necessary, but the fact that 1974 was a congressional election year obviously added to the incentive of many legislators. Members of Congress felt an urgency to show the nation that Congress was capable of purging many of the defects in the election process. And, of course, voting for reform legislation was one way that legislators could disassociate themselves from the Watergate violations. Even those congressmen who previously had supported election reform lukewarmly were now advocates of tough campaign legislation.

92

The end result of this congressional attention to the condition of the election process was passage in October 1974 of a law amending the Election Campaign Act of 1971. The new legislation was clearly the most comprehensive federal regulation of election campaigns in the nation's history. The bill enacted six major alterations in the way campaigns for federal office were to be conducted.

First, the act contained *limitations on direct campaign contributions to political candidates*. Previously, individuals could contribute funds to a political candidate almost without limitation. This created a political dependence on large campaign contributors. Americans had become increasingly suspicious of this situation, fearing that governmental officials would feel an obligation to those who contributed large amounts of money to their election. The new limitations dictated that no person or group could make direct contributions of more than $1000 to any one candidate for federal office. Registered political committees were restricted to contributions of $5000 per candidate. No person could exceed a $25,000 limit in campaign contributions to all federal candidates in any one year. These new limitations were radical changes from past election practices.

Second, the act imposed certain *individual expenditure limitations*. According to the act's provisions, no person could independently spend more than $1000 of his own funds in behalf of any candidate. This provision was designed to prohibit persons from avoiding the candidate contribution limitations by unlimited independent personal spending. Furthermore, the act curtailed a candidate's use of his own personal assets during a campaign. Office seekers were limited in the amount of personal or family funds they could use for campaign purposes. For presidential and vice-presidential candidates this limit was set at $50,000, for senatorial candidates, $35,000, and for House candidates, $25,000.

Third, the act made mandatory extensive *campaign disclosure procedures*. At various specified times during the campaign period, candidates were required to provide a full accounting of campaign income. The names and addresses of all persons contributing more than $10 had to be disclosed. In addition, the occupation and place of business of all those who contributed in excess of $100 were to be disclosed.

Fourth, Congress enacted *public financing of presidential elections*. This was perhaps the most significant section of the new legislation. No longer would candidates for public office be totally dependent upon private contributions. Instead, the law provided for a tax return check-off system whereby each individual taxpayer could annually designate that one dollar of his taxes go to the financing of presidential elections. These funds would then be distributed to serious candidates for the presidency. The goal of this provision was to give candidates the funding necessary to conduct a viable campaign without having to rely on large campaign contributors. This section of the act was a major victory for reform proponents, although many were disappointed that the act did not also provide for federal funding of congressional campaigns.

Fifth, the act imposed *campaign spending ceilings*. Through a complicated formula the total amount of money that could be spent in a federal election campaign was established. The formula included taking into account inflationary pressures and numbers of voters in relevant constituencies. While the final spending limitations were, therefore, subject to a certain amount of variation, the general ceiling levels were: $10 million for presidential primary campaigns, $20 million for presidential general elections, $100,000 for Senate primaries, $150,000 for Senate general elections, $70,000 for House primaries, and $70,000 for House general elections. These limitations were imposed in order to stop the skyrocketing costs of campaign activities.

Sixth, the act *established a Federal Election Commission*. This commission was given the authority to administer and enforce the act. The commission was to be composed of eight bipartisan members. Two commissioners each were to be selected by the Speaker of the House, president pro tempore of the Senate, and president of the United States. The clerk of the House and the secretary of the Senate were to be ex-officio members of the commission. The commissioners were subject to congressional confirmation. The commission could go to court to enforce the act, refer violators of the law to the Justice Department for prosecution, and pass certain regulations to implement the act.

Given the comprehensive nature of the legislation and the many changes it would produce in the way election campaigns were run, it was predictable that opponents of the reforms would take legal action to blunt its impact. It did not take long for the legal battle lines to form. In January of 1975, just three months after the passage of the campaign reform legislation, a suit was filed in federal court challenging the constitutionality of the statute. Joining in the legal action to strike down the statute were an assortment of individuals and groups with radically different positions on public issues. Parties to the suit included such conservative forces as Senator James Buckley, the Conservative party of the state of New York, the Mississippi Republican party, the American Conservative Union, and the Conservative Victory Fund. Other members of the unlikely alliance to have the law declared unconstitutional were liberal independent presidential candidate Eugene McCarthy, the New York Civil Liberties Union, and a long-time contributor to liberal causes, Stewart Mott.

Opponents of the new law brought with them to court a wide array of challenges to the reforms. The lower courts generally upheld the validity of the new law, which set the stage for a final hearing by the United States

Supreme Court. On November 10, 1975, the Court heard oral arguments in the case known as *Buckley* v. *Valeo*.[1] Almost three months later the Court issued a complicated and lengthy opinion resolving the constitutionality of the new regulations. The majority opinion itself devoted 137 pages to interpreting the validity of the act in light of basic constitutional provisions. In addition, five justices wrote separate opinions detailing their own individual views of various sections of the reform legislation. In the final analysis, the Court struck down several provisions of the act, but upheld others. The decision was sufficiently complex to allow both sides of the legal dispute to claim partial victory.

The limitations in individual contributions to political candidates were found to be constitutionally valid. Challengers had claimed that the First Amendment freedom of expression provisions should be interpreted to protect the right of a person to give his own money freely to a candidate or campaign committee. The Court, however, held that the law balanced these freedom of expression guarantees against the power of government to regulate bribery, corruption, and other possible weaknesses in the election process. In the final analysis, the Court held, "A limitation upon the amount that any one person or group may contribute to a candidate or political committee entails only a marginal restriction upon the contributor's ability to engage in free communication." The Court's majority reasoned that this marginal restriction was a reasonable price to pay for the improvements in the election system.

The Court, however, struck down restrictions on the amount of money a person could independently spend on behalf of a candidate as well as the limitations on the freedom of a candidate to spend his own personal funds. The majority found that an individual who directly expended funds in behalf of a candidate was exercising First Amendment rights, and Congress had no authority to restrict this variety of free expression. Therefore, the Court held that Congress has a legitimate interest in regulating the process whereby a person gives money to a candidate, but has no authority to regulate an individual who independently spends money in order to communicate his political feelings. In practice this means that, for example, an individual may not give a presidential candidate a donation of $1500 because this would be in violation of the $1000 contribution limit set by Congress. On the other hand, the same person could take the same $1500 and independently purchase newspaper advertising in behalf of the candidate. Since this latter action is a means of direct individual expression of a citizen's political views, Congress has no right to limit that expression. Hence, Congress is empowered to regulate campaign contributions to candidates but not restrict independent individual political expenditures.

The Court upheld the campaign reporting and disclosure sections of the act. Congress had for many years required a reporting of campaign contributions and expenditures. The only major difference between this reform legislation and previous statutes was the more comprehensive nature of the regulations. Since the new act imposed changes in the degree of regulation only, the constitutionality of this section was never in serious doubt.

To the joy of election campaign reformers, the Court gave its stamp of approval to public financing of presidential elections. Approval came in spite of two objections submitted by opponents of the act. First, opponents had argued that the federal government was becoming involved in an area normally reserved for the private sector. Second, the act was challenged on the grounds that it favored major parties over minor ones, allowing the established Democratic and Republican party candidates to obtain federal funds much more easily than minor party candidates. The Court essentially deferred to the judgment of Congress on this issue. In the words of the majority opinion: "Congress has concluded that the means [the Federal Election Campaign Act] are 'necessary and proper' to promote the general welfare, and we thus decline to find this legislation without the grant of power in Article I. . . ." The Court held that the principles of public financial aid to election campaigns did not contradict the Constitution, nor did the specific means of distributing those funds.

Opponents won at least a partial victory on congressional limits on campaign spending. The Court held that the ceilings imposed on spending for House, Senate, and presidential elections were unconstitutional. A law that prohibits a person from using funds in excess of a certain amount to bring his views to the American people is a clear violation of the First Amendment. However, the Court did conclude that such ceilings could be used as a prerequisite for obtaining federal dollars for a candidate's campaign. Therefore, candidates running for the presidency would be forced to make a choice. If they applied to receive federal subsidies for their campaign costs, Congress could validly impose spending limits. But if a candidate did not agree to accept government funds, relying totally on personal wealth or private contributions, Congress could not impose spending restrictions. In actual practice, all major candidates running for the presidency in the 1976 elections accepted the first alternative. Each agreed to limit spending and, in return, receive federal funds. Therefore, while Congress could not absolutely impose spending limitations, it could make the voluntary acceptance of such limitations financially attractive to presidential candidates.

Finally, on the creation of the Federal Election Commission, the Court handed down a twofold decision. First, the Court generally approved of the idea of a commission having investigative and enforcement powers over the execution of the Campaign Act. However, the Court held that the manner in which the commissioners were selected violated the Constitution. If the commission was to have enforcement powers, then it properly must be under the executive branch of government. And as a body empowered to enforce the law, its commissioners must be appointed by the president. To have the enforcement commissioners appointed by the legislature violated the principle of separation of powers. Hence, the Court ordered Congress to reconstitute the commission so that its members would be appointed by the president. Following the decision, Congress did in fact heed the High Court's instructions and modified the selection process to give the appointment power to the president, with Senate confirmation of the chief executive's nominees. This change brought the commission into compliance with the Constitution's separation of powers doctrine.

While the decision in *Buckley* v. *Valeo* provided support for positions taken by the reformers as well as the act's opponents, the clear edge goes to those who supported the act. In spite of the fact that the Court struck down individual spending limitations and absolute ceilings on campaign spending, most of the act remained intact. Public financing and limitations on contributions were the most important aspects of the legislation, and on both points the reformers were the clear victors.

The comprehensive nature of the Election Campaign Act amendments of 1974 is the most recent example of a growing trend of federal involvement in elections and voting. Voting has become one of the most important rights of American citizens. Congress has become increasingly active in passing legislation designed to protect the right to vote and to preserve the integrity of American elections. This increasing federal activity in the nation's electoral system will be the focus of the following pages.

The Constitution, Elections, and Voting

The Framers of the Constitution would undoubtedly look upon the Federal Election Campaign Act with disfavor. The entire constitutional status of the right to vote and the power of the federal government to regulate elections has undergone remarkable change since the Constitution was first ratified. The members of the Constitutional Convention focused some of their deliberations on the right to vote, but for the most part included very little dealing with the subject in the Constitution. One reason for this lack of attention to the right to vote was that under the original document there was to be very little voting for federal officials. The president and vice-president were to be selected by the electoral college, and the Senate was to be chosen by the various state legislatures. Only the House of Representatives was designed to be elected directly by the people. The Convention considered establishing qualifications for voters who would participate in the selection of federal representatives, but each of the states had their own voter requirements. Rather than create a separate federal electorate, the Framers provided in article I, section 2: "the Electors in each State shall have the Qualifications requisite for Electors of the most numerous Branch of the State Legislature." With this provision the Convention essentially left the matter of voter qualifications under the authority of the states. If a citizen was entitled to vote for state legislators, he was also able to participate in congressional elections.

By leaving undisturbed the standing voter qualifications of the states, the Convention indicated its general approval of the voter requirements then in effect. The electorate in 1787 in no way resembled the electorate of today. First, suffrage was restricted by sex. Only male citizens were permitted to vote. Practically no one questioned this limitation. Second, the right to vote was reserved for property-owners. The states varied as to how much property ownership was necessary to qualify one to vote, but usually freeholder status was required. And third, a majority of the states, most of them in the South, excluded blacks from participation in the election process. Hence, the early electorate in this country was generally male, white, and propertied.

Congress and the Regulation of Voting

The Framers, however, did leave the door ajar for possible congressional activity in regulating federal elections. Article I, section 4 reads: "The Times, Places, and Manner of holding Elections for Senators and Representatives, shall be prescribed in each State by the Legislature thereof; But the Congress may at any time by Law make or alter such Regulations." This provision maintained the notion that election regulation was primarily the responsibility of the states, but did allow for the possibility that Congress might need to enter the process at some future date. Congress first legislated on the authority granted by this provision in 1842 when it stipulated that members of the House should be elected from legislative districts rather than representing their respective states generally. Congress has also been responsible for designating a specific day (the first Tuesday after the first Monday in November of even numbered years) on which all states will conduct federal elections. Finally, under authority of the Times, Places, and Manner Clause, Congress has passed certain statutes designed to insure the integrity of the election process. These laws proscribed such activities as bribery, unlawful voting, obstruction of the elections process, and election fraud and prescribed such procedures as the secret ballot. The first time Congress legis-

Fifteenth Amendment applied only to general elections and not to primary elections. Since the primary elections for all practical purposes were the only important elections in one-party states, a state that prevented blacks from voting in the primaries effectively denied blacks any meaningful right to vote. On the basis of this reasoning, the state of Texas passed legislation in 1923 which openly stated that blacks could no longer participate in Democratic party primary elections. Four years later, however, the United States Supreme Court struck down this statute on the grounds that it violated the Equal Protection Clause of the Fourteenth Amendment.[3]

Denied the right to restrict voting in primaries, the Texas legislature passed a statute holding that political parties were empowered to draft qualification standards for voting in party primaries. The constitutional argument employed by the state legislature was that while the state cannot discriminate in authorizing the right to vote, political parties can. Parties are private organizations. The Fourteenth Amendment only prohibited a *state* from discriminating, not private parties. On the basis of this authorization by the legislature, the Democratic party of Texas ruled that blacks could not vote in party primaries. Once again there was a court challenge, and once again the Supreme Court struck down the state statute.[4] This time the Court held that the statute giving parties the power to discriminate was sufficient state action in itself to conflict with the Equal Protection Clause.

Texas politicians again went back to the drawing board. This time the Democratic party decided to prohibit black voting in primaries directly, without any state authorization to do so. In this way the party hoped to eliminate any "state action" whatsoever and, therefore, avoid any Fourteenth Amendment violations. This time the state of Texas was victorious. In 1935, a unanimous Supreme Court held that since it was a private party that was doing the discriminating without any involvement by the state, the Equal Protection Clause was not abused.[5]

The state's victory, however, was short-lived. In 1944, the Supreme Court ruled on the appeal of Lonnie Smith, a black Texan who had been denied the right to vote in the 1940 Texas Democratic primary.[6] The state argued that because the Democratic party was a private club it was free to limit participation in its affairs in any way it saw fit—including the right to discriminate on the basis of race. The Supreme Court, however, was convinced by attorneys representing Smith that its 1935 ruling was improper. The Court held that when a state regulates primary elections, recognizes party nominees as the only persons to be placed on the general election ballot, and imposes certain election procedures, the state becomes a party to the primary election. Hence, if there is racial discrimination in the party primaries, the state is indirectly involved in that discrimination. This involvement is enough to constitute "state action" under the meaning of the Fourteenth and Fifteenth Amendments. In so holding, the Court overruled its

1935 decision. Following this case, the status of primary elections was completely altered. No longer were primary elections considered the exclusive affairs of a private club. Instead, primaries were viewed as integral parts of the election system which must be conducted with the same respect given to civil rights as required in general elections.

Literacy Tests

Another device imposed by southern states to restrict black voting was a required literacy test. On the grounds that only those capable of intelligent voting should be allowed the privilege of casting a ballot, states such as Alabama, Georgia, Louisiana, Mississippi, North Carolina, South Carolina, and Virginia imposed literacy standards as a voter qualification requirement. Normally an individual who wished to register to vote was required to read and interpret a provision of the state constitution to the satisfaction of the voting registrar. As applied, these requirements were used to eliminate black voting. Not only was illiteracy more common among the black population, but even well-educated blacks commonly found themselves unable to satisfy the discriminatory standards of the local voting registrar. Congress made several direct attacks on the literacy test. In the 1964 Civil Rights Act, Congress provided that individuals who had completed six years of formal education would be exempt from all literacy tests. The 1965 Voting Rights Act further reduced the use of the literacy test, and in subsequent extensions of that act Congress banned states from employing literacy tests altogether. Congressional authority to impose such restrictions on the states was challenged in court, but the U.S. Supreme Court ruled that literacy tests represented an "unremitting and ingenious defiance of the Constitution . . . specifically designed to prevent Negroes from voting." Consequently, the Court held that congressional restrictions on literacy tests were justified means of enforcing the Fifteenth Amendment.[7]

The Poll Tax

Eleven states, all in the South, imposed a tax on the right to vote. The tax was minimal, not exceeding two dollars in most instances, but it did provide a barrier to voting. The poll tax, however, was only partially a means of racial discrimination. Estimates of the impact of the tax have concluded that more whites were discouraged from voting because of the tax than were blacks. Therefore, a poll tax measure had both racial and socioeconomic discriminatory effects. It applied to all potential voters who were unable or unwilling to pay for the right to vote. Congress made several attempts to outlaw the poll tax, but each attempt was blocked by southern senators. Finally, in

1962 Congress proposed a constitutional amendment that prohibited the imposition of a poll tax in federal elections. The Twenty-Fourth Amendment was ratified in 1964. The coverage of the amendment, however, was not sufficiently broad to please many people. It outlawed poll taxes as requirements in federal elections, but did not extend its prohibitions to state elections. The battle over the validity of the use of poll taxes as a requirement to vote in state elections was finally decided in the federal courts. In 1966, in *Harper* v. *Virginia State Board of Elections*[8] the Supreme Court ruled that poll taxes violated the Equal Protection Clause. In behalf of the Court, Justice Douglas concluded: "Voter qualifications have no relation to wealth nor to paying or not paying this or any other tax."

Congressional action supported by federal court rulings has virtually eliminated racial discrimination in the area of enfranchisement. Federal regulation of the elections and voting rights has become quite complex. The 1965 Voting Rights Act and its subsequent amendments have allowed for substantial federal involvement to insure that states do not engage in racial discrimination. It has taken several decades, but the nation has finally attained the objectives of the Fifteenth Amendment.

Residence and the Right to Vote

States have uniformly imposed residence requirements on the right to vote. For the most part, these regulations are reasonable actions designed to insure the integrity of the elections process. No one would seriously argue that a person should be allowed to vote in states or other representational districts of which he is not a resident. Occasionally, however, the judiciary has held residence requirements to be in violation of the Constitution.

Residence and the Right to Vote

The various states have often required that a person establish residency in a particular voting district for a stipulated period of time prior to becoming eligible to vote. It was not uncommon for a state to impose a one-year waiting period for voting in statewide elections and a thirty-to-sixty day waiting period for local elections. This waiting period was required in order for the states to complete the administrative tasks necessary to insure against voter fraud. It also was designed to enforce bona fide residence as a voting requirement. These restrictions were challenged in federal court by James

Blumstein, a professor of law. Blumstein had moved to the state of Tennessee in order to accept a teaching position at Vanderbilt University. He entered the state in June of 1970 and had expected to vote in August and November elections. However, when Blumstein attempted to register in July of 1970, he was denied his voting rights on the grounds that he had failed to satisfy Tennessee's one-year state and one-month county residence requirements. Blumstein sued, calling the restrictions an unreasonable regulation of the right to vote in violation of the Equal Protection Clause of the Fourteenth Amendment. In 1972, the United States Supreme Court issued its decision on Blumstein's litigation.[9] With Chief Justice Burger in dissent, the Court held that the one-year requirement was unconstitutional. According to the majority, an entire year was an unreasonably long period, and the state could accomplish its goals of preserving the purity of the election process by imposing a much more lenient residence period. The majority suggested that a thirty-day waiting period would be acceptable and would allow the state sufficient time to complete any administrative actions necessary to combat voter fraud or other assaults on the integrity of the process.

In a related matter, the Court struck down a Texas residence requirement in 1965. This state regulation was directed at military personnel. Texas feared that large numbers of military personnel transferred into the state for temporary periods would have an adverse effect on elections. This danger was particularly acute for local elections in areas with large military bases. State officials reasoned that members of the military, because of their expected short residence in the locality, might not vote in a responsible fashion and in a manner consistent with the long-range best interests of the community. Hence, the state enacted a statute that denied the right to vote to any members of the military who moved into Texas as long as they remained attached to the armed forces. Therefore, a person transferred into the state of Texas by the military was forever considered a nonresident, even though he might serve in the state for several years. Resident status could be gained only by terminating military service. The Court found these restrictions unreasonable and instructed the state to develop more precise tests to determine bona fide residence.[10]

Malapportionment and the One Man, One Vote Formula

A much different form of residence discrimination was tackled by the Supreme Court during the 1960s. This involved the controversial issue of malapportionment, a representational scheme that diluted the voting power of persons residing in urban areas. Apportionment is the process of constructing legislative or other representational districts. When legislative districts are correctly apportioned on the basis of population, each legislative district will be so drawn as to have approximately the same population size. Hence, each legislator will represent the same number of citizens. By the 1960s the legislatures in many states had become malapportioned. That is, population in certain legislative districts had become substantially larger than in others. Many states' congressional districts suffered from the same condition. This situation had developed largely because the state legislatures, which are responsible for drawing state and federal legislative district boundaries, had not modified their apportionment schemes to keep pace with population shifts. Many states had not reapportioned since the turn of the century. During the interim, massive changes had occurred in population trends. For the most part, this had taken the form of substantial migration from rural areas into the cities. This resulted in urban legislative districts that were disproportionately large in comparison to rural districts, thereby discriminating against urban residents. If, for example, a given urban district contains 1000 voters and a rural district only 100 voters, then a rural voter's impact on the state legislature is ten times greater than the voter who happens to reside in the urban district. Once malapportionment set in, the state legislators were often unwilling to correct it. The legislatures became dominated by rural interests, and they were unwilling to give up their power to the urban areas, which, of course, would be the natural consequence of reapportioning.

Unsuccessful at convincing the state legislatures to reapportion, urban voters went to the federal courts for relief. A test case on this issue, *Reynolds v. Sims*,[11] was decided by the Supreme Court in 1964. It involved a challenge to the apportionment of the Alabama legislature, which had become badly unbalanced. In the state house the largest district had become sixteen times more populated than the smallest district, and the most populated senate district was forty-one times larger than the smallest senate district. The citizens who filed the suit, largely residents from urban legislative districts, argued that the malapportioned legislature violated the Equal Protection Clause. By an eight-to-one vote, the Supreme Court struck down the Alabama legislative districting scheme on equal protection grounds. In doing so, the Court announced its famous "one man, one vote" formula, holding that legislative districts must be so drawn as to insure that they are as close as practically possible in terms of population size. In subsequent decisions, the Supreme Court applied the same formula to congressional districts, local government units, and even special governmental agencies such as school district commissions.

The Supreme Court in recent decades has approached denial of the right to vote and the dilution of the value of the vote with a suspicious eye. Only those residence requirements that are clearly reasonable have met the Court's standards of validity.

Property Qualifications and Voting Rights

The emphasis that the Framers put on the importance of property was not long-lived. The theory that only the propertied classes should vote began to lose support with the political era ushered in by Andrew Jackson and his common man philosophy. Property qualifications for voting were reduced or totally eliminated in most states. As the nation entered the twentieth century property qualifications were a thing of the past. Only the poll taxes, which were eventually erased by the Twenty-Fourth Amendment and subsequent Supreme Court action, remained as a reminder of the old theory that only the monied classes should be eligible to determine the nation's leaders and policies.

In the 1960s, however, the question of property qualifications was resurrected. In many states property-owners became increasingly dissatisfied with escalating property taxes. In most states property taxes are the chief means by which local governments finance special projects and improvements. Similarly, public educational systems in the majority of states are financially supported almost exclusively from property tax revenues. Normally, property taxes can be raised through public referendum procedures. A bond issue is placed on the ballot asking the voters to accept or reject the issuance of revenue bonds to finance government spending. The local bonds would be redeemed by increased property taxes. Therefore, the voters have a voice in property tax rates. What became increasingly upsetting to property-owners in many sections of the country was the fact that while all voters could cast their ballots on bond issues, the increased taxes were to be paid only by property-owners. Renters or other individuals who did not own real property, therefore, would freely vote in favor of better schools, modern sewer systems, increased park lands, and other improvements knowing full well that they would not be directly taxed to pay for increased spending levels. Studies conducted in several states found that it was not uncommon for a bond issue to pass, even though property-owners voted against the issue. The negative votes of property-owners were more than offset by the non-property-owners who overwhelmingly supported the new bonds. In response to this situation, property-owners in several states began pressuring the legislatures to enact property restrictions on the right to vote in bond elections. Several states responded to this pressure by passing the requested legislation.

The Supreme Court heard its first major challenge to these modern property restrictions in 1969 in the case of *Kramer* v. *Union Free School District*.[12] The particular statute in question was a New York state regulation that voting in school district elections would be restricted to people who owned or leased real property within the school district or who had custody of children attending the local public schools. The rationale behind the statute was to limit the electorate to those who had a direct interest in the school system, either because of being taxed to finance it or having children enrolled in it. Kramer was a bachelor who neither owned nor leased real property. He was denied the right to vote in elections dealing with public school issues. He sued on the grounds that the statute discriminated against him in violation of the Equal Protection Clause of the Fourteenth Amendment. The Supreme Court agreed, ruling that elections relevant to the public school system have a broad impact on the local community, and therefore it is unreasonable to restrict the right to vote in such elections according to the arbitrary system imposed by New York.

In the years immediately following the *Kramer* decision, the Court struck down several other property restrictions on the right to vote. A Louisiana statute restricting the right to vote to property-owners in elections held to approve the issuance of revenue bonds by a local utility was declared unconstitutional by the Court in 1969.[13] An Arizona regulation limiting the right to vote on questions involving general revenue bonds to those persons paying property taxes was struck down in 1970.[14] The city of Fort Worth, Texas was prohibited from excluding non-property-owners from voting on issuing bonds to construct a new library in a 1975 decision.[15]

The general rule that evolved from these decisions was that if an election can be classified as having a general impact on the community then it is unconstitutional to restrict the right to vote to a segment of the electorate, such as those that own property and pay property taxes. However, if an election can be classified as a "special interest" election, it may be possible to restrict the electorate. An example of such a special interest limitation involved a California law that was upheld by the Supreme Court in 1973.[16] The particular statute regulated voting in water storage district elections. It restricted voting to land-owners who were served by the district. Since only the land-owners received the services of the district and only the served land-owners were taxed for the benefits of the water district, it appeared reasonable to restrict the right to vote to those affected by the system. Since non-land-owners were not affected by the activities of the water district, they had no reasonable claim to demand a voice in district affairs. In the absence of conditions that make an election a special interest affair, however, the right to vote cannot be denied on the basis of property holdings.

Summary

The United States political system places a great importance on elections. At the federal level we select our legislators and chief executive directly or indirectly through democratic balloting procedures. At the state level we elect executives, legislators, and judges in addition to voting on many questions of public policy.

Two developments are significant in the historical growth of elections in America. The first is the expansion of the electorate. In the beginning of the nation's history the right to vote was largely restricted to the white, male, property-holding citizens. However, one by one the obstacles to voting have been eliminated. The striking down of these barriers has occurred through constitutional amendment, state and federal legislative action, and court decrees. Today factors that may disqualify a person from voting are indeed minimal. An American citizen who is a bona fide resident of a state and has attained the age of eighteen cannot be denied the right to vote as long as he properly registers with local voting officials and is not a convicted felon or mental incompetent.

The second major development in the area of voting rights and elections has been the increased activity on the part of the federal government. Our original Constitution left little authority to the national government to regulate elections. Yet through the adoption of several constitutional amendments a substantially expanded role for the federal government evolved. The Congress has seized upon this new constitutional authority as a means to improve the nation's election system. Congress has passed several statutes to insure that voting rights are not abridged and has enacted laws imposing comprehensive regulations for political campaigns. The goal of this federal activity has been the expansion of the electorate and the preservation of the integrity of the ballot.

Notes

1. 424 U.S. 1 (1976).
2. See Oregon v. Mitchell, 400 U.S. 112 (1970).

3. Nixon v. Herndon, 273 U.S. 536 (1927).

4. Nixon v. Condon, 286 U.S. 73 (1932).

5. Grovey v. Townsend, 295 U.S. 45 (1935).

6. Smith v. Allwright, 321 U.S. 649 (1944).

7. South Carolina v. Katzenbach, 383 U.S. 301 (1966).

8. 383 U.S. 663 (1966).

9. Dunn v. Blumstein, 405 U.S. 330 (1972).

10. Carrington v. Rash, 380 U.S. 89 (1965).

11. 377 U.S. 533 (1964).

12. 395 U.S. 621 (1969).

13. Cipriano v. Houma, 395 U.S. 701 (1969).

14. Phoenix v. Kolodziejski, 399 U.S. 204 (1970).

15. Hill v. Stone, 421 U.S. 289 (1975).

16. Salyer Land Company v. Tulare Lake Basin Water Storage District, 410 U.S. 719 (1973).

Further Reading

Aiken, Charles (ed.). *The Negro Votes.* San Francisco: Chandler, 1962.

Baker, Gordon E. *The Reapportionment Revolution.* New York: Random House, 1966.

Claude, Richard. *The Supreme Court and the Electoral Process.* Baltimore: Johns Hopkins University Press, 1970.

Elliott, W. E. Y. *The Rise of the Guardian Democracy.* Cambridge, Mass.: Harvard University Press, 1974.

Gillette, William. *The Right to Vote.* Baltimore: Johns Hopkins University Press, 1970.

Lewinson, Paul. *Race, Class, and Party.* New York: Grosset and Dunlop, 1964.

Marshall, Burke. *Federalism and Civil Rights.* New York: Columbia University Press, 1964.

McKay, Robert B. *Reapportionment.* New York: Twentieth Century Fund, 1965.

Ogden, Frederic D. *The Poll Tax in the South.* University, Ala.: University of Alabama Press, 1958.

Smith, C. E. *Voting and Election Laws.* New York: Oceana, 1960.

Strong, Donald S. *Negroes, Ballots and Judges.* University, Ala.: University of Alabama Press, 1968.

Williamson, Chilton. *American Suffrage from Property to Democracy, 1760–1860.* Princeton, N.J.: Princeton University Press, 1960.

Political Parties and
Interest Groups

Chapter six

The Regulation of Political Parties:
Williams v. *Rhodes*

The election year of 1968 found the nation bitterly divided. The government was firmly committed to a military defense of Vietnam. Thousands of American lives had been lost in Southeast Asia, and millions of American dollars were being sent abroad to ward off the advancing Communist forces. At home a frustrated American people were asked to contribute larger portions of their incomes through federal taxation programs to support the war effort and to maintain domestic programs. News from the war front did not encourage U.S. citizens. In spite of being better equipped and having greater financial resources, the Americans could not win significant battles. On American streets, crime was rising in spite of dramatically increased government spending on social programs of various kinds. The United States government was losing the respect of foreign governments and the confidence of its own citizens. No one appeared satisfied. From the liberals came the cry to pull out of Southeast Asia and concentrate on domestic needs. From the conservative quarter came the demand to unleash all of America's military might and successfully end the war once and for all. Many moderate, middle-class voters were disenchanted.

These cleavages in American public opinion manifested themselves in the form of protest and reaction. The antiwar forces, finding their basic support on the nation's campuses, were particularly active in promoting mass demonstrations in the streets calling for an end to the war effort.

110

Opposing groups also engaged in various forms of political protest. President Lyndon Johnson became a target of the antiwar movement, while being supported by the more military oriented groups. The president's status in the public opinion polls began to plummet as the war dragged on. He had been ushered into office with the full support of the American public in 1963 upon the assassination of John Kennedy and had been returned to the office in 1964 in one of the most massive landslides in political history. But by 1968 the tide had changed. Johnson had been expected to seek reelection in 1968, but pressures became too great and the demands of the war too severe. To the surprise of almost everyone, Lyndon Johnson announced in early 1968 that he would not seek the nomination of his party. The country would have to turn to another figure to lead it.

The Republican party responded by nominating former vice-president Richard M. Nixon. Nixon promised a return to normalcy. Pledging "peace with honor," Nixon appealed to the moderate sympathies of the American people. He urged extrication from Vietnam, but only upon terms that would allow the United States to leave Southeast Asia with its pride intact. Domestically, Nixon presented a platform heavily accented by traditional American values of self-reliance and limited governmental interference.

The Democratic party was badly split. The peace advocates generally supported Eugene McCarthy, a United States senator from Minnesota. The more conservative Democrats promoted the candidacy of Vice-President Hubert Humphrey. The party's national convention in Chicago was torn by dissent. Through television, violence in the streets surrounding convention headquarters was flashed to the nation. Democrats were bitterly divided and the party's wounds were not to heal until after the November election. The convention finally selected Vice-President Humphrey to lead the party. Humphrey argued for a general continuation of the programs of Lyndon Johnson. He refused to repudiate the war effort, but called for increased efforts to negotiate peace. The Humphrey Democrats called for increased, creative federal programs to deal with the nation's domestic ills. But the party was too badly split to present an effective campaign and ran poorly in comparison to Richard Nixon throughout the greater part of the campaign period.

Against this backdrop rose a third political force. It took the form of a new political party hastily created around the candidacy of Alabama governor George Wallace. Wallace's American Independent party appealed to those Americans who did not believe that the traditional parties could provide adequate leadership. Wallace, with a solid base of support in the southern states, attempted to move from being a regional candidate to one with a national following. He traveled the country articulating his message that there were few major differences between the Republican and

Democratic parties. Both, he claimed, represented the same approach to government, which had proven itself to be a failure. Wallace argued for a strong national defense, military victory in Vietnam, repression of criminal elements, and a drastic cutback in welfare spending. The Alabama governor knew that his chances of winning the presidency were slim, but he hoped to accomplish a strong showing at the polls in order to have an impact on American policies. Unfortunately for his supporters, Wallace ran into some difficult obstacles. Because he did not represent an established party, several states refused to place his name on the November election ballot automatically. Unless Wallace was able to gain ballot position in almost every state, his chance of accomplishing an impressive showing at the polls would be slight.

The American Independent party found that in many states difficult requirements needed to be met to gain access to the ballot. Wallace supporters had to engage in political and legal skirmishes in order to have the governor's name placed before the voters. The most important battle between the Wallace campaign and state election officials occurred in Ohio, and it was not settled completely until the United States Supreme Court entered the scene.

Ohio was a key state to the Wallace campaign. A large state in the nation's midsection, it was geographically northern, but had a substantial number of migrants from the rural south. The state had a large proportion of blue-collar workers, a segment of the population in which Wallace found a good deal of his natural constituency. But Ohio refused Wallace access to the ballot. The laws of the state were the most restrictive in the country, biasing the elections process in favor of the established parties. In order for a new political party to have a candidate placed on the ballot, the party had to obtain petitions signed by qualified electors totaling 15 percent of the number of ballots cast in the last gubernatorial election. Furthermore, the petitions had to be filed with state officials by February of the election year. This particular state law virtually eliminated the possibility that newly formed political parties would attain a place on the ballot. The major political parties, however, were treated in a much different fashion. As long as the established parties received the votes of 10 percent of the participating electorate during the last governor's election, the party's nominee was automatically placed on the following presidential election ballot. The Democrats and the Republicans, therefore, did not have to submit any petitions in order to secure a ballot position for the 1968 presidential election.

The American Independent party of Ohio was formed in January of 1968. This allowed less than one month to complete the process of obtaining the required petitions. Based upon the most recent gubernatorial election, the party was required to submit the signatures of 433,100 registered Ohio voters. Although it was virtually impossible for the party to gain the required number of signatures by the established deadline, party members set about the task of gathering the petitions. By June of 1968 the American Independent party had the signatures of 450,000 voters. State officials, however, refused to accept the petitions on the grounds that the deadline had passed by more than four months.

Rebuked by state authorities, the Wallace supporters turned to the federal courts for relief. In behalf of the Ohio American Independent party, Glen A. Williams, a party official, sued Governor James A. Rhodes and other state officers, requesting that the judiciary strike down the restrictive statutes. There were at least two ironies in this action. First of all, the federal judiciary was one of the primary targets of the Wallace campaign. At every campaign stop the Alabaman chastised the federal court system for its liberal rulings. Hence, the very judges whom Wallace criticized as being a source of America's state of disrepair were being asked by the candidate to remove obstacles to his campaign. Second, a companion suit was filed in the same district court by the Socialist Labor party. The Socialists were an old, established party, but were small in size. Official members numbered only 108 in the state; therefore, the party had extreme difficulty gathering the required number of signatures to obtain a position on the Ohio ballot for its presidential nominee. The Socialist Labor party, of course, represented a political ideology anathema to the Wallace philosophy. Consequently, George Wallace indirectly joined forces with the very elements of society he abhorred to ask the federal courts for assistance in his campaign.

The federal district courts were not obliging. The suit was filed in July of 1968. On August 29, the ruling of the special three-judge court convened to hear the case was announced. The court granted partial relief. It found fault with the Ohio election system, but not to the extent that the Wallacites had hoped. Rather than ordering the state to place the American Independent party and the Socialist Labor party candidates on the ballot, the court simply ordered the state to leave room on the ballot for write-in candidates. In essence, the court found nothing substantially wrong with the Ohio system except that it did not allow for write-in possibilities. The decision was not well received by the supporters of either party. Appeals were immediately filed with the United States Supreme Court.

The Court acted on these appeals immediately. Because the election was only weeks away, the justices expedited the process considerably, and the case was made the first item of the Court's business when its October 1968 session was called to order. The case was heard on October 7 and a decision was announced one week later. By a six-to-three vote the justices held in favor of Wallace, striking down the restrictive legislation of the state of Ohio.[1]

The state had relied on legal arguments based upon the Second Article to the Constitution. Section 1 of that provision states:

> Each State shall appoint, *in such Manner as the Legislature thereof may direct*, a Number of Electors, equal to the whole Number of Senators and Representatives to which the State may be entitled in the Congress. . . . (emphasis added)

According to the reasoning of the state of Ohio, this provision was intended to give the state absolute discretion over the manner in which presidential elections were to be conducted. The state of Ohio had decided to conduct its presidential elections by restricting placement on the ballot to those parties that represented serious political movements. This would eliminate the possibility of the ballot being cluttered by inconsequential political groups or short-lived political organizations. To require a party to demonstrate its significance by obtaining the signatures of 15 percent of the participating electorate and to submit those signatures ten months before the general election was not unreasonable.

Attorneys for Wallace argued that while the state had authority to regulate political parties and elections within reason, such regulation had to be within the limits set by the Equal Protection Clause of the Fourteenth Amendment. That provision holds that no state can deny any person equal protection of the laws. To treat members of established parties differently from members of newly created parties, according to the appellants' arguments, violated this constitutional mandate of equal treatment.

The Court's opinion, written by Justice Hugo Black, closely follows the logic presented by attorneys for the American Independent party. Black held that the right to form a political party was constitutionally protected by the freedom of expression and the rights to assembly and petition. However, according to the Court: "The right to form a party for the advancement of political goals means little if a party can be kept off the election ballot and thus denied an equal opportunity to win votes." The justices recognized the basic right of the state to regulate the electoral process, but held that the Equal Protection Clause was violated whenever the state treated persons differentially without a compelling reason to do so. While the goal of the state to protect the voters from an overburdened and unwieldy ballot was a reasonable one, the method of accomplishing this goal was excessive. As evidence, the Court noted that no other state required petition signatures from more than 5 percent of the electorate in order for new parties to attain a place on the ballot. And forty-two states had require-

Political parties and interest groups   115

ments of 1 percent or less. None of Ohio's sister states, according to the Court, had serious difficulties with minor parties cluttering the ballot. Hence, the Court concluded that the state of Ohio had applied measures far in excess of those necessary to accomplish its goal, and that these measures had the effect of suppressing those with minority political views from organizing and competing for the approval of the voters. In the words of Justice Black: "The State has here failed to show any 'compelling interest' which justifies imposing such heavy burdens on the right to vote and to associate."

George Wallace, therefore, received his requested assistance from the Supreme Court. He was placed on the Ohio ballot and ran an active campaign in that state. When the votes were counted, his American Independent party had garnered the ballots of 468,591 citizens of Ohio. In doing so, he compiled a respectable showing for a third-party candidate, but trailed both Richard Nixon, who captured the state's electoral votes, and Hubert Humphrey. Wallace's national campaign in 1968 was unsuccessful in terms of winning the presidency, but he did have a recognizable impact on American politics by serving as a spokesman for millions of discontented voters.

Political Association and the Constitution

In *Williams* v. *Rhodes*, the Supreme Court reaffirmed its support for the right of political association. It held that the nation's political system must be free of unreasonable restrictions on the right of the people to form effective political organizations and to compete for the approval of the voters. Furthermore, the Court recognized that the American political system must remain open for new political groups to express minority or unconventional political views. Government regulation of the political process may be necessary to preserve the integrity of that process, but the state cannot provide excessive advantages to the established parties at the expense of newly forming political movements. Only by following these principles can the nation's political process remain open to new political ideas and allow the opportunity for minority opinions to become majority views.

In contemporary politics a great emphasis is placed on political organization. Few campaigns for public office or popular movements for the adoption of a particular policy are successful without effective organizational efforts. In a nation the size of the United States political support for a person or an idea does not occur spontaneously, but only through persistent organized activity. The mobilization of the electorate is not an easy task. Because of these political realities, America abounds with political organizations. These normally take the form of political parties, campaign organizations, and interest groups. The first two are devoted to placing candidates in positions of public trust, and the third is dedicated to convincing the government to adopt policies and programs beneficial to the group's membership. The formation of parties, campaign organizations, and interest groups occurs relatively unrestrained by governmental regulation. The activities of these groups, however, are limited by both state and federal statutes. Because political organizations have a dramatic influence on the American political process, reasonable regulation to insure against corruption of the governmental system has been allowed by the courts.

Political parties and interest groups are not mentioned in any section of the American Constitution. Occasionally we need to remind ourselves that although political organizations are an established phenomenon in contemporary politics, they were looked upon with disfavor at the time our nation came into existence. President Washington was one of the foremost spokesmen for limiting the power and activities of political groups. He warned the nation on several occasions that "factions" represented a danger to the country. In spite of these warnings, political parties and interest groups began to form shortly after the formation of the Republic. Since those early years organized political movements have flourished.

The constitutional foundation for political parties and interest groups is found in the First Amendment, which guarantees the rights of speech, press, assembly, and petition. Taken together, these particular rights have been interpreted to protect a freedom of association. Both political parties and interest groups assemble individuals for the purpose of petitioning the government by various means of political expression. Hence, Americans are able to join political groups as freely as they may affiliate with nonpolitical organizations. Any governmental intrusion on the rights of Americans to join with other persons for the purposes of engaging in peaceful political activity is considered a direct violation of the First Amendment. This political right has been generally well observed by state and federal governmental units. There has been relatively little litigation involving the right to associate with political parties or interest groups. When such restrictions have been promulgated, they normally have been directed against organizations or movements considered dangerous to the American people or to our form of government. Such regulations have been particularly troublesome problems for the judiciary, but for the most part the courts have upheld the right of political association even for the most unpopular groups.

Freedom of Association and
Militant Political Groups

It is a universally recognized right of governments to take actions to preserve themselves. All political systems have had limitations on activities directed at the destruction of the government. For example, treason is considered a most serious criminal offense under all governmental systems. Similarly, most societies have declared espionage, sabotage, assassination, and related political acts to be crimes punishable by rather severe sanctions. It is not uncommon for governments to be faced with the formation of political parties or organizations dedicated to toppling the government. Some of these groups may be relatively public organizations, such as the American Communist party, or they may be secret, underground societies. Depending upon the nation's attitudes toward civil rights, various forms of governmental actions may be taken in response to opposition groups. In some nations the groups are made unlawful; in others imprisonment, exile, or even capital punishment may await members of subversive organizations. In the United States, however, the First Amendment protects freedom of association and, therefore, generally provides a barrier against the government outlawing certain groups or imposing criminal punishments against those who would join such groups. The United States government has more often directed its attack against militant political groups by declaring certain subversive actions to be criminal rather than providing penal sanctions for mere membership alone.

The Court and Communist Organizations

The United States has had laws against various kinds of subversive activities since the passage of the Sedition Act of 1798. However, serious attempts to control the activities of members of militant organizations did not begin until the years immediately surrounding the First World War. The war itself demonstrated to Americans that they could no longer feel safe simply because they were separated from the European countries by the Atlantic Ocean. The United States had become an active part of the world community in spite of the fact that a large segment of the population preferred to remain isolationist. The Russian Revolution of 1917 further prompted United States citizens to be concerned about the future. The communist philosophy was dramatically incompatible with the free enterprise capitalistic system which was firmly entrenched in the United States at that time. Many Americans feared that if the communist movement was sufficiently strong to destroy czarist Russia, it might one day turn its sights to the United States. The war and the threat of communist subversion encouraged Congress to pass the

Espionage Act of 1917 and the Sedition Act of 1918. There were several prosecutions under these acts and the judiciary was generally tolerant of the legislation.² The era of prosperity during the 1920s prompted the nation to reduce its fears of communist subversion. However, with the initiation of hostilities associated with World War II and the "cold war" that followed, the nation once again came under the grip of a "Red Scare."

During the 1940s and 1950s Congress passed several pieces of legislation designed to curtail the activities of the Communist Party. The most prominent was the Smith Act of 1940 and the Internal Security Act of 1950. Among other things, the Smith Act made it unlawful to teach or advocate the violent overthrow of the government of the United States, to distribute literature advocating the violent overthrow of the government, to organize any group of persons to teach, advocate, or encourage such violent overthrow, and to become a member of any group engaged in advocating the violent overthrow of the government. The Internal Security Act of 1950 required the registration of communist organizations (including the names and addresses of certain members) and an accounting of the groups' financial activities. There were several prosecutions under these acts. During the late 1940s and 1950s the nation was very concerned about the possibility of internal subversion. Investigations, often degenerating into "witch-hunts," were frequently held in Congress. The House Unamerican Activities Committee and the work of Senator Joseph McCarthy focused the nation's attention on domestic communism and made the purge of communist sympathizers a national fixation.

The federal legislation designed to attack communist organizations, however, was of questionable constitutionality. Not only was there the danger that the statutes curtailed freedom of speech and belief, but they also attempted to destroy political organizations, in possible violation of the freedom of association. The United States Supreme Court on several occasions was forced to wrestle with the competing values of internal security and First Amendment rights. By siding in favor of the restrictive legislation the judiciary ran the risk of preserving the government by trampling on precious First Amendment freedoms. On the other hand, ruling in favor of the protection of rights for persons engaged in subversive activities would be somewhat meaningless in the long run if such support allowed the communist movement to seize control of the government. It was not an easy time for the judiciary. The nation's judges were as divided on this question as was the country's citizenry. It is not at all surprising, therefore, that many of the judiciary's rulings on these questions appear somewhat contradictory.

One of the first significant questions facing the court focused on a provision of the Smith Act which made it a crime willfully to advocate or teach the duty or propriety of overthrowing the government of the United States by force or violence. Here the Court was faced with a direct threat to First Amendment guarantees of freedom of speech. If such teaching or advocacy was oral, how could the statute stand in light of the guarantee that "Congress shall make no law abridging the freedom of speech"? In two major decisions, *Dennis* v. *United States* (1951)[3] and *Yates* v. *United States* (1957),[4] the Court carefully attempted to answer this question. First, the Court made it clear that the act could not be applied to the mere discussion of the communist doctrine. Discussion alone was protected by the First Amendment against government encroachment. Second, the government could not constitutionally punish the teaching of an abstract philosophy or doctrine. In applying criminal sanctions to philosophical teaching the government was abridging freedoms of speech, belief, and thought. Finally, however, the Court upheld the right of the government to take action against the advocacy of action against the government. In advocating concrete action or inciting such action to occur either immediately or in the future, the perpetrators were sufficiently in the realm of conduct rather than pure speech to allow for the possibility of governmental interference.

A second major question dealt with the issue of membership. Could Congress validly outlaw membership in the Communist party or similar groups in light of the Constitution's protection of the right of assembly? The court confronted this question in 1961 by reviewing the cases of *Scales* v. *United States*[5] and *Noto* v. *United States*.[6] In a five-to-four vote, the Court upheld the conviction of Junius Scales for being a member of the Communist party in North Carolina. The minority branded the decision as a legalization of guilt by association, sending a man to prison who had committed no illegal act. In the *Noto* case, decided the same day as *Scales*, however, the Court unanimously ruled that the petitioner could not be constitutionally punished for his membership in the Communist party. A comparison of the two decisions gives us a good indication of the line of demarcation that the Court attempted to draw. The Court ruled in *Scales* that an individual could be punished by the government if he knowingly participated as an active member of an organization engaged in illegal advocacy of the violent overthrow of the federal government. Scales, the Court concluded, had the requisite knowledge and intent and, therefore, could be punished in spite of the fact that he had not engaged in any concrete action intended to destroy the government by force. Noto's conviction was reversed on the grounds that his membership was entirely different in character from that of Scales. Noto was a member of a communist group, but that group was devoted only to the teaching of the abstract theory of communism. It was not engaged in advocating violent overthrow of the government. Hence, whether one can be punished for his membership in a communist organization depends upon the distinction between teaching and advocacy outlined by the Court in *Yates* v. *United States*. Actively participating in a group that advocates violent overthrow can be restricted by the government, whereas punishing membership in a group that only teaches or discusses communist philosophy violates the First Amendment guarantees of speech and peaceful assembly.

Communist Registration Laws

The final major question facing the courts involving the anticommunist federal legislation concerned the question of registration of subversive groups. The 1950 Internal Security Act required communist organizations to register and to identify their officers. The Communist party challenged the validity of this statute claiming that it was a direct violation of the freedom of association and was a poorly disguised attempt to outlaw the party altogether. After several years of litigation, the Supreme Court finally addressed this issue in the case of *Communist Party* v. *Subversive Activities Control Board*[7] in 1961. In a narrowly drawn opinion the Court upheld the registration provisions. However, what appeared a victory for those in Congress who had promoted restrictive legislation against the Communist party actually proved a false triumph. The Communist party refused to comply with the registration law in spite of the fact that the Supreme Court had upheld its validity. This refusal triggered the applicability of another section of the Internal Security Act. This provision held that if a communist organization did not register as ordered by the government, then the individual members of the organization were required to register. Not surprisingly, no member came forward to register with the government. The Subversive Activities Control Board reacted to this situation by taking legal action to force two members of the party to register. The members refused to do so, claiming that the individual registration requirement violated the Fifth Amendment's right against self-incrimination. The members argued that if they were forced to file a document with the government admitting that they were members of a communist action organization, then they would be admitting that they had violated the Smith Act's criminal provisions against membership in a subversive group. In short, they argued, the government's registration requirement was forcing them to admit that they had committed a federal crime. To accept such reasoning would be to conclude that the registration provisions were in direct violation of the Fifth Amendment. The Supreme Court heard this very argument in *Albertson* v. *Subversive Activities Control Board*.[8] In its decision, the Court accepted the self-incrimination argument and declared the registration provisions unconstitutional.

The era of anticommunist public opinion has largely evaporated today. The fear of a communist takeover of the United States, which many have described as verging on national hysteria, has subsided. Many provisions of the restrictive legislation passed in previous decades have now been repealed by Congress. Other provisions, as we have seen, have been declared unconstitutional by the courts or have been interpreted so narrowly as to reduce their significance substantially. The years of governmental devotion to exposing and eliminating alleged communists in the United States were not good ones for the health of American civil liberties. Nonetheless, many of the decisions of the judiciary during this period explicated the meaning of the rights of freedom of speech and association.

The Constitution and Interest Groups

In almost every political campaign in the United States at least one of the competing candidates is likely to attack the influence of "special interests" in the governmental process. Such an appeal attempts to exploit the feeling of many Americans that pressure groups representing monied interests somehow control governmental decision making. In reality, there is nothing particularly sinister about interest groups. They are merely collections of individuals with shared concerns who group together for the purposes of collectively expressing their views regarding public policy. In contemporary American political life there are literally thousands of interest groups attempting to influence the decisions of local governments, state legislatures, governors, administrative agencies, and even the judiciary. While it is obviously true that some of the most powerful pressure groups represent the interests of the more wealthy classes, it would be hard to find an adult American whose concerns are not somehow represented by at least one pressure group. A person who belongs to a labor union, a professional association, a church, a social fraternity, a business group, a recreational association, or a charitable organization is almost assured of having representatives of such groups working in behalf of the groups' interests. Most citizens are not aware of the fact that they may actually hold membership in one or more interest groups.

Interest groups work in various ways to influence governmental policy. Groups such as labor unions with large memberships often emphasize to public officials the great electoral power the group possesses. Others with smaller memberships may attempt to mold public policy by providing information to public officials which is favorable to the group's interests. Still others may actively engage in litigation to convince the judiciary to interpret the law in such a way as to have a favorable effect on the group's membership. It is not uncommon for interest groups to provide funds and organizational support at election time to those candidates who are generally sympathetic to the group's objectives. Interest groups may appeal to public opinion through mass demonstrations or public relations techniques. Many pressure groups will have paid representatives, known as lobbyists, constantly contacting political leaders in behalf of the groups' concerns.

It is important to keep in mind that in spite of the fact that we often view interest groups with a degree of skepticism and even alarm, interest group activity is protected by the Constitution. In the first place, the right to organize into such groups is clearly guaranteed under the First Amendment's protection of the right to free assembly. And second, the activities of the interest groups fall under protections of speech, press, and especially petition. Interest groups cannot be prohibited by the government without running afoul of the Constitution. To legislate that lobbyists could no longer attempt to influence legislators would be to ignore fundamental First Amendment rights. This, of course, does not mean that certain limitations cannot be placed on the activities of interest groups and their representatives. Congress has legislated in this area on several occasions. Lobbyists, for example, are required to register with the government and to disclose certain activities and contributions. While Congress cannot stop interest group efforts to influence policy, it can at least require that such attempts occur as often as possible in the public spotlight.

The judiciary has not been required to enter the political process to protect the rights of interest groups on many occasions. For the most part our nation has been quite tolerant of pressure group activity, largely because our officials realize that lobbying efforts generally have a positive effect on the governmental process. However, there have been instances in which the government has attempted to curtail the formation of such groups, expose the membership of interest groups, or restrict the legitimate activities of such organizations. Usually these restrictive actions have been taken against interest groups that represent unpopular causes. Traditional interest groups, like traditional political parties, have rarely been the victims of repressive regulation.

An interesting example of attempts to prohibit the formation of certain interest groups is provided by the case of *Healy* v. *James*.[9] In September of 1969, students at Central Connecticut State College attempted to form a chapter of the Students for a Democratic Society (SDS). The SDS was a national organization whose membership consisted primarily of college and university students. It was dedicated to promoting radical political objectives including admittedly left-wing approaches to civil rights, peace, and income redistribution. On several campuses the "lobbying activities" of the group allegedly included violence, arson, and vandalism. Fearing that such activities might occur on the Connecticut campus if the SDS were recognized, Don James, president of the college, refused to allow the group to form. The students took this issue to the federal courts, claiming that First Amendment rights of assembly and speech had been violated by the college. A unanimous Supreme Court held that the college had deprived students of their right to freedom of association. In the absence of clear evidence that the group would engage in unlawful behavior, a state college cannot deny students the right to organize. An individual has the right to join with others to further political beliefs. Mere disagreement by the college with the student group's philosophy is no legitimate reason to deny official recognition to the group.

In several instances states have attempted to expose the members of certain interest groups in much the same way as the federal government tried to expose members of the Communist party. Most notable among these attempts were those of several southern states against the National Association for the Advancement of Colored People. The NAACP has been one of the most active and successful of the civil rights interest groups. During the 1950s several southern states implemented various measures to blunt the effectiveness of the NAACP. One strategy was to gain access to membership lists of NAACP chapters and publicly identify participants in the organization. Individuals having their membership exposed would then be susceptible to private community pressures of various kinds. On several occasions the Supreme Court ruled that forcing a legitimate group to submit a list of its members violated the constitutionally protected right of association. The Court declared void the membership identification strategies of states such as Alabama,[10] Arkansas,[11] and Florida.[12] These decisions were made in spite of a rather embarrassing 1928 precedent in which the Court had ruled that New York authorities could validly require membership lists to be submitted by the Ku Klux Klan.[13]

State and local governments have also attempted to attack interest group effectiveness by limiting the variety of activities that can be legitimately practiced. In doing so, the government runs the risk of violating the First Amendment. Individuals have the protected liberty of petitioning government for redress of grievances alone or in concert with other individuals. Restrictions on freedom of expression or petition can only be justified if tied to a compelling state interest. The judiciary has been called upon to arbitrate disputes between groups of individuals and governmental units over the question of legitimate governmental regulation of organizational activities. For example, the state of Virginia passed a regulation making it unlawful for

attorneys to encourage litigation. This statute prohibiting improper solicita-
tion of legal business was actually directed at the Virginia chapters of the
NAACP, which were active in encouraging minority individuals to assert
their civil rights in the courts. The Supreme Court struck down this statute,
agreeing with the NAACP that litigation can be a valid form of political expression.[14] In the context of the civil rights movement, filing lawsuits is one
of the primary means of petitioning the government for redress of grievances.
Similarly, the Court has upheld the right of labor unions to make known
their grievances by public picketing,[15] allowed racial groups to have non-
discriminatory access to public streets for demonstration of their views on
public policy,[16] and permitted religious groups to distribute handbills on the
public streets.[17] Unless pressure group strategies include activities that en-
danger the public safety, disrupt governmental business, infringe on the rights
of others, or are corrupt practices, the judiciary has been reasonably vigilant
in protecting organized expression and petition.

Employment and Political Associations

While it is clear that Americans have the constitutional right of freedom of
association, the Constitution does not necessarily protect an individual from
disadvantages that may be the consequence of holding certain group memberships. Quite often by being an active member of a particular organization, a
person may forfeit certain opportunities. Frequently employment possibilities
may be decreased because of group associations. We would be reluctant, for
example, to allow an active participant in the Communist party to be employed in a sensitive position with the Central Intelligence Agency. An individual may have a constitutional right to join any group of his choice, but he
does not necessarily have the constitutional right to a specific position of employment. Both federal and state governments have enacted regulations that
restrict employment on the basis of group membership. Some of these statutes have been within the guidelines set by the Constitution, and others have
transgressed the boundaries of constitutionality.

The Hatch Act: Government Employees
and Politics

Perhaps the most well-known federal restriction on freedom of association
as it relates to employment is the Hatch Act. This particular piece of legisla-

tion was passed by Congress in 1939 and was designed to reduce the influence of partisan politics on the government bureaucracy. It was one step in the government's attempt to keep the civil service system as immune as possible from partisan influences. The Hatch Act essentially prohibited federal civil service employees from engaging in partisan political activities. Such employees cannot hold office in a political party, take an active part in political campaigns, or become involved in any political management work. In essence, the act deprives a large portion of federal employees from exercising freedom of expression and association as it relates to politics. To violate the act is to place one's job in jeopardy. There have been two major court challenges to the validity of the Hatch Act. The first, *United Public Workers* v. *Mitchell*,[18] was heard by the Supreme Court in 1947. The Court upheld the Hatch Act by a single vote, ruling that it was within the power of Congress to enact such legislation in order to preserve the efficiency and integrity of the governmental process from partisan corruption. A second offensive against the Hatch Act was considered by the Court in 1973 in *Civil Service Commission* v. *National Association of Letter Carriers*.[19] Again, the Court approved the act against constitutional challenge. Congress was seen as sufficiently empowered to restrict the political activities of civil service workers in order to insure effective and fair operation of the administration of governmental programs. Recently, Congress has been urged by several groups to repeal the Hatch Act.

Loyalty Oaths

During the 1950s, another issue of freedom of association and government employment received national attention. This involved the question of the constitutionality of required loyalty oaths as a prerequisite for governmental positions. Many governmental units had required employees to swear that they upheld the Constitution of the United States, opposed violent overthrow of the government, and had never been a member of a subversive organization. At first the Court upheld such loyalty oaths.[20] But in 1952 the Court struck down an Oklahoma statute that prohibited government employment for all those who would not swear that they had never been a member of various communist-oriented groups.[21] The major defect in the Oklahoma regulation, according to the Court, was that it proscribed even innocent membership, in which an individual might have joined a subversive group not knowing the actual character of the organization's objectives. Following the 1952 Oklahoma case the Supreme Court, under the liberal leadership of Chief Justice Earl Warren, struck down numerous loyalty oath statutes, finding that such requirements violated the constitutionally protected rights of speech and association. However, in 1972 a more conservative Court under Chief Justice Warren Burger signaled a new approach to the loyalty oath question. In *Cole* v. *Richardson*,[22] the Court held a Massachusetts loyalty oath to be constitutionally valid. The oath required government workers to swear to uphold and defend the constitutions of the United States and the state of Massachusetts and to oppose overthrow of the government by force. According to the rationale of the Court's majority, this particular oath was permissible because it did not proscribe any protected right of expression or association. Since there is no constitutionally protected right to overthrow the government by violence, no right was violated by requiring employees to denounce forceful overthrow.

Employment Disqualification

Finally, there is the question of whether employment can be denied a person because of his associational memberships. Those who fear domestic communist influences have always been particularly concerned with infiltration of the defense establishment and educational institutions. In response to these fears the federal government passed a provision that made it unlawful for any member of a communist-action organization to engage in any employment in any defense facility. Many states passed regulations prohibiting communists from accepting employment as instructors in state educational institutions. In 1967, the Supreme Court handed down two decisions affecting government policies of this variety. In the first, the Court struck down a New York statute designed to eliminate communists from educational positions.[23] The act was challenged by two professors from the State University of New York at Buffalo. The Court held that mere membership in a communist-oriented group without evidence of specific intent to further any unlawful aims was not sufficient justification for terminating a professor's employment. The New York regulations were in violation of the right to freedom of association.

In the second decision, the Court was forced to examine the validity of federal action against a communist employee of a defense facility.[24] The employee, Eugene Robel, served as a machinist at a Seattle shipyard facility. The Court struck down the government regulation on the grounds that the statute was overbroad, that it did not distinguish between various degrees of membership in the party and did not apply only to defense positions that were of a sensitive nature. Hence, before the government can remove a person from his employment on the grounds that he holds membership in a communist-oriented group, it must show that the membership is an active one coupled with intent to carry out illegal actions and that the position occupied would be adversely affected if filled by a subversive.

Summary

Political organizations perform an integral function in our American republic. Political parties and interest groups provide the means by which American citizens can join with others of similar political persuasions to exert influence on government. These groups exist and operate in relative freedom because of the constitutional guarantees of freedom of expression, assembly, and petition. These protections allow our political system to remain relatively open, so that new political groups and movements can test their ability to capture the allegiance of the American people. The Supreme Court has been called upon on several occasions to interpret the meaning of these constitutional guarantees in light of governmental regulation of various political organizations and interest groups. For the most part, our government has been relatively inactive in placing restrictions on established, traditional political organizations. When the government has imposed sanctions on certain types of groups, they have usually been militant political parties, subversive organizations, or interest groups which for one reason or another represented an unpopular cause or clientele. The Supreme Court has applied our constitutional guarantees of freedom of association and expression to traditional groups as well as to splinter organizations and those dedicated to an alien ideology. In general, the Court has followed a policy of protecting organizational activity unless the government can demonstrate that the members have gone beyond the limits of constitutional protection.

Notes

1. Williams v. Rhodes, 392 U.S. 23 (1968).
2. See, for example, Schenck v. United States, 249 U.S. 47 (1919); Frohwerk v.

United States, 249 U.S. 204 (1919); Debs v. United States, 249 U.S. 211 (1919); Abrams v. United States, 250 U.S. 616 (1919).

3. 341 U.S. 494 (1951).
4. 354 U.S. 298 (1957).
5. 367 U.S. 203 (1961).
6. 367 U.S. 290 (1961).
7. 367 U.S. 1 (1961).
8. 382 U.S. 70 (1965).
9. 408 U.S. 169 (1972).
10. NAACP v. Alabama, 357 U.S. 449 (1958).
11. Bates v. Little Rock, 361 U.S. 516 (1960).
12. Gibson v. Florida Legislative Investigation Committee, 372 U.S. 539 (1963).
13. New York ex rel. Bryant v. Zimmerman, 278 U.S. 63 (1928).
14. NAACP v. Button, 371 U.S. 415 (1963).
15. Thornhill v. Alabama, 310 U.S. 88 (1940).
16. Cox v. Louisiana, 379 U.S. 536 (1965).
17. Johnson v. Texas, 318 U.S. 413 (1943).
18. 330 U.S. 75 (1947).
19. 413 U.S. 548 (1973).
20. See Garner v. Board of Public Works of Los Angeles, 341 U.S. 716 (1951).
21. Wiemann v. Updegraph, 344 U.S. 183 (1952).
22. 405 U.S. 676 (1972).
23. Keyishian v. Board of Regents, 385 U.S. 589 (1967).
24. United States v. Robel, 389 U.S. 258 (1967).

Further Reading

Abernathy, Glenn. *The Right of Assembly and Association.* Columbia: University of South Carolina Press, 1961.

Chase, Harold W. *Security and Liberty.* Garden City, N.Y.: Doubleday, 1955.

Cohn, R. *McCarthy.* New York: New American Library, 1968.

Cook, Thomas I. *Democratic Rights versus Communist Activity.* Garden City, N.Y.: Doubleday, 1943.

Davis, David B. *The Fear of Conspiracy.* Ithaca, N.Y.: Cornell University Press, 1972.

Fellman, David. *The Constitutional Right of Association.* Chicago: University of Chicago Press, 1963.

Gardner, David P. *The California Oath Controversy.* Berkeley: University of California Press, 1967.

Goodman, Walter. *The Committee: The Extraordinary Career of the House Committee on Unamerican Activities.* New York: Farrar, Straus, and Giroux, 1968.

Horn, Robert A. *Groups and the Constitution.* Stanford, Calif.: Stanford University Press, 1956.

Iverson, R. W. *The Communists and the Schools.* New York: Harcourt, Brace, 1959.

Rice, Charles E. *Freedom of Association.* New York: New York University Press, 1962.

Vose, Clement E. *Caucasians Only: The Supreme Court, the NAACP, and the Restrictive Covenant Cases.* Berkeley: University of California Press, 1959.

Part 3

The Constitution and Governmental Institutions

Congress

The President and
His Administration

The Judiciary

Congress

Chapter seven

Congressional Membership:
Powell v. *McCormack*

One of the most interesting and controversial figures ever to serve in the United States Congress was Representative Adam Clayton Powell, Jr. On occasion a most effective legislator, Powell was more well known for his unconventional and flamboyant behavior than for his congressional accomplishments. Powell's rise to power began in 1937 when he succeeded his father as pastor of the Abyssinian Baptist Church in Harlem, one of the nation's largest congregations. From this position Powell became an extremely influential and popular figure and was elected to the House of Representatives in 1944 after receiving the nominations of both the Democratic and Republican parties. He was continually reelected to that office by overwhelming margins. By 1961 he had acquired sufficient seniority to assume the chairmanship of the House Committee on Education and Labor, becoming the second black person in history to chair a congressional committee.

During Powell's quarter of a century in Congress his career was anything but serene. He seemed to thrive on controversy and enjoyed the attention the sensationalist press gave him. He lived an opulent life and refused to conform to the normal protocols of congressional conduct. He had occasional brushes with the law, including a standing feud with the Internal Revenue Service which at one point led to his indictment on violations of the tax code. In addition, Powell's tenure as chairman of the Education and Labor Committee was not a happy one for other members of that group. His leadership tactics as well as his rather unpredictable conduct made him an extremely unpopular chairman. Ultimately, Powell's unconventional life style, conflicts with the law, and loss of support from his colleagues led to his downfall.

The beginning of the end for Powell occurred in 1960 when he charged on television that a sixty-three-year-old widow, Mrs. Esther James, was involved in collecting graft payments for corrupt New York City police officers. Mrs. James filed two suits against Powell for defamation of character and other infractions. In the first suit the court ordered Powell to pay $211,739 in damages, and in the second, Powell was obligated for damages of $155,785. Although both judgments were ultimately reduced by a substantial amount, the net result was that Powell was legally ordered to assume a rather large financial responsibility. Powell paid the assessed amount of the first suit, largely from royalty money he earned from his record "Keep the Faith, Baby." However, Powell balked at paying the second damage award. Because of this refusal, New York courts found him in contempt of court on four separate occasions. To avoid arrest on the contempt charges, Powell remained in Washington. He traveled back to New York State only on Sundays to preach at his church. Fortunately for Powell, New York law provided that the official processing papers could not be served on Sundays. Hence, Powell was safe from being penalized on the contempt citations as long as he entered the state only on Sundays. Later, when this particular legal requirement was altered, Powell fled to his vacation residence in the Bahamas.

During the Eighty-Ninth Congress (1965–1966), the House Administration Committee initiated an investigation of Powell's activities. While no formal action was taken against Powell by the committee, evidence suggested two major violations of congressional rules. First, on Powell's frequent trips to the Bahamas he was usually accompanied by a female staff member. The travel was allegedly financed by government money. And second, Powell kept his estranged wife on the payroll at an annual salary in excess of $20,000. Furthermore, his wife did not work in the congressman's home district or in Washington, D.C., as required by law, but resided in Puerto Rico. While the committee did not recommend punitive actions against Powell at that time, the information gathered by the investigation insured that ultimately the House would have to address this apparent misconduct.

Powell did not have to wait long for the House to act. He was reelected in the November 1966 elections, but shortly thereafter the Democratic members of the House voted to strip him of his chairmanship. Furthermore, when the House was about to be sworn into office in January of 1967, Powell was asked to step aside and not take the oath, pending an investigation into charges made against him. Thereupon the House voted 364 to 64 to establish a select committee to conduct an investigation into Powell's behavior. Powell was not allowed to take his seat until the investigation was completed, although he was granted his salary and other financial benefits.

The select committee held hearings during February of 1967. Powell was invited to attend three separate committee sessions. On the first, he refused to answer any questions except those pertaining to his age, citizenship, and residency. By so confining his response to the committee's inquiry, Powell was setting the groundwork for a subsequent lawsuit. Powell's position was that the United States Constitution provides in article I, section 2, clause 2:

> No person shall be a representative who shall not have attained the age of twenty-five years, and been seven years a citizen of the United States, and who shall not, when elected, be an inhabitant of that state in which he shall be chosen.

The House, Powell claimed, did not have the authority to refuse to seat a duly elected representative unless he failed to meet the three criteria written into the Constitution. According to Powell, Congress was without the power to remove any of these constitutional requirements, nor was it empowered to add requirements to those set in the Constitution. Since he met the age, citizenship, and residence requirements, Powell argued that Congress could not validly refuse to allow him his seat. Following this first committee session, Powell refused to attend any subsequent hearings.

On March 1, 1967, the committee reported to the House. It had reached four major findings. First, Powell met the three constitutional requirements to sit in the House. Second, Powell had misbehaved with respect to the New York contempt matter. Third, he had engaged in the wrongful use of public funds. And fourth, Powell had submitted false financial expenditure reports. On the basis of these findings, the committee recommended that Powell be censured, stripped of his seniority, and fined $40,000.

The House, however, was not about to let Powell be dealt with so leniently. In three votes the House imposed much greater sanctions. First, by a vote of 222–202 on a procedural question, the House in effect refused to accept the committee's recommended punishment. Second, in a 248–176 vote the House amended the committee report by including a provision that would exclude Powell from the United States House of Representatives. And finally, the House voted 307–116 to accept the committee report as amended by the exclusion provision. The governor of New York was then notified that the seat to which Powell had been elected was officially vacant, requiring that a special election be held to select a replacement.

Adam Clayton Powell was not one to accept such a judgment from his colleagues graciously. His response was twofold. First, he filed as a candidate in the special election and was reelected by his constituency by a six-to-one margin. The House again refused to seat him, upon which a third election was held that Powell again won by a substantial margin. At this point, the House agreed to seat Powell at the beginning of the Ninety-First Congress in January 1969. While he had succeeded in regaining his seat, Powell's two-year exclusion from the House cost him twenty-two years of seniority, because House rules calculate seniority on the basis of continuous service.

Powell's second response was to file suit in federal court asking that the judiciary declare the actions of the House in violation of the United States Constitution. Both the federal district court and the court of appeals for the District of Columbia ruled against Powell, holding that the judiciary was without power to hear the case. The judges claimed that the Powell matter was a political question rather than a legal issue, that it was a matter of internal business of the House, and, therefore, it would violate the principle of separation of powers for the judicial system to rule on an internal House matter.

Convinced of the validity of his constitutional argument, Powell took his case to the United States Supreme Court. His appeal stressed the identical points he had made from the very beginning: the Constitution set the requirements for membership in the United States House, and Congress had no authority to do any more than judge whether or not those specific requirements had been met. To exclude him from his seat for reasons other than age, citizenship and residency, according to Powell, was a violation of the Constitution.

Attorneys representing Congress argued several points. First, they reiterated the separation of powers position taken by the lower courts, that the judiciary had no jurisdiction to rule on matters of internal congressional politics. Second, the House attorneys relied on article I, section 5, clause 1 of the Constitution, which stipulates: "Each house shall be the judge of the elections, returns and qualifications of its own members." And third, stress was placed on the words found in article I, section 5, clause 2: "Each house may determine the rules of its proceedings, punish its members for disorderly behaviour, and with the concurrence of two-thirds, expel a member." Supporters of the congressional action, therefore, were arguing that the Court should not accept this case in the first place because it did not constitute a proper legal question, but that if the Court did rule on Powell's appeal, it should decide in favor of the exclusion action. After all, the House was simply judging the qualifications of one of its members as provided for by the Constitution, and by two-thirds vote it had decided to punish Powell by excluding him from his seat.

On June 16, 1969, the Supreme Court issued its decision.[1] By a seven-to-one vote the Court held in favor of Powell. The majority opinion was announced by Chief Justice Earl Warren. The Court failed to find merit in the arguments advanced by congressional spokesmen. First, it held that while the issue presented obviously had an effect on the internal workings of the House, the basic question dealt with an interpretation of the federal Constitution, a task demonstrably within the power of the Court to address. Second, the Court ruled that the only qualifications necessary to assume a seat in Congress were those established by article I, section 2, clause 2: age, citizenship, and residence. Third, as to the constitutional provision granting the House the power to judge the qualifications of its members, the Court held that this section referred only to those required qualifications stipulated in article I, section 2, clause 2. Hence, Congress was empowered only to rule on whether or not an elected member met the age, citizenship, and residency requirements. Fourth, the Court addressed itself to the question of the authority of the House to expel a member upon two-thirds vote. The Court acknowledged this prerogative of the House, but concluded that the House did not *expel* Powell. Instead, the House *excluded* him from taking his seat. The two actions, expulsion and exclusion, are entirely different processes. The House and Senate may expel a member for any reason of misbehavior upon which two-thirds of the appropriate house can agree. However, expulsion applies only to seated members. Since Powell was excluded from his position (i.e., never seated) it was impossible to expel him. Had Congress desired to be rid of Powell, the House should have officially seated him and then expelled him for misbehavior. But the House did not choose to follow this correct action. Instead, it had excluded him from his seat in spite of the fact that he satisfied every constitutional requirement for the seat.

The announcement of the Court's decision in the *Powell* case signaled the end of the public careers of two prominent Americans, both of whom were variously loved and hated and always controversial. The first, Adam Clayton Powell, returned to the House having been vindicated at least on the constitutional issue he presented. But Powell was not the Adam Clayton Powell of old. He was disgraced and had lost all of his effective power. His magic was gone in his home district also. He offered his candidacy for reelection in 1970, but was defeated in his own party's primary. For the first time in a quarter century Harlem was to be represented in the House by someone other than Adam Clayton Powell. Shortly thereafter Powell died. The second career that was about to end was that of Chief Justice Earl Warren. Warren's opinion in *Powell* v. *McCormack* was his last. In ceremonies held in the Supreme Court chambers eight days after the *Powell* decision was announced, Earl Warren officially retired from office, having served as leader of the Court for a sixteen-year-period marked by numerous historic decisions.

The Court's decision in *Powell* v. *McCormack* reflects the position that the membership qualifications of article I form the sum and substance of the requirements for legislative positions. Congress cannot alter these qualifications either by addition or deletion. For the House members must possess the previously noted requirements of having attained their twenty-fifth birthday, been a citizen of the United States for seven years, and resided in the state they are to represent. Senators must be at least thirty years old, have nine years of United States citizenship, and when elected inhabit the state from which they are chosen. Other than these requirements, it is only necessary for the designated legislator to have won his seat according to the proper election regulations.

The Constitution and
Congressional Elections

The original Constitution provided for the selection of federal legislators in two ways. Members of the House were to be elected, as they are today, directly by the people for terms of two years. However, members of the United States Senate were selected by the various state legislatures for terms of six years. In 1913, the system for senatorial selection was altered with the implementation of the Seventeenth Amendment, which provided for the direct election of senators. The ratification of this amendment was promoted by a rising tide of public opinion in favor of more democratic governmental processes. Agrarian groups and labor organizations were particularly active in promoting this reform.

The Constitution gives each house of Congress the authority to judge the election of its members.[2] Occasionally the House and the Senate are called upon to settle a dispute between rival candidates over contested election results. Traditionally these disputes have been settled by majority vote of the particular house, and usually votes have demonstrated straight political party balloting. However, in the most recent case of a disputed election a different course of action was taken.

Following the 1974 election for the United States Senate from the state of New Hampshire, the results were uncertain. The original election-night count found Republican Louis Wyman ahead of Democratic candidate John Durkin by 355 votes. Durkin, however, demanded a recount, the results of which indicated that Durkin had won by ten votes. An investigation by the state ballot commission later reversed the recount vote and declared Wyman the victor by two votes. At issue was the status of some 32,000 challenged ballots. By any calculation the New Hampshire election was the closest balloting for a Senate position since ratification of the Seventeenth Amendment. Durkin appealed the state ballot commission decision to the United States Senate, which had to make a final judgment as to the proper winner of the election. The Senate first referred the question to its Committee on Rules and Administration. Under normal circumstances Durkin would have been declared the winner because of clear Democratic majorities on the committee and in the Senate generally. However, the committee was hopelessly tied in a series of four-to-four votes, caused by Democratic senator James Allen of Alabama, who voted with the three Republican committee members. Because of the committee deadlock, the matter was referred to the Senate floor. Here the Democratic members attempted to use their majorities to declare Democrat Durkin the winner. They were thwarted in this attempt by defections by some southern Democratic senators and because of a Republican filibuster. Finally the deadlock was broken and the Senate voted to decide the issue by calling for a special election by New Hampshire voters. The decision to hold a second election for the seat was considered a victory for Wyman because of the high levels of Republican registration in the state. However, in the special balloting, New Hampshire voters gave 53.6 percent of their ballots to Durkin, the Democrat. On September 18, 1975, the issue was finally settled when John Durkin was sworn in as a United States senator, some ten months after the original election.

Congressional Immunity

A final note regarding congressional membership should be made about the special immunities granted to federal legislators by the Constitution. In order to insure an independent legislative branch and to protect the free flow of open debate, congressmen were granted certain privileges in article I, section 6. First, members of Congress may not be arrested while attending a session of Congress or going to or returning from such legislative sessions. Exceptions are made for felonies, treason, and breach of peace. The purpose of this provision was to protect legislators from arrest on minor, politically inspired civil or criminal charges which would keep them from attending to congressional business. Second, the Constitution states that members of Congress cannot be questioned in any other place about any speech or debate in the legislature. This protects legislators from threats of suits for libel, defamation, or other charges which might otherwise be filed against a representative for what he says during the conduct of his official duties.[3] Such a protection allows legislators to engage in frank, open debate without fear of reprisals by lawsuit.

The Powers of Congress

The Framers of the Constitution expressed their faith in the legislative branch of government by devoting the first article of the document to its powers and limitations. The men who drafted the Constitution committed far more re-sources to delineating the functions of the legislative branch than for either the executive or judicial institutions. The legislature was considered the primary branch of government. The members of the convention appeared somewhat uncertain about the powers of the judicial branch, and many were fearful of giving excessive power to the executive. This left the legislature as the governmental branch in which the Framers placed their greatest trust.

Congress is empowered with the federal government's legislative author-ity. This, of course, refers to the power to enact laws in behalf of the national government. The Constitution specifically states that legislative proposals must receive the approval of majorities of both houses of Congress before they become law. The legislative power is subject to the executive's authority to veto legislation, but even if the president exercises the veto, Congress has means at its disposal to overrule the chief executive's action.

Perhaps the most important portion of article I is found in section 8, where the specific legislative powers of the Congress are enumerated. In serial fashion the Framers listed those areas of regulation that were to be delegated to the legislative branch. Even a casual reading of section 8 conveys the un-mistakable message that the convention attempted to take all areas of regulation that applied to nationwide problems and delegate such authority to the national legislature.

The Taxing and Spending Powers

One of the most significant powers granted to Congress is the authority to tax and spend. As noted in chapter 1, the Articles of Confederation collapsed in part because of the inability of the central government to raise revenue in order to deal with the national debt. Hence, it is not surprising that the Framers included taxation as the first of the enumerated powers. The orig-inal version of the Constitution specifically acknowledged taxes such as duties, imports, excises, and capitation taxes. It was not until 1913 that Congress was given the power to levy taxes based on income. This added taxation power was granted with the ratification of the Sixteenth Amendment. Today the federal government receives less than 10 percent of its income from the original taxation sources (duties and excise taxes). More than half of federal revenues are derived from personal and corporate income taxes. The re-mainder of the federal treasury is filled through mandatory insurance taxes (for example, social security) and governmental borrowing.

It is important to note that the Constitution grants the legislature the power to tax and spend for the national defense and for the general welfare. Therefore, the real purpose of a taxation measure may not be the raising of revenue, but may well be to promote some noneconomic result or to give the federal government a basis for regulating in an area not otherwise delegated to it by the Constitution. Similarly, Congress may use the spending power to promote the general welfare in spheres of activity not otherwise delegated to the federal government. For example, today Congress is active in spending large sums of money to improve education and promote agriculture in spite of the fact that education and agriculture are nowhere mentioned in the Constitution. Hence, the taxation and spending powers can be used to expand the role of the federal government.

Regulation of Commerce and the Economy

Another reason for the fall of the Articles of Confederation was the inability of the central government to control the economy and regulate commerce. Under the Constitution multiple economic powers were transferred to the Congress. For example, Congress is given the power to borrow money in the name of the United States government, to legislate regarding bankruptcies, to coin money and regulate its value, and to fix standards of weights and measures. Each of these specific powers gives the federal government a foothold in the area of economic regulation. Without them a uniform system of commerce and the economy would be impossible.

The most important of the economic powers granted to the Congress is the right to regulate "commerce with foreign nations and among the several states." The commerce power has become one of the most expansive of all federal powers, allowing the government to legislate over a wide variety of activities. The commerce power has been one of the most frequently litigated sections of the Constitution. In almost every period of our history important commerce power questions have been submitted to the Supreme Court. For the most part, these questions can be reduced to three basic issues: What constitutes commerce? What constitutes interstate commerce? And for what purposes may Congress validly regulate commerce?

To the first question the answer has become relatively clear. From the very beginning the Supreme Court held that commerce meant much more than the simple act of a commercial transaction.[4] Chief Justice Marshall ruled with respect to the Commerce Clause that "these words comprehend every species of commercial intercourse. . . ." Hence, the fields of transportation, navigation, communications, and others fall under the category of commerce, in addition to the more traditional forms of business transactions. Commerce, in the constitutional sense, must be interpreted very broadly. The power of Congress to regulate commerce, therefore, is a very broad power.

The second major question of what constitutes interstate commerce is especially significant. It is clear from what we know of the Constitutional Convention that the Framers intended to grant Congress the power to regulate commerce among the states, but intended the regulation of intrastate commerce to remain within the purview of the respective states. Therefore, the question often arises as to where intrastate commerce ends and interstate commerce begins. The judicial response to this question has evolved over the years. During the earlier periods of our nation's history the judiciary took the position that until goods entered the flow of interstate commerce they were under the regulatory authority of the states rather than the federal government. Under this interpretation interstate commerce was seen more in terms of transportation and distribution than as an overall economic activity. By following this philosophy of the Commerce Clause, the Supreme Court ruled that manufacturing,[5] production,[6] processing,[7] and mining[8] were all stages of the commercial process that occurred intrastate and, therefore, were exempt from the federal power of regulation. It made no difference to the Court if the goods produced during these stages were destined for ultimate delivery in other states or if the production-manufacturing stage had a substantial impact on interstate economics. The controlling fact was whether or not the commercial stage in question occurred exclusively within the boundaries of a single state. Since a mining operation, for example, was a stationary economic activity confined within a single state, it was part of intrastate commerce and, therefore, under the exclusive authority of the state to regulate. Once the ore produced by the mine was extracted from the ground and put on railroad cars bound for destinations in other states, then and only then did interstate commerce begin and with it the regulatory power of the Congress was activated. In times of economic prosperity this view of the Commerce Clause did not have a substantial adverse impact on the economy. However, when the Great Depression set in following the 1929 stock market crash, Congress found itself paralyzed to enact substantial legislation to move the nation back to economic security. The Supreme Court on numerous occasions struck down federal legislation designed to cope with the economic crisis of the 1930s on the grounds that Congress had regulated intrastate aspects of the commercial process and, therefore, had gone beyond the limits set by the Constitution.

A substantial change in the Court's approach to the commerce power occurred in 1937. The country at that time remained in the grips of the Depression. Franklin Roosevelt had been swept into office in 1932 by a huge electoral margin, promising commercial regulation that would bring better economic days to the nation. However, with the Court adverse to his congressionally enacted proposals, Roosevelt was having difficulty attacking the nation's economic ills. He had hoped to appoint new, liberal-thinking justices, but it was not until October 1937 that the first Roosevelt appointee, Hugo Black, assumed a position on the bench. In the meantime, Roosevelt made the Court a political issue, blaming it for blocking meaningful attempts to bring the Depression to a swift conclusion. His most striking attack on the Court was his notorious Court-Packing Plan, in which he proposed that the Court be expanded to as many as fifteen justices. The sole purpose of the plan was to permit Roosevelt to appoint New Deal supporters to the bench to the extent that they would outnumber the economic conservatives who were hostile to Roosevelt's regulatory programs. While the 1937 Court-packing proposal was not passed by Congress, it presented a sufficient threat that justices who held key "swing votes" on the Court began to reevaluate their positions and became more favorable to Roosevelt's legislative proposals. Dramatically, in 1937 the Court's majority began taking a new approach to the commerce power. First, the Court ruled that steel production could be regulated by the federal government;[9] shortly thereafter the Court allowed Congress to regulate manufacturing[10] and agriculture.[11] It became clear that the Court's new view of interstate commerce included in that classification any economic activity that had an impact on interstate commerce regardless of whether or not that specific activity occurred exclusively within a single state's boundaries.

The Court's interpretation of what constitutes interstate commerce continued to broaden as the nation entered the 1950s and 1960s. By the conclusion of the Warren Court years there were very few economic activities which did not fall under the Court's definition of interstate commerce. For example, hotels and motels were considered interstate commerce because they served interstate travelers,[12] restaurants fell into that classification because much of the food served was grown or processed in other states;[13] and even an obscure Arkansas recreational club was ruled to be in interstate commerce because some of the food served was brought in from other states, and some of the club's patrons were interstate travelers.[14] Under present interpretations of commerce, it is doubtful that the Court would define any serious enterprise as being intrastate commerce. Rare indeed would be the commercial concern that served only intrastate patrons, used only intrastate-produced materials, did not engage in interstate business correspondence, or did not link itself to the interstate telephone system. Any one of these characteristics would undoubtedly be sufficient to establish the interstate nature of the commercial activity. Therefore, the Court radically changed its position on the commerce power. Prior to 1937 most commerce was considered intrastate and therefore outside the regulatory power of the Congress. Today Congress has been granted regulatory authority over almost every economic activity through the expansion of the Court's definition of interstate commerce.

The third major commerce power question that has periodically faced the Court involves the purposes for which Congress may validly regulate commerce. The Court's response to this question has been relatively consistent. The Commerce Clause makes no reference to the purposes or motives of commercial regulation. Therefore, Congress may regulate interstate commerce for almost any purpose or motive whatever. As long as the regulation does not violate the Bill of Rights or other constitutional protections, congressional power is absolute and entire. Hence, commerce can be regulated for noncommercial reasons. As early as 1902, for example, the Court upheld on the basis of the Commerce Clause the right of Congress to regulate interstate lottery activities.[15] The purpose of this legislation was obviously not commerce, but to promote certain standards of morality. Nonetheless, the congressional action was valid under the commerce power. Similarly, the Court has validated under the authority of the Commerce Clause the right of the Congress to prohibit the exploitation of child labor[16] and to enact statutes making certain forms of racial and sexual discrimination unlawful.[17] Clearly, the commerce power is one of Congress's most important authorities. Along with the taxing and spending powers, it has expanded the role of the federal government far beyond that envisioned by the men who wrote the Constitution.

Congress and the Military

Along with the fiscal powers of taxation, spending, and economic regulation, section 8 of article I gives Congress a number of powers dealing with military matters. Congress is given the responsibility for raising armies and navies, for providing economic support for military forces, for establishing rules by which the armed forces operate, and for providing the necessary military forces to quell domestic insurrections. Furthermore, the Constitution delegates to the legislative branch the right to declare war. While Congress has been active in each of these areas, normally it acts upon the recommendation of the president. Given the fact that the chief executive has primary responsibility for the nation's foreign policy, the Congress has usually been content to exercise its military powers consistent with the foreign policy positions of the executive branch. Even the power to declare war, which the Framers thought sufficiently important to transfer to Congress from its traditional place under the executive branch, has never been invoked unless the president supported such action. Furthermore, the president has on occasion waged war without a congressional declaration. The most prominent example of such action was the Vietnam War effort, which was conducted by the United States over the administrations of three different presidents without a formal war declaration ever being issued by Congress.

Miscellaneous Powers of Congress

In addition to the foregoing powers granted to the legislative branch, Congress was authorized to exercise a number of other rights which do not neatly fit into any particular category. However, several of these miscellaneous rights constitute substantial powers. For example, Congress has been granted the authority to regulate naturalization and immigration policy for the United States. In a nation that has grown largely because of population movements into its boundaries, immigration and citizenship matters have been of great importance. The Supreme Court has allowed Congress wide latitude in exercising this power, permitting Congress to establish whatever conditions it deems necessary for the entry of foreigners into the United States. Article I grants the Congress the right to establish and maintain a postal system. This function was given to the federal government in order to promote nationwide communications rather than relying on fragmented state-sponsored postal operations. The Constitution allows Congress to impose regulations regarding copyrights and patents in such a manner as to promote the practical arts and sciences. This provision permits the legislature to enact regulations that make it economically desirable to engage in the production of new ideas and designs and in doing so to promote the advancement of science and invention. Congress has the power to create a lower court system for the nation's judiciary. Article III, the portion of the Constitution dealing with the judicial branch, only stipulates that there shall be one Supreme Court. The creation of additional inferior courts is left to the discretion of the Congress. Finally, Congress has been granted the power to develop and regulate the nation's capitol and other federally owned lands. Therefore, the District of Columbia, military bases, United States territories, and other parcels of federally controlled land are regulated by the Congress. At first glance these miscellaneous powers may appear insignificant, especially in comparison with the fiscal and monetary powers of the Congress. In effect, however, the exercise of these particular responsibilities has a dramatic influence on the way our nation operates and the conditions of living within our borders.

The powers described in this section are those enumerated in the Constitution. It should not be forgotten that in addition to these enumerated powers the Constitution gives Congress the authority to make laws "necessary and proper for carrying into execution the foregoing powers." This, of course, is the basis of the implied powers doctrine discussed in chapter 2. Congress was not explicitly granted the authority to create a national bank, but the bank was a useful and convenient way to carry out the fiscal powers enumerated in article I. Therefore, the creation of the national bank was constitutionally valid. The Framers specified certain powers that Congress was entitled to exercise and added the Necessary and Proper Clause to allow Congress a degree of flexibility in executing its enumerated powers.

Legislative Investigation

One implied power that deserves special mention at this point is the authority to conduct legislative investigations. The very act of legislating assumes intelligent behavior based upon as much credible information as possible. So important is the right to investigate that the Supreme Court has held that investigative authority is inherent in the legislative function itself.[18] Congressional investigations, however, must be kept within proper limitations. The ultimate purpose of such investigations must be a valid legislative objective. Congress may investigate in order to gather information about the need for new legislation, the effectiveness of past legislation, or alternative approaches to a particular legislative goal. Congress cannot investigate for the sake of investigation, but must be able to demonstrate that the investigation is tied to a legitimate congressional activity. The investigative power must also be exercised in a manner consistent with the dictates of the Bill of Rights and other guaranteed liberties.[19] If a congressional committee orders a person to testify, the committee must observe the rights of the witness to First Amendment freedoms and to the privilege against self-incrimination. Furthermore, the questions presented to the witness must be pertinent to a valid legislative investigation that the committee has been properly authorized to conduct.[20] Investigations are necessary legislative activities. Congressional committees are armed with powers to compel persons to testify and to produce relevant materials, but the scope and method of the investigation must be confined to reasonable limitations.

Delegation of Congressional Authority

It goes without saying that the world today is a much different one than existed at the time the Constitution was drafted. It is a much more complex world presenting problems calling for more technical expertise and varied experience than ever anticipated at the time of the formation of the Republic. When the Constitutional Convention drafted article I there was the reasonable expectation that the powers granted to the Congress would be exercised by the Congress. Today it is impossible for Congress to execute all of its responsibilities by itself. For example, Congress is empowered to manage all federally owned lands. Yet Congress could not be expected to devote its attention to such things as the proper speed limits and camping regulations in Yellowstone National Park. It is reasonable to allow Congress to delegate some of its lawmaking authority—in the case of Yellowstone, to the National Park Service. This, however, presents a constitutional question beset with many problems. Can the legislature give up its legislative power? Can Congress delegate its legislative authority to agencies of the executive branch without violating the principle of separation of powers? Obviously, the Framers had reason to give certain powers to the Congress and not to the president. Is it therefore valid for the Congress to pass its constitutionally granted powers to the chief executive? If so, under what limitations is such a delegation permissible?

These questions are not easy ones. The Supreme Court first authorized legislative delegation in 1825 when Chief Justice Marshall declared it permissible for Congress to delegate insignificant legislative actions.[21] Congress, for example, may pass a piece of legislation that establishes certain standards and allow an administrative agency to "fill in the details" while administering the act. The judiciary has traditionally required that whenever Congress delegates a portion of its legislative powers to an executive agency it must stipulate the goal of the legislation and be specific regarding the limits of the administrative law-making authority. Occasionally when such firm standards were not imposed by Congress, the Court has declared the legislative delegation of authority in violation of the Constitution.[22]

In today's world, however, conditions demand a considerable degree of legislative delegation. In fact, the rules and regulations promulgated by federal administrative agencies each year far outnumber the laws passed by Congress. Nonetheless, these agencies have been created by Congress and can be abolished by Congress if they go beyond their established authority. Furthermore, Congress has the power to modify any administrative rule handed down by these agencies. The courts have realized the need for such legislative delegation and over the past four decades have been reluctant to strike down any statute on the basis of the improper delegation question. Clearly this particular aspect of legislative power is at variance with the intentions of the Framers. The men who attended the Philadelphia Convention would most surely have been astonished, for example, by the Economic Stabilization Act of 1970 in which Congress gave the president the power to impose wage and price controls on the American economy. It is doubtful that the convention would have approved wage and price controls at all, but they surely would have been horrified to see the president exercise such power. However, the conditions of the twentieth century demand many things that were not foreseen by our ancestors. Fortunately, the Constitution is sufficiently flexible to allow the nation's governmental system to keep pace with the changing world.

Congress and the Separation of Powers

The powers the Constitution grants to Congress are normally exercised for the purposes of initiating or maintaining certain public policies. The legislative power is essentially one of converting into legal prescriptions the political priorities of the American people. No matter what programs the president prefers or the specific policies supported by public opinion, few alterations in the actions of the government can be executed without the approval of Congress.

The manner in which Congress exercises its authority has a major impact on the activities of the executive and the judicial branches. As we noted in chapter 2, the Framers of the Constitution believed in a system of separation of powers and gave each branch the constitutional authority to check many of the operations of the two branches. Consistent with the separation of powers doctrine, Congress has certain general and specific grants of power that are capable of restraining the executive and the judiciary.

Congress and the Executive Branch

Congress has a great deal of influence on the shape and powers of the executive branch. The legislative power of Congress, for example, must be exercised for the creation of every executive agency and department. Each agency created has its powers specifically defined by federal law passed by Congress. The various departments are organized into a hierarchy determined by Congress. The president is powerless to change this organization of the federal bureaucracy in the face of congressional opposition. In addition, the number of federal employees attached to the executive is set by Congress. So too are the qualifications and standards that must be used in the employment of these persons. As we have seen, Congress, through various civil service statutes like the Hatch Act, can place employment conditions on persons working for the executive. Individuals selected to fill key policy-making positions under the president can take office only after receiving the approval of the United States Senate. And finally, Congress through its investigative powers may maintain continuous supervision and oversight of the activities of the executive branch. These congressional checks limit what could otherwise develop into an administrative bureaucracy with excessive amounts of power.

Congress also controls to a certain extent the policy making activities of the executive. No matter what political and legislative platform to which the president may have been pledged during his election campaign, he cannot initiate any of these policy preferences without congressional approval. This congressional approval normally requires two distinct actions. First, the new policies and all the required machinery to implement them must be authorized by the legislature. This authorization action, in effect, gives a congressional stamp of approval to the principle espoused by the proposed policy. The second action required is usually an appropriations grant. Almost all program modifications call for some change in the level of federal spending in a particular policy area. Any changes in funding levels must be approved by Congress. This power of the purse is often cited as Congress's most effective power. Congress also has a policy check on the executive through the confirmation process. If the Senate does not approve of the qualifications of a particular presidential appointee and believes that the nominated individual will adversely affect particular governmental interests, it can refuse to approve the nominee. The supervision and oversight power also allows Congress to monitor how members of the executive branch execute the policy legislation passed by the legislature. If that administration is not to the liking of Congress, the legislature may alter the powers of the agency, program authorization, spending levels, or the procedures the agency is required to follow.

The president has the primary responsibility under the Constitution for the nation's foreign policy, yet Congress is not without influence in the nation's foreign affairs. Any presidential policies that require personnel or federal appropriations must clear the Congress. An appropriate example of this is the country's foreign aid programs. Foreign spending levels are proposed by the president, but the funds do not become available without congressional appropriation actions. Congress may modify the general levels of aid to be distributed or may direct that aid be increased or reduced to specific nations in order to reflect Congress's attitude toward the actions of those countries. The Framers gave the United States Senate the power to ratify treaties. The president is powerless to pledge the United States to treaty commitments without Senate ratification of the treaty provisions, as illustrated by the recent controversy over ratification of the Panama Canal Treaty. In recent decades presidents have avoided the use of treaties by entering into executive agreements with foreign heads of government. This practice has sharply reduced the intended role of the Senate over the nation's alliances with foreign powers. The Senate confirmation power has an impact on foreign policy, since key foreign policy positions, including all ambassadors, can be filled only with persons acceptable to a majority of the Senate. Finally, in the event that the president wishes to initiate hostilities against a foreign power, Congress has certain war powers. The declaration of war, the raising of military forces, the numbers of military forces, and appropriations for necessary arms and equipment are all the responsibility of Congress. In times of crisis Congress has tended to approve presidential recommendations in these areas, but the threat of a legislative check is a very real one. Furthermore, the decisions that Congress makes as to the national defense posture during times of peace have a substantial bearing on the conduct of a war effort when hostilities are initiated.

The final major check that Congress may exercise over the executive is the power of removal. The Constitution stipulates that a president can be removed only by the congressional action of impeachment.[23] The removal power is a two-stage process. First, the House of Representatives must bring formal impeachment charges against the incumbent. If a congressional investigation into the activities of the president produces evidence that he has engaged in "treason, bribery or other high crimes and misdemeanors," the House by majority vote may charge the president with impeachable offenses. Such charges are then referred to the United States Senate, which must determine whether the president is in fact guilty of the charged offenses and whether, therefore, he should be removed from office. The Senate proceedings take the form of a trial with the chief justice of the United States as the presiding officer. The concurrence of two-thirds the senators present and voting is necessary to remove the president. No American president has ever been removed from office. However, on two occasions the Congress has come very close to exercising the removal power. In 1868, after House impeachment, the Senate failed by a single vote to convict and remove President Andrew Johnson. And in 1974, the House investigated the activities of President Richard Nixon. The evidence against Nixon was so incriminating that impeachment and conviction seemed highly probable. In response to these realities, Nixon became the first president of the United States to resign his office. While no president has been officially removed by the Senate, the possibility of impeachment and conviction is always present. The same impeachment power extends to the vice-president and other civil officers of the United States government. Fortunately for the stability of our governmental system, it has not often been necessary to invoke the Constitution's impeachment provisions.

Congress and the Judiciary

The legislature's methods of checking the activities of the judicial branch are not as extensive as those that can be applied to the executive departments. Nonetheless, the checks can be very powerful. First, the Congress has broad authority to shape and support the judiciary. The Constitution is relatively silent regarding the court system's structure. It provides for only one Supreme Court and inferior courts which Congress may from time to time create. Congress, then, creates courts and creates the judgeships necessary to staff those courts. To what extent Congress gives financial support to the courts greatly determines the type of justice system which the federal government will maintain. Salary levels must be sufficiently high to attract quality attorneys to fill judgeships; resources must be available to give the judges necessary support facilities; there must be sufficient courtroom space constructed; and funds need to be devoted to auxiliary personnel such as law clerks, marshals, and clerical assistants.

Second, Congress can have a direct impact on judicial policy making.

The legislature's law-making power can be used to block or modify the implementation of judicial decision. If Congress disapproves of the manner in which the judges are interpreting the law, it can change the law. If Congress is not satisfied with the judiciary's interpretation of the Constitution, it can propose a constitutional amendment to alter the meaning of the document. Congress has resorted to this action on several occasions. For example, in 1866, Congress proposed the Fourteenth Amendment, which in effect reversed the Supreme Court decision of *Dred Scott* v. *Sanford*[24] with respect to the meaning of state and federal citizenship; and in 1909, Congress proposed the Sixteenth Amendment, giving the legislature the authority to tax incomes. This amendment was proposed in direct response to the Court's ruling in *Pollock* v. *Farmers Loan and Trust*[25] which had substantially curtailed congressional taxing power. The Constitution also gives Congress the power to regulate the Supreme Court's appellate jurisdiction. Theoretically, the national legislature can define the Court's jurisdiction in such a manner that certain types of cases can never come before the Court. On occasion this theoretical power becomes a practical one. For example, in 1868 the Supreme Court was about to decide a case involving a challenge to the federal Reconstruction Acts following the Civil War. Rather than risk the possibility that the Court might rule the acts unconstitutional, Congress passed a statute stripping the Court of its jurisdiction to hear the case.[26]

Finally, the Congress has a role in the judicial selection and removal process. All federal judges are nominated by the president, but before taking office they must be confirmed by the United States Senate. When the Senate perceives serious weaknesses with the nominee or has substantial reservations about his stands on matters of legal policy, it is empowered to reject the president's choice. Such was the case in 1930 when President Hoover's appointment of John J. Parker to be a Supreme Court justice was rejected by the Senate because of the nominee's views on labor and civil rights. Similarly, in 1969 and 1970, Richard Nixon's nominations of Clement Haynsworth and G. Harrold Carswell to join the Court were defeated, the first because of alleged ethical violations and the second because of a lack of judicial ability. In addition, Congress controls the removal power. Impeachment and conviction by Congress is the only way in which a federal judge can be removed from office against his will. The removal power has been infrequently invoked. Less than ten federal judges have been impeached by the House, and only one-third of those were convicted by the Senate.

The checks that the Constitution authorizes Congress to exercise against the other branches of the government have been reasonably effective. While it is true that some of the intended checks have lost their potency (e.g., the power to declare war and the treaty ratification authority), the overall impact has been quite successful. The executive and judicial branches have been kept within reasonable limits by the Congress without suffering excessive losses of power through the abusive use of the checks granted to the legislature.

Summary

The Constitution discusses the national legislature in significant detail. The membership qualifications, powers, and procedures are all well outlined. Surprisingly enough, the constitutional provisions regulating Congress have remained largely intact throughout the nation's history. The Sixteenth Amendment, authorizing substantial new taxing powers to Congress, and the Seventeenth Amendment, mandating popular election of United States senators, have significantly altered the structure and powers of the Congress. Additional constitutional amendments have granted the legislature power to enforce certain civil liberties, but these have not dramatically changed the institution. It is to the credit of those attending the Constitutional Convention that the framework established at that time has not required radical surgery. Perhaps this has been the case because the Framers gave careful consideration to the legislative power and had learned by the failures of the Congress under the Articles of Confederation experience. For whatever the specific reasons, the Constitution has given Congress ample power to cope reasonably well with national needs. In addition to explicit grants of authority, certain sections of article I allow for a broad range of legislative actions. Particularly important among these are the taxing and spending powers, the Commerce Clause, and the Necessary and Proper Clause. Not only has the legislative institution been capable of dealing successfully with a majority of the country's problems, but it has also served well the check and balance function which the Framers assigned to it.

Notes

1. Powell v. McCormack, 395 U.S. 486 (1969).
2. Article I, section 5, clause 1.
3. See, for example, Gravel v. United States, 408 U.S. 606 (1972); Doe v. Mc-Millan, 412 U.S. 306 (1973).

4. Gibbons v. Ogden, 9 Wheaton 1 (1824).

5. United States v. E. C. Knight, 156 U.S. 1 (1895).

6. Hammer v. Dagenhart, 247 U.S. 251 (1918).

7. Schechter Poultry Corporation v. United States, 295 U.S. 495 (1935).

8. Carter v. Carter Coal, 298 U.S. 238 (1936).

9. National Labor Relations Board v. Jones and Laughlin Steel Corporation, 301 U.S. 1 (1937).

10. United States v. Darby Lumber, 312 U.S. 100 (1941).

11. Wickard v. Filburn, 317 U.S. 111 (1942).

12. Heart of Atlanta Motel v. United States, 379 U.S. 241 (1964).

13. Katzenbach v. McClung, 379 U.S. 294 (1964).

14. Daniel v. Paul, 395 U.S. 298 (1969).

15. Champion v. Ames, 188 U.S. 321 (1903).

16. United States v. Darby Lumber, 312 U.S. 100 (1941).

17. See, for example, the Civil Rights Act of 1964, as amended.

18. McGrain v. Daugherty, 273 U.S. 135 (1927).

19. Watkins v. United States, 354 U.S. 178 (1957).

20. Barenblatt v. United States, 360 U.S. 109 (1959).

21. Wayman v. Southard, 10 Wheaton 1 (1825).

22. See, for example, Panama Refining v. Ryan, 293 U.S. 388 (1935).

23. See also Amendment Twenty-Five, which provides for removal of presidential powers and transfer of power from a chief executive who resigns or becomes disabled.

24. 19 Howard 393 (1857).

25. 158 U.S. 601 (1895).

26. Ex Parte McCardle, 6 Wallace 318 (1868).

Further Reading

Benson, Paul. *The Supreme Court and the Commerce Clause, 1937–1970.* New York: Dunellen, 1970.

Berger, Raoul. *Congress versus the Supreme Court.* Cambridge, Mass.: Harvard University Press, 1969.

Berger, Raoul. *Impeachment: Constitutional Problems.* Cambridge, Mass.: Harvard University Press, 1973.

Erlich, Walter. *Presidential Impeachment.* St. Charles, Mo.: Forum Series, 1974.

Gallagher, Hugh G. *Advise and Obstruct: The Role of the United States Senate in Foreign Policy Decisions.* New York: Delacorte, 1969.

Harris, Richard. *Decision.* New York: Dutton, 1971.

Javits, Jacob K. *Who Makes War.* New York: Morrow, 1973.

Lee, R. Alton. *A History of Regulatory Taxation.* Lexington, Ky.: University of Kentucky Press, 1973.

MacNeil, Neil. *The Forge of Democracy.* New York: McKay, 1963.

McGreary, M. Nelson. *The Development of Congressional Investigative Power.* New York: Octagon, 1966.

Morgan, Donald G. *Congress and the Constitution: A Study of Responsibility.* Cambridge, Mass.: Harvard University Press, 1966.

Murphy, Walter F. *Congress and the Court.* Chicago: University of Chicago Press, 1962.

The President and
His Administration

Chapter eight

Executive Power and the Constitution:
United States v. *Nixon*

On July 8, 1974, the United States Supreme Court convened in an extraordinary summer session in order to hear oral arguments in the case of *United States* v. *Richard M. Nixon, President of the United States*.[1] To many observers this litigation represented the culmination of the nation's most serious constitutional confrontation. Never before had the country's three governmental branches been so involved in a struggle which was to test the strength of our constitutional system. It was a credit to the nation's stability and commitment to the rule of law that the most important issue in this conflict was to be decided in the highest court of the land. In nations with less faith in constitutionalism similar issues would be decided by military takeover or violence in the streets.

The events that led to this historic Supreme Court session began in the early morning hours of June 17, 1972, when the headquarters of the National Democratic Committee located in the Watergate Office Building in Washington, D.C. was illegally entered. Eight persons were immediately involved in the break-in. Five individuals actually conducted the illegal entry: James McCord, a security coordinator for the Committee to Reelect President Nixon and a former FBI and CIA agent, and four Cuban Americans who were active in Florida-based anti-Castro organizations. Serving as a lookout for the operation was Alfred Baldwin, a former FBI agent and employee of the Committee to Reelect the President. Located in a nearby hotel and maintaining radio contact with the burglars were Howard Hunt and G. Gordon Liddy.

154

Hunt was a former CIA agent, and Liddy had been previously with the FBI. Both had done investigative work for the executive branch and were associated with the Nixon Reelection Committee. Unfortunately for the eight conspirators, a night watchman contacted police, who apprehended the suspects and placed them under arrest.

The break-in and arrest caused a moderate public stir at the time, generated primarily by the fact that the nation was in the middle of a presidential election campaign and the crime itself had obvious political overtones. What made the incident even more intriguing was the linkage between the conspirators and the Nixon reelection effort and possibly the White House itself. The Democrats, of course, charged the Republicans with instigating illegal political activities. At the time, however, the Watergate break-in did not loom as a major campaign issue with the American people. Richard Nixon's reelection bid was hardly slowed by the publicity surrounding the event, and in November he scored one of the nation's greatest electoral victories, smothering attempts by Democratic senator George McGovern to unseat him.

The trial of the Watergate break-in suspects began on January 8, 1973. During the seven-month interim between the crime and its subsequent trial, substantial evidence, direct as well as circumstantial, had been published in the press leading to the conclusion that the Watergate break-in was not an isolated activity by a few overzealous Nixon supporters. Instead, there was probable cause to believe that the Watergate operation was only one example of a broad, coordinated effort to carry out political "dirty tricks," that the break-in was orchestrated by persons of influence within the president's reelection team, that knowledge of the break-in might have gone to the White House itself, and that high White House officials might have been engaged in an effort to cover up the connection between those who actually carried out the illegal entry and their White House superiors. There were claims of obstruction of justice, payoffs, and promises of executive clemency. The investigative reporting and the media coverage of the break-in as well as the mysterious events surrounding it captured the nation's attention. The country looked forward to the trial, anticipating that it would bring forward information that would resolve all the doubt and conflicting interpretations of the Watergate affair.

Those who hoped that the trial would clarify matters were to be disappointed. Most disappointed of all, however, was U.S. District Judge John J. Sirica, the presiding judge. Sirica was determined to learn the exact nature and extent of the criminal activity. The cases made by the prosecution and defense attorneys appeared to Sirica to be much more of a cooperative effort to hide the facts than to constitute a true adversary trial. Often Sirica was compelled to ask questions of the witnesses on his own and to admonish the participating attorneys for failing to pry the entire truth from the witnesses. Frustrated at the trial's end by his failure to gain a clear picture of the Watergate operation, Sirica made one last attempt to encourage the defendants to relate everything they knew about the Watergate break-in. After the suspects were found guilty, Sirica announced that he would postpone final sentencing until he was able to give a full consideration to the matter. He noted, however, that one of the factors he would take into account in determining the defendants' sentences would be the extent to which they cooperated with authorities to bring about a full disclosure of the details of the Watergate affair. In order to demonstrate the seriousness with which he considered this matter, he announced provisional sentences for the Watergate defendants of up to thirty-five years. Sirica was obviously determined to crack what appeared to be a deliberate cover up.

Sirica's strategy was already paying dividends. James McCord had delivered a letter to the judge expressing his willingness to tell everything he knew about the Watergate operation and related activities. The government agency to which McCord was to tell his story was the United States Senate Select Committee on Presidential Campaign Activities, chaired by Senator Sam Ervin of North Carolina. The Ervin Committee was officially established during the course of the Watergate trial. Once Sirica had acted in behalf of the judicial branch, it was the federal legislature which was to occupy the attention of the American public. During the summer of 1973, the committee conducted public televised hearings investigating the Watergate crime and related campaign activities. The results of this investigation were staggering. The Watergate break-in appeared insignificant in comparison to the sum total of wrongdoing uncovered. Evidence of several break-ins, illegal surveillance, payoffs, obstruction of justice, illegal campaign contributions, and illegal or unethical activities by members of the FBI, CIA, the Internal Revenue Service, and the Justice Department was presented to the committee members. The disclosures implicated high-ranking members of the Nixon reelection organization and White House personnel as well. What remained unclear at the end of the investigation was to what extent the president was aware of these activities and what his exact role might have been.

Without doubt the most significant piece of information the Senate investigation produced was that Richard Nixon had installed tape-recording devices in order to keep a permanent record of all discussions and telephone conversations that occurred in the White House. The revelation that the White House had been "bugged" by the president was astounding. Persons who had communicated with the president or his key advisors either in person or on the telephone now learned that their supposedly confidential conversations were actually tape recorded without their knowledge and that the tapes were stored somewhere in the control of the White House. For the purposes of the investigation, the presidential tapes constituted an invaluable source of evidence necessary to establish the precise role of the president and his key officials in the Watergate-related activities.

During the next year the Nixon tapes became the paramount topic in the Watergate investigations. The Senate committee made every attempt to gain access to relevant tape recordings in order to evaluate the conflicting testimony that had been presented to it. Also interested in the tapes was the office of the special prosecutor. Congress had created the position of special prosecutor when it appeared certain that criminal activities had occurred. The special prosecutor's function was essentially executive in nature, but as established, the office was somewhat insulated from the control of the Justice Department, which would normally handle such criminal investigations. The special prosecutor (first Archibald Cox and later Leon Jaworski) in cooperation with Judge Sirica had empanelled a special federal grand jury to determine if formal criminal charges (indictments) should be issued against any of the alleged participants in the questionable campaign activities. The special prosecutor's office desired the tapes to determine where criminal responsibility rested and to use as evidence before the grand jury and in subsequent criminal trials.

By late 1973, a third governmental body directed its attention to Watergate developments and the White House tapes. This group was the Judiciary Committee of the United States House of Representatives. The Judiciary Committee was focusing its efforts on investigating the specific activities of Richard Nixon to determine whether the president should be impeached. To the House committee the tapes were a prized source of information to discover the exact role of the president in order to determine if he had engaged in "high crimes and misdemeanors."

Therefore, at least three governmental groups were attempting to gain access to the tapes. First, the Senate investigating committee made several legal moves to be given copies of the recordings in order to decide what kinds of campaign legislation might be necessary to preserve the integrity of future elections. Second, the office of the special prosecutor desired the tapes to carry out its mission of obtaining possible indictments and convictions of persons involved in illegal activities. And third, the House Judiciary Committee wanted access to the tapes in order to conduct its investigation of possible impeachable offenses by the president. The president, however, was not receptive to making available the tape recordings themselves or transcripts of the recorded conversations.

The final round in this emerging confrontation began on March 1, 1974. On that date the Watergate grand jury issued formal criminal indictments against seven men who allegedly had engaged in a conspiracy to defraud the United States government and to obstruct justice through their various roles in the Watergate affairs. The indicted included former United States attorney general John Mitchell, the White House chief of staff, H. R. Haldeman, Nixon's chief advisor for domestic affairs, John Ehrlichman, Nixon White House advisor Charles Colson, and three other persons associated with the White House. In addition, the criminal indictments charged Richard Nixon as an unindicted conspirator in the Watergate break-in cover-up attempts. These indictments set the stage for a major criminal trial charging corrupt activities by the highest-ranking officials in the Nixon administration. To many experts it constituted the most significant charges of executive wrongdoing in the nation's history.

On April 18, 1974, Judge Sirica granted Special Prosecutor Leon Jaworski's motion to issue a subpoena ordering the president to produce specified tape recordings relevant to the upcoming criminal trial. This order set the power of the judiciary against the will of the executive. Judge Sirica was demanding that the head of the executive branch of government deliver up certain records. The defendants in the criminal trial supported this move, hoping that the tapes would provide information beneficial to their cases. The legislature supported the action of the special prosecutor (in addition to initiating its own legal action) with the anticipation that if Judge Sirica's order proved successful Congress might also gain access to the recorded material.

President Nixon's reaction was for the most part negative. He claimed that the principle of executive privilege allowed him to retain confidential presidential records. To allow open access to these conversations would be to place in jeopardy certain secret materials relevant to the safety and defense of the United States. Furthermore, Nixon claimed that the doctrine of separation of powers protected the president from being compelled by the judicial branch (or the legislative branch for that matter) to produce certain documents. To uphold Sirica's judicial order, the president argued, would be to make the executive branch subservient to the judicial branch. The separation of powers doctrine dictates that each branch is independent within its own sphere of authority and cannot be ordered about by the other branches.

While standing on the claim of executive privilege, President Nixon on April 30, 1974, released transcripts of some forty-three conversations. Twenty of these conversations were among those mentioned in Judge Sirica's subpoena. Nixon released these transcripts "voluntarily." The transcripts of the taped conversations were not whole and complete; they were substantially edited by the White House. Furthermore, not all of the conversations ordered produced by Sirica were released by the president. Nixon, however, argued that to release the additional tapes would be to release information that must remain secret in the best interests of national security. Furthermore, the executive, and the executive alone, was qualified to decide which conversations could not be released and what editing was necessary in the conversations voluntarily made public.

Three weeks later, on May 20, 1974, Judge Sirica escalated the battle with the president. He held that the president had not complied fully with his subpoena and therefore ordered the president to produce within eleven days all the required documents, including the original tape recordings. Sirica based his order on the conclusion that the special prosecutor had made a compelling case that the taped conversations were required to guarantee a fair trial of the Watergate cover-up defendants. Furthermore, Sirica ruled that the judiciary, not the executive, was the final arbiter of the question of whether or not executive privilege could be validly claimed.

The significance of Judge Sirica's order could not be overestimated. A U.S. district court judge was ordering the president of the United States to produce evidence that might well lead to the convictions of his own personal and political advisors and could possibly implicate the chief executive in impeachable offenses which would drive him from office. Sirica was placing the interests of a fair trial over Nixon's claimed interests of the presidency, the rule of law over the rule of a single officeholder. Given the importance of the issues involved in this conflict, it was clear that Sirica's order would be appealed to the United States Supreme Court. Only four days after Sirica issued his final order, both Nixon and the special prosecutor petitioned the Supreme Court to review the judge's actions. The Court agreed to review the issues involved under special procedures for expediting significant and pressing cases.

United States v. *Nixon* loomed as an especially important decision from the standpoints of both constitutional law and practical politics. In a constitutional sense, the Court was asked to balance several different values and powers. Most important was the question of executive privilege. While several presidents at various points in history had claimed executive privilege, the judiciary had never ruled on whether the doctrine was constitutionally correct. Whatever the Court decided in this particular controversy would be the only major precedent on the question and would have a significant bearing on the separation of powers doctrine. Politically, the litigation probably would determine the fate of the Nixon administration. In spite of the many principles involved in the Watergate controversy, there were still a great many partisan-based hostilities. It was perhaps inevitable that politics would enter the picture. Yet it was left to the Court, supposedly our least political institution, to arrive at a final decision in the tapes controversy.

On July 24, 1974, the Supreme Court announced its decision in a majority opinion written by Chief Justice Warren Burger. The vote was unanimous (with Justice William Rehnquist not participating) and generally in favor of the position taken by the office of the special prosecutor. The Court held that the claim of executive privilege was not well taken by President Nixon in this instance. Executive privilege is not mentioned anywhere in the Constitution. Instead, proponents of executive privilege claim that it is derived from the separation of powers doctrine. The Court found that indeed there was some basis to the executive privilege theory, but that the privilege was not an absolute one which could be invoked by the president at will. The Court recognized the necessity for the president to enjoy confidentiality in his communications and documents; however, legitimate governmental needs may at times outweigh the need for confidentiality. One such need is the interest of the judicial branch in seeing that criminal trials are carried out with fairness and full information. Presidential privilege may have a constitutional base, but so too does the defendant's right to a fair trial. It is, therefore, necessary for the Court to balance the need for executive privilege and the need for full information for a fair trial. In this instance, the Court ruled in favor of a disclosure of the subpoenaed materials. This decision was based on the fact that the special prosecutor had demonstrated a compelling need for the information if the trial was to be a fair one, and because the president had failed to show that any specific national interest would significantly suffer by a release of the tapes.

The Court, however, did not simply order that the tapes be made public. The majority found merit in the president's argument that extraneous material was perhaps mixed among those conversations that dealt with information relevant to the trial. Therefore, the Court generally upheld the suggestion of Judge Sirica that the subpoenaed tapes be given to the trial judge for scrutiny in secret. The trial judge would then be empowered to edit out those sections of the tapes which bore no relevance to the upcoming trials. The Court held emphatically that it was the duty of the judiciary, not the executive, to make the final decision as to whether executive privilege could be validly claimed and also to decide which materials were relevant to the pending judicial hearings.

From a practical point of view the decision of the Supreme Court meant that President Nixon was ordered to deliver the requested tapes and transcripts to Judge Sirica. Sirica would then listen to the taped conversations and release those portions of the conversations relevant to the criminal charges against the Watergate defendants. Once these conversations were made public, of course, they could be used by other governmental bodies such as the House panel considering the impeachment of the president. Given the importance of the tapes and the damning evidence that many thought was contained in the recorded conversations, there was some speculation that Richard Nixon might refuse to obey the Supreme Court's ruling. Had he chosen to do so, the nation would have entered a period of serious constitutional strain. After all, it is the executive branch which is empowered to enforce the laws and the decisions of the courts. The judiciary itself has no enforcement powers. Had Nixon not complied with the Court's ruling voluntarily, no governmental force could have compelled him to do so. Fortunately for the country, Nixon obeyed the order of the Court. The tapes and related documents ordered by the trial court were delivered to Judge Sirica, who edited them in private and finally released the portions of the recorded conversations relevant to the Watergate trials.

What followed, of course, is well known. The tapes Nixon had withheld from Judge Sirica demonstrated that the president had known about attempts to cover up the Watergate break-in. This evidence implicated the president in obstruction of justice violations. The conversations were sufficiently incriminating for the House Judiciary Committee to vote to recommend to the full House that the president be impeached. It was clear to Richard Nixon that the release of the tapes had sealed his fate. It was certain that the House of Representatives was about to impeach him, and the probability was very high that the Senate would convict him of high crimes. He would be forced from office, the first American president to be relieved of his position. Therefore, rather than undergo a painful and debilitating impeachment proceeding and Senate trial, Nixon resigned from the presidency on August 8, 1974. Several months later, John Mitchell, John Ehrlichman, H. R. Haldeman, and the other Watergate cover-up defendants were found guilty. Judge John Sirica had finally accomplished what he had set out to do. He got to the bottom of the Watergate break-in and its related activities. Had it not been for his efforts to expose the cover-up attempt, the nation might not have ever known the extent of the illegal activities and the number of high-ranking individuals involved in wrongdoing.

The Supreme Court's decision in *United States* v. *Nixon* is especially significant for placing the powers of the presidency in proper perspective. The Court's opinion is a strong statement for the position that our governmental leaders, no matter what high office they might hold, are still under the authority and the limitations of the law of the country. The Court had reaffirmed the principle that this is a nation of laws and not of men.

Presidential Selection and Tenure

No other section of the Constitution has undergone so many changes as the one dealing with the selection and tenure of the president of the United States. These changes have been adopted both by constitutional amendment and through custom and practice. On four different occasions the nation has ratified constitutional modifications that alter the way our president is chosen and the conditions under which he is to serve. These changes represent one-quarter of the constitutional amendments passed following the addition of the original Bill of Rights.

The office of the presidency was a subject about which there was considerable bargaining and compromise at the Constitutional Convention. There were proponents of a strong executive and those who favored a weak executive. Some preferred a short tenure, others a long term of office. Presidential selection alternatives divided the delegates. There was even some support for a plural executive rather than the single presidency upon which the Convention quickly agreed. The delegates resolved each of these issues, but the final product of their efforts was not completely workable.

Qualifications and Selection of the President

The Framers first placed certain qualifications in the Second Article.[2] No one could become president of the United States unless he met three rather specific requirements. First, the office was restricted to natural-born citizens. All persons born in the United States or born abroad of parents having United States citizenship are considered natural-born citizens. This provision bars naturalized citizens (individuals who originally held the citizenship of another country but subsequently attained citizenship in the United States) from assuming the presidency. Second, no person is eligible for the office unless he has attained the age of thirty-five. And third, eligible candidates must have resided in the United States for a period of fourteen years. These three requirements are obviously minimal ones and impose no substantially restrictive barriers to the office.

After considerable debate on the question of presidential selection procedures, the Constitutional Convention decided upon a compromise. Under the proposed system there would be popular elections in each state for the office of "elector." Each state received a number of electors equal to the number of representatives it had in the United States House and Senate. Once selected by the people, these electors would cast their votes for their preferred choice among the various presidential contenders. Theoretically the electors could exercise their independent judgment regarding the best possible candidate, but practically speaking many delegates to the Constitutional Convention realized that the electors would become publicly pledged to a particular candidate prior to the election. As a group these electors became known as the electoral college, a collection of individuals with no other purpose than the selection of the leaders of the executive branch of the government.

Under the original version of the Constitution each elector was empowered to cast two electoral votes. When these electoral votes were counted, the candidate with the most votes from a majority of the electors would become president. The candidate with the second highest number of votes became the vice-president. This system worked well for the first two presidential elections, largely because there was overwhelming agreement upon George Washington and John Adams to hold the top two slots in the executive branch. However, the election of 1796 began to demonstrate some of the problems associated with the original election regulations. In that year, John Adams received the largest number of electoral votes, and Thomas Jefferson was the recipient of the second greatest total. According to election procedures at that time, Adams became president and Jefferson vice-president. However, these two were political rivals representing different political parties. It became apparent that such divided control of the executive branch might lead to potential difficulties. In the following presidential election of 1800 an even more serious defect revealed itself. In that campaign Jefferson and his vice-presidential running mate, Aaron Burr, were attempting to unseat the incumbent president, John Adams. A majority of electors selected that year favored the Jefferson-Burr ticket, and accordingly each of these electors cast one vote for Jefferson and one for Burr. The result was that Jefferson and Burr each received the identical number of electoral votes in spite of the fact that it was generally understood that Jefferson was running for the presidency and Burr for the second spot. Because both received the same number of votes, the election was referred to the House of Representatives for a final determination of the outcome. Thirty-six ballots were required before the House agreed upon Jefferson to become president and Burr, vice-president.

After the 1796 and 1800 elections, it was clear that some revision of the presidential selection system was necessary. Therefore, before the 1804 elections took place, Congress proposed and the states ratified the Twelfth Amendment. That amendment made several alterations in the method of executive selection. First, it stipulated that the members of the electoral college would cast their votes separately for president and vice-president. This modification corrected the defects in the original document which led to the 1796 and 1800 difficulties. No longer would the vice-president simply be the runner-up in the presidential race, but would be independently elected. Second, the amendment provided that if no presidential candidate received a majority of the electoral votes, the House of Representatives would select the president from the top three candidates. Voting in the House of Representatives would be according to states, with each state having a single vote and a majority of states required to elect the president. Third, if no vice-presidential candidate received a majority of votes, the election would be referred to the United States Senate for resolution. The Senate would select the vice-president from the two candidates for that office who had received the greatest number of electoral votes. Each senator would have one vote in this process. Fourth, the Twelfth Amendment provided that no person could assume the office of vice-president unless he met the requirements necessary to become president. This modification corrected a defect in the original document, which had neglected to establish any minimum qualifications for the vice-president. The Twelfth Amendment substantially clarified and improved the constitutional scheme for the selection of the president and vice-president.

The Electoral College

The system employed today is largely identical to that imposed by the Twelfth Amendment.[3] However, custom and practice have modified the process to a certain extent. Today the electoral college is largely symbolic, having little independent authority. It has become almost automatic for all of the electoral votes from a given state to be cast for the presidential and vice-presidential candidates who receive a plurality of the state's popular votes. Under some states' statutes the electors are required to vote consistent with the popular vote outcome. It is infrequent that an elector will violate the understanding that electoral votes should be cast in accordance with the prevailing will of the voters, but it does occur. For example, in 1976, although Gerald Ford carried the popular vote in the state of Washington, one elector cast his vote in the electoral college for former California governor Ronald Reagan. The Reagan vote was the lone exception to the rule that electoral votes should follow the lead of the popular voting within the state. Although electors have not often violated the public trust by failing to vote with the will of a plurality of the state's voters, critics of the electoral college system frequently cite the fact that such independent voting is possible as a major defect in the presidential selection process.

A more common criticism of the electoral college focuses on the practice of granting all of the state's electoral votes to the winning popular vote candidate, regardless of the margin of his victory. It makes no difference, for example, if a presidential candidate obtains 100 percent of the state's vote, or 51 percent, or even 10 percent. If he leads all other presidential contenders in the state, he gains all of the state's electoral votes. Conversely, a losing candidate in a particular state will receive no electoral votes in spite of the fact that he may have been the electoral choice of several million voters within that state. This winner-take-all formula has prompted many to support reform of the electoral college system, both in the interests of fairness and because under the current system it is possible for a candidate to receive the largest number of the nation's popular votes but lose in the electoral college.[4]

The most radical of the proposals for change promote the replacement of the electoral college with the direct popular election of the president. More moderate reforms suggest that electoral votes be apportioned on the basis of a candidate's popular vote percentage in each state. Still other suggestions would allow the popular-vote winner in each congressional district to receive one electoral vote.

After each presidential election, there is movement in Congress to propose a constitutional amendment to reform the presidential selection system. However, each attempt has lost enthusiasm and died, only to be resurrected again following future elections. No reform has yet been adopted, although following the 1976 presidential campaign the reformers were again arguing more strenuously than ever for a constitutional amendment modifying the executive-selection process.

Presidential Tenure

During the debates at the Constitutional Convention a substantial amount of discussion was directed at the question of presidential tenure. The delegates finally agreed to a presidential term of four years. This was judged time enough for an officeholder to accomplish his goals, but not too long to allow the incumbent to accumulate excessive power. The Constitution in its original form, however, placed no limitation on the number of terms a president could serve. Requiring a president to return to the people and the electoral college for approval before serving beyond a four-year period was thought a sufficient check, and the imposition of an absolute limitation on the number of years of possible service was considered unnecessary. However, on two occasions the nation has found it advisable to revise the presidential tenure provisions of the Constitution. The first modification was enacted with the ratification of the Twentieth Amendment, which has proven of relatively minor consequence. This amendment, which became part of the Constitution in 1933, changed the beginning of a newly elected president's term from the original date in March following his election to the present inaugural date of January 20. The second modification, however, was of greater significance. In 1951, the Twenty-Second Amendment became operative, limiting any president to a maximum of two full terms in office. The amendment was largely a reaction to Franklin Roosevelt's unprecedented four consecutive terms of office. Prior to Roosevelt's tenure, no President had violated the two-term tradition initiated by President Washington following the end of his years of service in 1797. Since the tradition of limited terms had broken down, it appeared prudent to impose a constitutional limitation to insure against the emergence of a long-serving president who might develop into a near monarch.

Presidential Succession

There are several conditions under which a president can be forced to leave office before completing his elected term. He may die, resign, be impeached and convicted, or become incapacitated to the point of being unable to discharge the duties of office. The original Constitution briefly discussed what was to occur when such situations arose. The Second Article notes that whenever the president shall be forced from office for whatever reason the duties of the position will fall on the vice-president. This succession provision was not employed until 1841, when Vice-President Tyler assumed the presidency following the death of William Henry Harrison only one month into the president's tenure. Since the beginning of the Republic, eight presidents have died in office, and the vice-president has been required to assume the highest executive office in each case. On no occasion have both the elected president and vice-president died, leaving a void in executive leadership. However, the Constitution has provided that Congress shall have the power to enact a statute regulating succession beyond the office of vice-president. The succession acts passed by the national legislature list a number of governmental officials in line to assume the presidency beyond the office of vice-president. First in line of succession is the Speaker of the House, followed by the president pro tempore of the Senate, the secretary of state, and the other cabinet officials.

In 1967, the required number of states ratified the Twenty-Fifth Amendment to the Constitution which was designed to clarify the subjects of presidential removal and succession. The original Constitution was reasonably clear as to the procedures to be followed in the case of the death, resignation, or impeachment of the president, but the question of presidential disability was not completely answered. Unlike the other conditions under which the president might be forced to leave office, there may be substantial disagreement over the question of whether the incumbent has lost his ability to carry out his constitutional duties. For example, President Garfield clung to life for almost three months following an attack by an assassin; President Wilson suffered a severe illness while in office which substantially restricted his activities; and President Eisenhower was the victim of both heart attack and stroke. In each case there was question as to the extent of the presidential disability and whether the vice-president should assume control of the executive branch. Yet the Constitution did not define incapacitating disabilities. The Twenty-Fifth Amendment remedied this situation by providing that upon a written declaration signed by the vice-president and a majority of the cabinet an incumbent president would be considered unable to discharge his duties and the vice-president would assume the presidency. If the president opposes the declaration of incapacitation, Congress is empowered to decide the issue. In such cases, two-thirds vote by both houses is necessary to remove presidential powers from the incumbent. Thus far, there has been no necessity to invoke these provisions, but should such a situation arise the Constitution is now prepared to deal with the matter.

Another provision of the Twenty-Fifth Amendment provides for the appointment of a vice-president should the incumbent, for whatever reason, be unable to complete his term. Under the amendment's regulations the president may fill a vacancy in the office of vice-president by appointing an individual to that position, subject to confirmation by a majority of both houses of Congress. While this amendment has been in force only slightly longer than a decade, these provisions have already been used on two occasions. When Vice-President Spiro Agnew resigned in 1973, President Nixon nominated Michigan Congressman Gerald Ford to assume the office of vice-president. Then, after Nixon resigned the presidency in 1974 in order to avoid impeachment and Vice-President Ford became president, Nelson Rockefeller of New York was nominated to fill the vacancy created by Ford's promotion.

Presidential Powers

The office of the president has undergone a substantial growth in power over the history of the nation. The powers the Constitution accorded to the president were relatively weak by contemporary standards, and no constitutional revision has significantly added to those powers.[5] Hence, the growth in the office has been primarily in the area of informal authority. Through custom and practice the role of the chief executive has been expanded. Strong presidents have assumed authority in actions of questionable constitutionality. Yet each addition of power was treated as a precedent for future administrations. Men such as Abraham Lincoln, Woodrow Wilson, Franklin Roosevelt, John Kennedy, and Lyndon Johnson were responsible for some of the most significant increases in executive authority. Furthermore, as world conditions and technology have changed, increases in executive authority have become necessary. The executive branch has several advantages over the legislature in dealing with world affairs. The executive is able to act much more swiftly when situations demand a quick response, and the executive branch has at its disposal much more competent information and technological competence than does the Congress. Therefore, especially in the area of foreign affairs, the president has taken a commanding position over the other branches of the government. The wisdom of having a single executive in general command of foreign policy was recognized by the Framers, as it is today. As early as President Washington's 1793 Neutrality Proclamation the superiority of the chief executive in foreign relations was recognized.

Administrative Powers of the President

The executive authority is essentially an administrative power. Theoretically, the responsibility of the president and his administration is to execute the laws of Congress. Congress is empowered to set policy, and the president has the duty of making sure that these policies are carried out and enforced. Over the decades the enforcement power has grown substantially. No longer is the president simply expected to carry out the provisions of the law, but he is empowered to use substantial discretion in executing the law. Through the process of legislative delegation, discussed in chapter 6, the executive branch is given a great deal of law-making power which it couples with the ability to enforce legislative policy. The president is the head of a vast bureaucracy of administrative agencies entrusted with executing the law. The manner in which he shapes that administration and the policies he sets for the execution of the law have a significant bearing on the implemented policies of the federal government.

As head of the executive branch the president has substantial powers to appoint personnel to carry out the administrative function. Generally speaking, the president has the appointment authority over administration positions which share in the exercise of executive powers. Such executives take a part in setting policy and have a substantial degree of discretion. Nondiscretionary positions under the executive branch (such as clerical workers and other positions that do not share in the policy-making function) may be filled by means other than presidential appointment, normally through civil service merit selection procedures. For those positions over which the president enjoys the nomination power, the Senate has the ability to check the chief executive, since the Constitution requires confirmation of such appointments. Certain positions, such as members of the White House staff, are exempt from the confirmation requirement. The power to hire policy-making personnel also assumes the right to remove such employees. Members of the executive family who are responsible to the chief executive serve at his pleasure and may be removed by him at his discretion.[6] The president's appointment and removal power allows him to administer the federal government according to his own preferences and priorities without substantial opposition from within the executive branch itself.

The President and Foreign Policy

While the Constitution recognizes a role in foreign affairs to be played by both the legislature and the president, it is clear that the president has the primary authority in shaping the nation's course in international relations. That the foreign policy power should essentially reside within the executive branch was the predominant theory at the time the Constitution was drafted, and the years have not diminished the foreign policy responsibilities of the president. In fact, as the nation has grown, the role of the chief executive in the formation of foreign policy has become even larger. That the president should be the nation's spokesman in the area of foreign affairs has been recognized by the Supreme Court. In one important ruling which greatly expanded the position of the chief executive, the Court described the president as "the sole organ of the federal government in the field of international relations" and defined his authority as "plenary and exclusive."[7]

The president's foreign policy authority stems from several constitutional grants of power. First, the president has the power to appoint all ambassadors who represent the United States in the conduct of its foreign relations. The Senate holds confirmation power over these appointments, but historically Congress has been extremely reluctant to reject a president's choice. Furthermore, the president receives the ministers and ambassadors who represent the world's other states. The authority to receive ambassadors implies the power to recognize foreign governments and to set the conditions under which the United States will conduct normalized relations with foreign powers. The power to appoint and receive ambassadors places the president in a position of being the primary spokesman for the federal government in foreign affairs and the official to whom foreign governments communicate in conducting relations with the United States.

Second, the president has certain military powers. The Constitution grants him the position of commander in chief of the military forces. While it is true that Congress shapes the military by having responsibility for raising armies, setting the size of the military, providing financial support for personnel and equipment, and declaring war, the president is exclusively in charge of using and commanding the military forces. The military can be employed as a means of implementing the president's foreign policy. Activist presidents have commonly deployed military forces to protect American interests, with or without the full support of the Congress. Congress has attempted to curtail presidential authority over the military on several occasions, but was not successful until the nation became critical of the war in Vietnam. Dissatisfied with the manner in which Presidents Johnson and Nixon used the military forces in Southeast Asia, Congress passed the War

Powers Act of 1973. This act provided that the president could deploy military forces only under three conditions: (1) by a declaration of war, (2) pursuant to obtaining congressional authorization, and (3) in times of national emergency. Furthermore, the act provides that if the president commits military forces under conditions of national emergency, he must so inform Congress within forty-eight hours and cannot continue to deploy American troops beyond sixty days without congressional approval. While this act limits the president to a certain extent, the chief executive retains military command and in most instances the restrictions imposed are minimal ones. The president is still fully capable of using America's military might as an instrument of foreign policy creation and execution.

Third, the President has the power to enter into agreements with foreign countries. These agreements usually take one of two possible forms. First, permanent compacts normally are classified as treaties. The chief executive is empowered to negotiate treaties with foreign powers, but such agreements do not take effect until they are approved by a vote of two-thirds of the United States Senate. Second, the president may enter into executive agreements with foreign countries. Originally executive agreements (made between the president and the head of another nation's government) were designed to apply only to minor matters which did not require a formal treaty. In recent decades, however, presidents have used the executive agreement power to enter into compacts with foreign powers involving major issues. The primary advantage to the executive agreement alternative is that such agreements do not require congressional approval, although recent legislation has stipulated that the executive branch inform the Congress of all such agreements to which the administration has committed itself. Both treaties and executive agreements are recognized by the courts as the law of the land and have precedence over conflicting state statutes.[8]

The power over foreign policy is one of the president's most important responsibilities. The growth in the office of the president has largely been tied to the growth in the importance of foreign affairs. As the nation has become an active and significant participant in international relations, the president's role has been enhanced. As long as the nation remained primarily concerned with domestic matters, the role of the president was relatively weak, but as world affairs became more crucial to American interests the president has become a much more important and influential figure.

Legislative Powers of the President

The president also possesses certain legislative powers, and, like presidential authority in foreign affairs, the executive role in the law-making process has grown considerably over the years. The chief executive functions in both the initiation and evaluation stages of the legislative process. The Constitution makes the president responsible for reporting to Congress from time to time on the "state of the union." It has become customary for the incumbent chief executive to issue a major address to a joint session of Congress each year, giving the lawmakers his evaluation of the problems and conditions facing the federal government. In addition to this state of the union message, the president periodically reports to Congress on the budget, the economy, and other important functions of the national government. Originally Congress reacted to these messages by initiating legislation designed to cope with the problems emphasized by the president. However, over the past several decades the executive branch has become more and more active in the legislative initiation stage. Not only does the president report to the Congress on the state of the union and the various spheres of federal responsibility, but he also sends Congress his legislative recommendations. The members of Congress then react to these proposals by enacting appropriate ones into law. Congress has come to expect legislative leadership from the executive branch. It is now considered an established function of the president to recommend specific pieces of legislation as well as a general legislative program to deal with the major problems facing the country. As the role of the president has grown in this regard, the legislative initiation and creativity of Congress has tended to diminish.

The Constitution requires that the president evaluate every piece of general legislation passed by Congress. When a bill is passed by Congress it is sent to the president for his approval. The president is given ten days, excluding Sundays, in which to react to the bill. Three alternatives are open. First, if he approves the bill he may sign it, in which case the proposed legislation becomes law. Second, he may refuse to sign the bill. If he follows this second course, the bill will become law without his signature after the ten days have elapsed, providing that Congress is still in session. If Congress has adjourned during this ten-day period and is no longer in session, the bill dies. This has become known as a "pocket veto." The president normally will refuse to sign a bill to indicate that he has moderate objections to it or disapproves of a particular provision of the act, but for political or other reasons does not wish to reject the bill in toto. His third alternative is to veto the bill. A veto occurs when the president fails to sign the bill within the allotted ten days and returns it to Congress with an explanation of his specific objections. A veto kills the proposed legislation unless Congress is able to override the president's rejection. Overturning a veto requires that the bill be repassed by both houses of Congress by a two-thirds majority. Congress is normally unsuccessful in override attempts. Approximately 90 percent of all vetos are sustained, with the actual proportion, of course, varying widely according to the president's popularity and the political party distribution in Congress.

Finally, it should be noted that the president's veto power must be applied to the bill as a whole. The president, unlike many state governors, does not possess the item veto power, which would enable him to reject specific provisions of a proposed law.

The Constitution admonishes the president to "take care that the laws be faithfully executed." Regardless of whether the chief executive is acting within his administrative, foreign policy, or legislative powers, he remains subject to the laws of the land and is expected to enforce those laws. This enforcement power extends to laws passed by Congress and administrative agencies, as well as to judicial orders. The president has the responsibility to see that the law is followed and may be required to use military force to insure that the rule of law is maintained. Such was the case in 1958 when President Eisenhower was forced to send military troops into Little Rock, Arkansas to enforce school desegregation orders imposed by the federal courts.

The Supreme Court and Presidential Power

Occasionally a president may take actions that violate the spirit and the letter of the law. In most instances these actions are taken in what the president considers the best interests of the nation. However, the constitutional mandate that the president faithfully execute the laws does not allow for a violation of the rule of law even if the end result is advantageous to the country. Two examples illustrate this point. In 1952, during the height of the Korean War, the nation's steel workers announced that they were about to strike. Since steel production was necessary for the war effort, it was obviously in the best interests of the nation to keep the steel mills in operation. However, negotiations had broken down and no solution to the labor stalemate appeared likely. In order to deal with this situation, President Truman ordered his secretary of commerce to seize the steel mills and operate them in the name of the United States government. The mill owners obviously objected to the governmental take-over and immediately initiated court action to reverse Truman's orders. The Supreme Court struck down the president's actions, holding that however good his motives, Truman had violated the law of the land.[9] No provision in the Constitution could be construed to authorize such activity on the part of the chief executive.

A second example involves the fiscal policies of President Richard Nixon. One of the president's primary objectives in the economic sphere was to curtail inflation. In order to do so, he placed great emphasis on the reduction of governmental spending. Congress, however, continued to spend federal funds on programs it considered important to the well-being of the nation. Nixon therefore embarked on a policy of impoundment of federal funds. This action largely consisted of ordering certain administrative departments to spend less than the full amount appropriated by Congress. In so doing, Nixon effectively reduced federal spending in spite of Congress's refusal to do so. Nixon's actions could not be considered "faithful execution of the laws." Hence, several suits were introduced in the federal courts challenging the right of the president to withhold congressionally appropriated monies. The resulting court decisions overwhelmingly disapproved President Nixon's course of action, including one Supreme Court decision unanimously striking down the president's impoundment of federal pollution control appropriations.[10]

In spite of the fact that presidential powers have dramatically expanded over the years, the chief executive must still confine his actions within constitutionally permissible boundaries. On several occasions the judicial branch has been called upon to rule on contentions that the president has violated the authority granted him by the Constitution. As the Framers of the Constitution realized, the power of the executive is susceptible to great abuse. For this reason the judicial branch has striven to insure, as it did in *United States* v. *Nixon*, that the federal government remains ruled by laws and not by political incumbents.

The President and the Separation of Powers

The president plays an important role in the separation of powers doctrine. The chief executive is authorized to use several of his powers to check the actions of the Congress and the court system. For the most part the presidency has carried out this task quite well.

The President and Congress

The most obvious check the president may exercise over the legislative branch is the veto. No matter what legislative policy is enacted by the Congress, the president may block the implementation of that law through the use of the veto power. Of course, the legislature is fully equipped to reverse the president's action, but as a matter of practical politics overriding vetoes is not an easy task. The veto is an effective instrument of blocking legislative actions that are perceived as unreasonable or unwise.

Additional legislative authority held by the president often shapes the actions taken by the legislature. Not only does the president inform the Congress regarding the state of the union and recommend specific pieces of legislation, but the executive branch has become the Congress's most valuable source of information. The growth of the various administrative agencies and departments has seen a corresponding growth in the research and intelligence activities of the executive branch. Congress does not have the information-gathering facilities or capacity to provide all of the technical and sensitive knowledge necessary to legislate effectively. Hence, the executive branch is capable of shaping the actions of the legislature through the control of information to Congress. In recent years there have been periodic battles between the Congress and the president's administration over the amount and completeness of information distributed to the legislature by the executive and the president's obligation to provide full disclosure regarding administrative actions.

In the foreign policy field, the president clearly has certain checks on the legislature. Through the power to enter into executive agreements, the president may accomplish foreign policy objectives that may not be fully approved by Congress. And as commander in chief of the military the chief executive may take actions that commit the United States in advance of congressional authorization. The use of his power to recognize foreign governments may well circumvent congressional policy preferences.

Perhaps the most important check on the legislative branch can be found in the president's obligation to enforce and administer the acts of Congress. The individuals whom the president selects for his various administrative positions have a great bearing on the way the laws of the United States are administered. A president may vigorously enforce certain statutes and virtually ignore others. For this reason, Congress is always vigilant on questions of confirmation of key presidential appointees. A recent example is provided by President Carter's nomination of former federal judge Griffin Bell to be attorney general. There was considerable dissatisfaction in the Senate regarding the Bell appointment because many feared that he would not enforce federal civil rights legislation vigorously.

The President and the Judiciary

The chief executive possesses some very real checks on the judiciary. Perhaps the most important of these is the appointment power. Under the Constitution, all federal judges are appointed by the president. The variety of individuals he selects for the bench has a direct relationship to the kind of justice system the nation will enjoy. Especially with respect to appellate court positions, the president will take great pains to nominate judicial personnel who approach judicial and legal policy from the same philosophy and perspective as the president. Since the courts have such wide jurisdiction over matters of civil rights, governmental powers, and the economy, the president's authority to shape the judiciary through the appointment process is a considerable power.

The enforcement power the president enjoys over the legislative branch also extends to the judicial branch. The courts have no enforcement powers of their own. They must rely on voluntary compliance to implement their decisions and orders. In the absence of voluntary conformity to judicial rulings, the president and his administration are called upon to enforce the law as interpreted by the courts. For the most part, our presidents have been reasonably faithful when called upon to lend support in favor of compliance with court rulings. The success of the civil rights movement owes much to the vigorous enforcement by the Department of Justice of the desegregation orders of the courts. Should the executive branch be at odds with the judiciary over some line of legal policy, the president could order a general lack of support for enforcement among his administrative departments. In such situations the court system would be hard pressed to obtain full conformity with its rulings.

Finally, the president has the power to pardon. The president's power to pardon allows him to grant a complete dismissal of criminal charges against an individual. Normally a presidential pardon will be issued after an individual has been convicted of a given offense. A pardon rescinds the conviction, eliminates the punishment, and restores the convicted person to his full civil rights. A presidential pardon may also be issued while an individual is on trial for criminal offenses, or even before official criminal accusations are issued. Such was the case when President Gerald Ford issued an unconditional pardon to former President Richard Nixon with respect to any crimes that may have been committed during the Watergate-related events. The president's power to pardon is total and complete. He is able to attach any conditions to the pardon that he may desire. The pardon may be issued for a single person or may be granted to an entire class of individuals, such as President Carter's pardon of Vietnam era draft-evaders. The power to pardon is based on the Constitution itself.[11] The sole limitation on the pardon power is that it extends only to federal crimes and not to persons charged with violations of state law.[12] Therefore, the power of pardon may be used prior to trial to protect an individual from judicial action or may be employed following conviction if the chief executive believes the action taken by the courts against a person is unjust or excessive.

Summary

Many students of American government would forcefully argue that the president is clearly the most important political institution in the United states. This predominance of the executive branch is due to the great growth in power that agency has enjoyed over the years. The executive has made significant leaps in power and status without constitutional modifications in its official powers and responsibilities. This growth in political power has largely been accomplished by the development of the great informal powers of the office, by the increasing importance of foreign policy, which is largely the domain of the presidency, and the significant enlargement of the federal bureaucracy as a means of coping with modern societal and worldwide conditions.

The presidential selection system has been at various times severely criticized. Correspondingly, the nation has seen it necessary to make certain modifications in the constitutional provisions governing the selection and tenure of the chief executive. The selection process remains controversial today. There is considerable support in Congress and among the general population for the elimination of the electoral college system and the substitution of direct popular election of the president. Reform movements dedicated to modifying our executive selection procedure are periodically mounted, but as yet have been unable to maintain a sustained and successful effort to achieve national acceptance of a constitutional amendment to impose such a change.

The president and his administration hold a number of checks over the legislative and judicial branches. The president's legislative powers, including the veto, and the discretion he has in enforcing legislative policy give him a considerable influence in the public policy process. Similarly, the president may influence the judicial branch. Not only does he have the power to enforce court rulings and circumvent certain judicial actions through the pardon power, but his power to appoint federal judges significantly shapes the American system of justice.

Notes

1. 418 U.S. 683 (1974).
2. Article II, section 1, clause 5.
3. The only additional constitutional modification in the electoral college system oc-

curred with the ratification of the Twenty-Third Amendment in 1961, giving electoral votes to the District of Columbia. The number of electors granted to the District is based upon the same formula as that for the states, except in no case may the District have more electoral votes than the least populated state.

4. This situation did in fact occur in the 1876 election when Rutherford Hayes became president although his opponent, Samuel Tilden, received more popular votes; and again in 1888, when the more popular Grover Cleveland lost in the electoral college to Benjamin Harrison.

5. The specific grants of power to the president may be found in article II, sections 2 and 3.

6. See, for example, Myers v. United States, 272 U.S. 52 (1926); Humphrey's Executor v. United States, 295 U.S. 602 (1935); and Wiener v. United States, 357 U.S. 349 (1958).

7. United States v. Curtiss-Wright Export Corporation, 299 U.S. 304 (1936).

8. See United States v. Belmont, 301 U.S. 324 (1937).

9. Youngstown Sheet and Tube v. Sawyer, 343 U.S. 579 (1952).

10. Train v. City of New York, 420 U.S. 35 (1975).

11. See Ex parte Grossman, 267 U.S. 87 (1925); and Schick v. Reed, 419 U.S. 256 (1974).

12. The pardon power cannot be used to reverse or eliminate impeachment actions.

Further Reading

Berger, Raoul. *Executive Privilege: A Constitutional Myth.* Cambridge, Mass.: Harvard University Press, 1974.

Burns, James M. *Presidential Government.* Boston: Houghton Mifflin, 1973.

Fenno, Richard F., Jr. *The President's Cabinet.* Cambridge, Mass.: Harvard University Press, 1959.

Henkin, Louis. *Foreign Affairs and the Constitution.* New York: W. W. Norton, 1972.

Hirschfield, Robert S. (ed.). *The Power of the Presidency.* New York: Aldine, 1973.

Jackson, Carlton. *Presidential Vetoes, 1792–1945.* Athens: University of Georgia Press, 1967.

Koenig, Louis W. *The Chief Executive.* New York: Harcourt, Brace and World, 1968.

Polsby, Nelson W. *Congress and the Presidency.* Englewood Cliffs, N.J.: Prentice-Hall, 1971.

Reedy, George E. *The Presidency in Flux.* New York: Columbia University Press, 1973.

Schlesinger, Arthur M., Jr. *The Imperial Presidency.* Boston: Houghton Mifflin, 1973.

Scigliano, Robert. *The Supreme Court and the Presidency.* New York: Free Press, 1971.

Young, Donald. *American Roulette: The History and Dilemma of the Vice-Presidency.* New York: Holt, Rinehart and Winston, 1965.

The Judiciary

Chapter nine

The Significance of the Judiciary
in a Free Society: *Ex parte Milligan*

During the 1973 Senate Watergate investigation hearings, Committee Chairman Sam Ervin of North Carolina remarked that the most significant decision ever handed down by the United States Supreme Court was *Ex parte Milligan*.[1] Ervin, at that time the Senate's most highly regarded expert on the Constitution, was referring to an 1866 ruling stemming from events during the Civil War. The decision itself is especially important because of the value it places on a strong commitment to the court system and not allowing the integrity of the judiciary to be compromised for reasons of expediency. Furthermore, the ruling emphasizes that the courts are necessary to protect basic civil liberties during times when strong tides of public opinion might favor their temporary suspension.

The principal in this litigation was Lambdin P. Milligan, a relatively prominent Indiana attorney. During the 1850s, Milligan was active in legal and social circles in Indiana. He had developed a successful practice, often representing railroad interests. He became increasingly interested and active in politics, and there are reports that he secretly harbored ambitions of one day becoming governor of his state. However, Milligan had neither the ability nor the political following to attain that high position, and his activities were somewhat curtailed by persistent health problems. As the nation moved ever closer to an outbreak of hostilities between the North and the South, Milligan became one of many Indiana citizens who actively supported the Confederate cause. He was a promoter of the interests of states' rights and held favorable attitudes toward slavery. Since many of the settlers of Indiana had migrated from southern or border states, Milligan found substantial numbers who shared his views and were willing to organize to advance the Confederate cause. Of course, when war finally broke out Indiana remained in the Union, much to the disappointment of the Southern sympathizers.

Some of the more militant Confederate supporters in the North (known as "Copperheads") engaged in conspiratorial activities designed to assist the war efforts of the South. One of the more prominent of these movements was the Northwestern Conspiracy, which aimed at bringing the Northwestern states (Illinois, Missouri, Indiana, and Iowa) into the Confederate ranks, or at a minimum to force these states to abandon active support for the Union cause. Several secret societies developed within these states to promote the ends of the Northwestern Conspiracy. There was substantial evidence to indicate that Lambdin Milligan was a member of such a conspiratorial group, although the extent of his participation was never fully known.

Copperhead activities in the North presented a very real problem to the Northern war effort. President Lincoln placed great emphasis on breaking up any secret societies committed to the Southern cause and pursued a policy of bringing swift action against Northern residents who engaged in any activities of espionage, sabotage, or conspiracy to aid the enemy. Those suspected of being involved with pro-Southern organizations were subjected to harsh treatment by Lincoln's military officials. Civil liberties were ignored. There were arbitrary arrests, illegal searches and seizures, and suspects were held in custody without enjoying the constitutional right of a speedy and public trial. Lincoln's actions generally gave the maintenance of the Union priority over the civil rights of suspected traitors. He was willing to take otherwise unconstitutional actions in order to preserve the Union.

On September 24, 1862, President Lincoln took one of his most extreme steps in his attack against disloyal Northerners. He issued an executive order suspending the writ of habeas corpus and proclaiming that any person charged with disloyalties would be tried by military commissions under the rules of court-martial. The impact of this order on the American theory of civil liberties could hardly be overestimated. The writ of habeas corpus was a right that had been adopted by the United States from old English concepts of law. The right to habeas corpus was recognized in England's Magna Carta as well as in the American Constitution. The habeas corpus procedure allows a person who has been arrested or detained to challenge the validity of his detention in a court of law. Therefore, habeas corpus constitutes one of the nation's most important rights, for it provides a judicial check against arbitrary denials of freedom. Lincoln's order essentially meant that those persons arrested for disloyal activities no longer had a judicial means of challenging the legality of their incarceration. Furthermore, Lincoln's action allowed such persons to be tried by military tribunals according to the rules of court-martial procedures. This denied defendants the right to have their charges adjudicated in a civilian court. To President Lincoln, of course, these serious actions were necessary in order to cope with the rising rate of treasonous activity on the part of those Northerners supporting the Southern cause.

Lincoln's suspension of the right to habeas corpus was of questionable constitutionality. The United States Constitution provides in article I, section 9: "The Privilege of the Writ of Habeas Corpus shall not be suspended, unless when in Cases of Rebellion or Invasion the public Safety may require it." The first constitutional objection to Lincoln's action was the argument that the president is not empowered to suspend the writ of habeas corpus. While the Constitution is not specific as to the proper agency empowered to take such an action, it is assumed that since the habeas corpus provision is found in article I that the Framers intended Congress to have this authority and not the president. This objection to Lincoln's action lost some of its force in March 1863 when Congress passed a statute ratifying the president's suspension order. The second objection referred to the extent of the president's command. This argument held that even if otherwise valid, President Lincoln's action could apply only to those areas of the country included in the theater of war. In those areas in which hostilities had not broken out and normal governmental processes continued uninterrupted, it was argued, the president's order should have no force.

In their attempt to flush out rebel supporters in the North, federal agents maintained surveillance on Lambdin Milligan. They kept records of his speeches and activities. They found evidence that Milligan had joined with others in a Confederate-oriented group called the Sons of Liberty which was alleged to be involved in the Northwestern Conspiracy, that he had attempted to recruit men to support Confederate activities in the North, and that he had engaged in efforts to block the recruitment of personnel into the Union armies. In October of 1864, military investigators arrested Milligan in his Indiana home. The orders for the arrest had come from the commanding general of the Union forces in Indiana, Alvin P. Hovey. Milligan was incarcerated until his trial on October 21. On that day he was brought before a military tribunal and found guilty of disloyal activities which had given aid and comfort to the enemy and of inciting insurrection in the Northern states. The military commission found Milligan guilty of these charges and sentenced him to be hanged on May 19, 1865. Prior to his scheduled execution the war ended. Efforts were made to convince the president to pardon Milligan or reduce his sentence. Overtures were first made to President Lincoln, and then, following Lincoln's assassination, to President Andrew Johnson. Finally, Johnson granted Milligan a reduction in sentence from death to life imprisonment.

However, Milligan was not satisfied with a sentence that committed him to spend the rest of his days behind bars. He was convinced that his arrest and subsequent trial before a military tribunal were in violation of the United States Constitution. He firmly held that the military authorities had no legitimate jurisdiction over him. After all, Milligan had never been a member of the Union armies, nor had he joined the Confederate military. He was never engaged in any war-oriented activities and had never even resided in a war zone area. Therefore, Milligan asked, on what basis did the military authorities have jurisdiction over a civilian? Milligan pursued this question in the federal courts, claiming that his arrest, conviction, and sentence violated his basic civil liberties.

Milligan's appeal was heard by the United States Supreme Court in April of 1866. The Court was presented with a simple issue: Did the government have the power to suspend the right to habeas corpus in an area that was not an active war zone and, in so doing, commit civilian persons to trial by military tribunals? Milligan and his attorneys claimed that the procedures used were a direct violation of the accused's civil liberties and an abuse of the powers granted to the federal government. The government countered by arguing that in times of war or national emergency the powers of the federal government are expanded to include actions not permissible in more peaceful times. Lincoln's actions, the government contended, were necessary for the preservation of the Union and the elimination of disruptive actions directed against the Northern military strategy. The entire case focused on the propriety of the actions rather than the guilt or innocence of Lambdin Milligan.

When the United States Supreme Court issued its decision in this case, the vote was unanimous. The Court declared the actions of the government against Milligan unconstitutional and ordered that he be released from prison. The Court adopted the rationale presented by lawyers for the convicted Milligan. They concluded that Milligan was not a resident of one of the rebellious states, not a prisoner of war, not a member of the Union military forces, and had never been a member of the Union armies. He had been arrested in his home in Indiana by military forces of the United States government, and he had been charged, tried, convicted, and sentenced to be hanged by a military tribunal, which had been organized by the military commander of the state of Indiana. If the military had authority to act against Milligan in this way, its power to do so certainly did not rest on any association that Milligan had with the Union or Confederate forces. Under what authority, then, could Milligan be considered subject to military jurisdiction?

The Constitution, according to the Court's rationale, demands that persons charged with crimes be granted certain procedural safeguards. Among these are the right to a grand jury hearing, the right to an impartial trial, and the right to be tried by a jury of one's peers. It was clear that Milligan had not been granted these rights. The Constitution allows that in certain cases of national emergency the normal rights accorded to the criminally accused may be suspended. But were such conditions in existence at the time the government proceeded against Milligan? The Court gave a negative response to this key question. The situation in Indiana at the time of Milligan's arrest and trial was one of relative peace and order. The civil government of the state was operating, and most important, the civil courts were conducting business in a normal fashion. There were no military hostilities anywhere near Milligan's residence. There was simply no military emergency or crisis situation facing the area of Indiana at that time. Therefore, the Court reasoned, there was no justifiable reason for the government to suspend normal rights accorded the criminally accused. There was no compelling reason to avoid the civil courts as the proper tribunals for the trying of civilians charged with criminal offenses and to substitute military commissions in their place. The facts simply did not lead to the conclusion that the safety of the people required military law in the state of Indiana. And only when such a grave situation exists does the Constitution permit the suspension of the basic civil liberties and procedural rights to which the nation has committed itself.

The *Milligan* decision was an important one for the status of the American judiciary. First, it emphasized the need for judicial protection of basic civil liberties. Unless the civil courts are operative citizens of the United States have no legal recourse if their fundamental rights are violated. Therefore, the preservation of the judiciary is crucial to the preservation of the American system of rights and liberties. Second, the decision made clear that the normal judicial processes cannot be abbreviated or replaced with more expedient methods of dispensing justice unless a demonstrable and compelling national emergency requires such action. Only in the most extreme cases can such alternatives be justified. And third, the decision made it clear that the perception of the president that such extreme measures were necessary was not sufficient justification for by-passing the civil court system. To allow Lincoln to engage in such activity (admittedly for sincere reasons) would establish a precedent that future presidents could decide when and under what conditions military justice could be imposed on the nation. To allow such arbitrary power to rest in the hands of a single chief executive would be to opt for an unreasonably dangerous interpretation of the Constitution.

Ex parte Milligan stands today as an example of the nation's confidence in the judicial system as the final arbiter of governmental authority. It also represents the distrust of the American system in military rule over civilian matters and the potentially abusive exercise of power by the president. The courts have been established and have been given the responsibility to evaluate the actions taken by the political branches of the government and to decide if such actions are warranted and within the bounds of the Constitution. The judiciary is the most important institution for the protection of civil liberties and the nation's adherence to the principles adopted at the Philadelphia Convention of 1787.

The Federal Judiciary: Court Structure and Judicial Selection

The basic structure and powers of the federal court system are found in article III of the United States Constitution. The provisions contained therein provide a relatively sketchy description of the judicial branch. Article III is a rather short, four-hundred-word statement which allows Congress substantial powers to mold the judiciary within the general guidelines set by the Constitution. Neither the detail nor the comprehensiveness found in the first two articles of the Constitution are found in article III.

The Framers were faced with three possible alternatives when they turned their attention to the creation of the judiciary. Since each of the states had reasonably well functioning judicial systems, the Convention could have declined to create a central judiciary and allowed the states to have responsibility for interpreting laws and distributing justice. A second possibility was to abolish the state court systems and establish a comprehensive set of federal courts to handle the country's adjudication needs exclusively. The final alternative was to allow the state courts to continue in operation, but to establish a federal judiciary with a jurisdiction distinct from that of the state courts. It was this final option that the Framers selected, perhaps because it was the most politically acceptable plan and also because it contributed to the separation of powers theory upon which the national government was forged.

An Independent Judiciary

The Constitution reflects a national commitment to a strong and independent judiciary. There are at least three significant provisions in article III which were designed to insure that the courts would be relatively free of the political pressures to which the executive and legislative branches were susceptible. First, the individuals who serve as federal judges enjoy their positions for terms of "good behavior." Essentially, this provision dictates that a federal judge who retains his competence and conforms to the established standards of judicial ethics may serve in his position for life. Other than death or voluntary resignation, only impeachment and conviction by Congress can remove a federal judge. Second, the selection system for recruiting federal judges divides responsibility between the executive and legislative branches. The president is empowered to nominate individuals for federal judgeships, but the Senate is required to confirm such appointments before the office is officially conferred. Finally, the Constitution provides that Congress may not reduce the salary of any judge during the period of his tenure. These three measures insulate the federal judge and allow him to rule on cases in a manner that he thinks equitable and legally proper. Life tenure means that the judge is not obliged to return to the electorate or any agency of government in order to maintain his position. This at least partially protects the judges from public opinion and certain political pressures.[2] The divided system of judicial selection means that the judge enters office not beholden to a particular individual or a single governmental body for his position. The protected salary rule prohibits the Congress from using compensation reductions as a method of forcing judges to hand down decisions that meet the favor of the national legislature. The Framers' intention to create a strong and independent judiciary has been well realized. In fact, it is not at all uncommon for politicians to claim that federal judges enjoy excessive freedom and independence.

The Federal Court System

Article III is noticeably silent on the question of the structure of the federal court system. The Constitution stipulates only that there shall be one Supreme Court and such inferior courts as Congress may from time to time ordain and establish. The entire federal court system, below the Supreme Court, is the creation of Congress and not the Constitution. Today that judiciary is essentially a three-tiered system, with a level of trial courts, a cluster of intermediate appellate courts, and the Supreme Court resting at the top of the judicial hierarchy.

At the lowest levels of the court system are the federal district courts. These courts are the primary trial courts of the federal system. Judges at the district court level are responsible for hearing cases on original jurisdiction, that is, a suit is first heard in these courts. There are currently ninety-three United States district courts distributed among the various states, the federal territories, and the District of Columbia. Each state is granted at least one district court, with many states being allotted additional courts depending upon the amount of judicial business carried out in that particular state. Currently no state has more than four district courts. Each district court has jurisdiction over a particular geographical area known as a federal judicial district. The district courts hear trials of federal cases arising out of their respective judicial districts. These cases include both civil and criminal disputes. Presently there are slightly more than four hundred district judges, who are apportioned among the various districts on the basis of caseload. District court trials are heard by a single judge with the assistance of a jury when necessary. The number of district courts and the number of district judges, as well as how these courts and judges are apportioned among the states, are established by Congress. In 1977, Congress began serious deliberations on a bill designed to increase the number of district judges by approximately 25 percent.

Above the district courts are the federal courts of appeals. Congress has created eleven such courts, each having jurisdiction over a particular region of the country known as a federal judicial circuit. To each of the circuit courts of appeals is assigned a number of judges, currently ranging from three to fifteen. The number of appeals courts and the size of each is established by Congress and subject to modification whenever Congress deems such changes necessary. In 1977, Congress initiated work on a proposal to increase the number of judicial circuits and expand the number of appellate judges by a third. The primary duty of the courts of appeals is to decide appeals from the various district courts within their respective circuits and appeals from federal administrative agencies. The courts of appeals are collegial courts. Judges hear cases as a group rather than using the single-judge method practiced in the trial courts. Commonly the courts of appeals decide cases in panels of three judges, but on especially significant appeals, all of the judges of the circuit may participate in the decision-making process.

At the pinnacle of the judicial hierarchy is the United States Supreme Court. The Constitution notes that there shall be such a court, but fails to establish its size or to describe the parameters of its jurisdiction. These matters are left to the discretion of the Congress. The size of the Court has varied historically from five to ten members. The current number of Supreme Court justices is nine, a size that has remained unaltered since the days of President Grant. The jurisdiction of the Supreme Court is almost exclusively appellate, but the Constitution does stipulate that the tribunal will function as a trial court in cases involving foreign ambassadors or in which states are a party. The bulk of the Supreme Court's duties consists of deciding appeals from the federal courts of appeals as well as from the various state supreme courts. During the first half of the Supreme Court's history it was required to reach a decision on almost every case filed before it. However, especially since 1925, there has been a substantial increase in the discretionary jurisdiction of the

Court. Today the vast majority of cases taken to the Supreme Court are given a complete hearing only if the Court decides that the appeal involves significant legal and social issues. Each year more than five thousand cases are filed with the Supreme Court, and it is obviously impossible for the Court to decide each one. The discretionary power of the Court to control its own docket allows the justices to confine their resources to reaching decisions on only the most important suits. The Supreme Court acts as a collegial body with all nine justices normally participating in each decision.

In addition to the three basic levels in the federal court structure, Congress has established certain specialized courts that have very narrow areas of jurisdiction. For example, the national legislature has brought into being military courts, courts empowered to hear customs and patent cases, tribunals having jurisdiction over minor criminal and civil matters in the District of Columbia, and a court to decide suits involving claims against the United States government. These courts of specialized jurisdiction have been established in order to take a substantial load off the United States district courts and because of the necessity to develop courts capable of nurturing expertise in the more technical areas of the law.

Nomination and Confirmation of Federal Judges

All federal judges attain their positions in the same fashion. They are first nominated by the incumbent president and then approved by the United States Senate. The Constitution mentions no requirements for becoming a federal judge. The president is free to nominate any person regardless of ability, background, or qualifications. In practice, however, certain attributes are informally required. Potential federal judges must be members of the legal profession and must have demonstrated substantial legal ability at some point during their careers. Furthermore, nominees must be of the proper judicial temperament and must have demonstrated sound character and ethical standards. To be seriously considered, of course, nominees must be politically acceptable to the president and to a majority of the Senate.

The president normally takes a number of criteria into account in searching for appropriate persons to fill judicial vacancies.[3] First, he usually confines his choices to members of his own political party. This tradition was started by President Washington, who filled the federal courts from the very beginning with members of his own Federalist party. The custom continues today, with more than 90 percent of all federal judges being of the same political party as the appointing president. By confining nominations to members of his own political party, the president may repay certain political debts and is usually more certain that the prospective judge shares with the president certain political and ideological values. Second, the president will be concerned with the legal philosophy of the potential judge. Since courts have the power to review the validity of the president's programs and actions, it is crucial to the chief executive to select jurists who are sympathetic to the president's philosophy of government. Third, the president will normally attempt to give representation to certain geographical, religious, and ethnic groups. His appointees often include members from each region of the country, from among the various racial and ethnic groups, and from major religious movements. Fourth, the chief executive will attempt to designate individuals who have superior credentials. No president wants to be described in history as filling the federal judiciary with less than competent jurists. Finally, the president must make certain that his appointees are acceptable to important public officials and party leaders. In the appointing of district judges, who serve in a particular state, the president will consult with the members of the Senate from that state as well as important state party officials. In the selection of lower federal judges, local politics and the recommendations of the appropriate senators are extremely important factors. If a president selects his federal judges wisely, taking into account these various criteria, he will normally have little trouble getting his appointments confirmed by the Senate.

Before an appointee is nominated and confirmed he must undergo a complete investigation by at least three independent groups. First, the Justice Department screens potential nominees for each judgeship. This investigation includes a reasonably comprehensive evaluation by the Federal Bureau of Investigation as well as by other components of the attorney general's office. Second, the American Bar Association's Committee on the Federal Judiciary conducts an investigation of its own into the qualifications and backgrounds of those being seriously considered for a post in the federal court system. Upon completing this investigation, the ABA issues a recommendation regarding the acceptability of the potential judge. This recommendation is usually given considerable weight because it represents the evaluation of the organized legal profession. Finally, the nominee is subjected to an investigation by the Judiciary Committee of the United States Senate. This investigation is conducted by Senate staff members and often includes public hearings on the nominee. During such hearings individuals or groups who either oppose or support the nomination are given an opportunity to express their views.

Federal judicial selection is a rigorous process. Before obtaining a position on the bench the federal judge must undergo scrutiny by the chief executive himself, the Justice Department, the American Bar Association, and the United States Senate. Furthermore, if he is to serve in a particular state, the nominee must be acceptable to the senators from that state if they are of the same political party as the president. Without such support the nomination may die under the informal rule of "senatorial courtesy." Persons surviving this process are normally well qualified. The net result has been a judiciary that historically has been staffed by exceptionally qualified personnel. Instances of demonstrably unqualified persons or individuals who may engage in illegal or unethical activities have been exceedingly rare.

Judicial Power

The Constitution vests the judicial power of the United States in the federal court system. But the document itself is rather unclear as to the exact meaning of the term "judicial power." Therefore, the term is normally interpreted according to the standard, traditional functions of the judiciary in the history of Anglo-American law. The most fundamental of these functions is the power to decide legal cases and controversies.

The Case and Controversy Rule

The term "cases and controversies" has a rather technical meaning. According to judicial interpretations, the courts are powerless to impose judgments on disputes that do not meet the rather demanding standards of what has become known as the "case or controversy rule." These standards include four basic requirements, all of which must be met before a given dispute qualifies for a court hearing on the merits of the case. First, the parties to the dispute must be adversaries. The courts will entertain only disputes brought before the judiciary by hostile parties. Friendly individuals or groups who are separated by no significant conflicts of interest cannot bring a legal action before the judiciary. Second, the parties to a suit must have a substantial legal interest in the outcome of the dispute. No one can be a party to a legal suit unless he is an involved participant in the dispute. If the parties are not substantially affected by the resolution of the case, they may not act as adversaries in the legal confrontation. Third, the dispute must be a controversy growing out of a real set of facts. Courts will not hear cases based upon hypothetical situations. Nor will they entertain questions anticipating what might happen in the future. Judges restrict their attention to real disputes that exist in fact. This portion of the case or controversy rule also means that the courts may not be used to give the legislature or the executive advisory opinions as to the legality of pending laws or actions. Fourth, the dispute brought before the judiciary must be capable of being resolved through an enforceable determination of legal rights. The courts can decide only questions that can be answered through an interpretation of the law. Gerald Ford, for example, could not sue Jimmy Carter requesting the court to declare Ford the winner in the 1976 presidential election on the grounds that he was the better candidate. The decision as to who should hold a particular office and who is the best qualified candidate is essentially a political one and not one based upon law. Gerald Ford's suit could not be decided by the courts because it fails to present an issue that could be resolved by an enforceable determination of legal rights. Such a dispute is to be answered by the electorate and not the judiciary.

The Federal Question Requirement

If a legal dispute meets the case or controversy rule, it has the potential of being heard and decided by the federal courts. However, before the national judiciary can rule on such a dispute it must also present a "federal question." It is the presence of the federal question which makes a legal dispute relevant to the national courts rather than falling under the jurisdiction of the courts of a particular state. The federal question requirement can be met in one of two ways. First, a case may present a federal question if the dispute rests upon the interpretation or application of certain federal laws. For example, if the dispute arises under the United States Constitution, congressional statutes, federal administrative regulations, or United States treaties, the federal courts have jurisdiction. Furthermore, any case resting upon admiralty or maritime law is considered a federal question. So too are suits involving land claimed by two or more states. Second, a case may be considered to present a federal question because of the nature of the parties involved. The Constitution stipulates that the federal courts have jurisdiction over disputes involving any of the following as a party: the United States government, state governments, and accredited representatives of foreign nations. Furthermore, the federal courts may hear diverse citizenship disputes, that is, suits between citizens of different states. Therefore, if a legal dispute qualifies as a case or controversy and presents a federal question, then the United States courts have jurisdiction over the litigation and are empowered to resolve the conflict. Other court suits are more appropriate for a hearing in a state court.

Powers of the Courts

In resolving cases and controversies the courts are authorized to exercise certain traditional powers. For example, courts are empowered to issue injunctions, which are orders mandating that individuals or groups refrain from engaging in unlawful activities. Other judicial orders or writs may compel persons to carry out the obligations imposed by the law. For persons who refuse to obey court commands or otherwise show disrespect toward the judiciary, the judges may impose contempt citation punishments of fines or imprisonment. Appellate courts exercise a certain degree of rule-making authority, including the ability to designate procedural regulations for the presentation and hearing of litigation. The judiciary also exercises considerable control over the legal profession by setting standards for admission to the bar, admitting attorneys to practice, assigning various tasks to lawyers (such as representing indigents in criminal cases), and disciplining lawyers who violate the rules of proper professional conduct.

Of course, the most extreme power the judiciary may exercise in the course of deciding cases and controversies is the power of judicial review. Judicial review is the one major authority of the courts that cannot be found in the Constitution itself. While the roots of this particular judicial action can be seen extending deep into the history of British legal experience, the actual foundation of judicial review was accomplished through the rulings of the judiciary itself. The courts were not given the power to review the actions of the legislative and executive branches for constitutional infirmities; nor were they given the authority to strike down statutes and administrative actions. The judiciary seized the power. Through one bold, decisive ruling the judicial branch acquired its most potent power. The events and circumstances leading up to the decision in *Marbury* v. *Madison* were reviewed in chapter 1 and need not be repeated here. It is sufficient to note that the logic of Chief Justice Marshall's opinion has withstood the test of time. The power of judicial review exists today in the same form as it did when formally recognized in 1803. The Supreme Court wields the power in a reasonably judicious fashion. Fears that the courts would impose a form of judicial tyranny, cancelling out at will the actions of the legislature and the presidency, have not materialized. The power has been used regularly, however, and it provides a constant threat to lawmakers who would be tempted to stretch the boundaries imposed by the Constitution and to presidents who would become overzealous in their executive actions. Even the Supreme Court under Chief Justice Warren Burger, normally considered a fairly conservative group of justices, struck down twenty-seven federal laws during its first seven years of operation. Instances in which the Court has voided state statutes have been even more numerous.

Judicial Self-Restraint

For the most part the United States Supreme Court has proceeded somewhat cautiously in the exercise of the power of judicial review. In so doing the Court has developed a set of principles governing the review power that are commonly referred to as the principles of judicial self-restraint. Observance of these standards has meant that the Court has not generally struck down legislation arbitrarily or irresponsibly. Instead it has normally acted only when imposing judicial review remained as the best alternative available to reaching a fair and equitable resolution of a legal dispute. Among the principles of self-restraint are the following. First, the Court will not anticipate a question of constitutional law in advance of the necessity of deciding it. In practice this means that the Court will hear only those issues in a dispute which are absolutely necessary for the resolution of the suit. The Court will not project its ruling to cases or controversies that might arise in the future. Second, the Court will not hand down a constitutional ruling that goes beyond the precise facts in the case at hand. By confining its decisions to the narrow factual circumstances in the instant case, the Court reduces the necessity of handing down frequent sweeping constitutional rulings. Third, the Court will not decide a question of constitutional law if the dispute can be resolved on any other grounds. Therefore, if the judges are able to avoid exercising the power of judicial review by deciding a case on procedural, technical, or narrow statutory grounds, they will do so. Fourth, in determining the validity of a statute or other governmental action in the face of a constitutional challenge, the Court will give the benefit of the doubt to the governmental action. The burden of proof clearly rests with those who wish the law or action to be struck down. An act is presumed constitutional unless it is clearly proven to be otherwise. These principles of self-restraint, along with a judicious application of the case or controversy rule, means that the Court relies on the power of judicial review in far fewer cases than might otherwise be expected. The Court thereby avoids many potentially damaging political conflicts with the citizenry and the other agencies of government. Furthermore, judicial restraint has the impact of enhancing the position of the Court on those occasions in which a statute or governmental action must be voided because of constitutional infirmities.

The relatively sparing use of the power of judicial review, of course, has not insulated the courts from rather severe criticism in those instances in which the public or certain governmental officials have felt that the judicial branch has gone too far in its rulings. When the courts have struck down statutes in order to impose racial integration, eliminated criminal procedures that violated Bill of Rights protections, removed prayer from public schools, or upheld the rights of certain unpopular political groups against repressive governmental actions, the response of the public has often been intensely critical and fairly widespread. Yet the judiciary has survived well throughout the years because it has normally used its powers of judicial review in a reasonably prudent fashion. Furthermore, members of the federal bench have been relatively astute politically, realizing when it has been better to avoid political clashes with the Congress, the president, or the people rather than recklessly to attempt to impose politically unacceptable rulings.

Limitations on the Power of the Judiciary

When considering the powers of the judicial branch, two factors must be kept in mind. First, the judiciary is essentially a passive institution. This characteristic distinguishes it from the legislative and executive agencies of government. Congress, for example, may take up any subject it desires at almost any time it wishes to do so. It may initiate legislation whenever it perceives a need for the consideration and possible enacting of any statutory proposal. Similarly, the executive branch is free to initiate a wide variety of activities whenever the president or other key administrative officials consider it wise to do so. The courts, on the other hand, are unable to initiate actions. The judiciary is dependent upon others to create its business agenda. Until a case is filed before a court presenting a particular legal issue, the courts are powerless to rule on that specific question. If, for example, no one had challenged the validity of the 1974 amendments to the Election Campaign Act, the judicial branch could never have declared portions of that act unconstitutional as the Supreme Court did in *Buckley* v. *Valeo,* discussed in chapter 5. What questions the courts decide, therefore, are largely dependent upon parties other than the judges themselves.

A second significant factor regarding the courts is that the judiciary has virtually no enforcement powers. When a court hands down a ruling, it assumes that the parties affected will comply with the dictates of the decision. Virtually all court rulings receive the voluntary compliance of those involved. This compliance may be the result of a general degree of support for the specific ruling or may be due to the feeling that it is the responsibility of the citizen to obey the legal determinations of a court of law. At times compliance with court decisions is somewhat difficult to obtain because of widespread dissatisfaction. Recent court rulings involving the busing of school children, for example, prompted negative reactions among various segments of the citizenry. This led to mass demonstrations and the boycotting of public schools in some cities. Historically, however, the judiciary has been very successful at attaining compliance with its legal holdings. In those instances in which court decisions are flagrantly disobeyed, where resistance is unmoveable, the court must rely on the enforcement powers of the executive branch. In the final analysis the president may be required to dispatch military troops to insure that the rulings of the courts are adhered to. Examples of such actions have been extremely rare. The lack of enforcement powers works as a restraint against radical court actions. The judiciary is well aware that it must keep active opposition to its rulings to a minimum. The authority of judicial review and the other powers of the courts must be used in a sufficiently prudent manner to encourage voluntary compliance. The courts must keep in mind what is politically acceptable and those kinds of rulings that will lead to negative consequences.

The Judicial Branch and the Separation of Powers

The specific provisions included in the Constitution allowing the legislative and executive branches to exercise certain checks against the other agencies of government have no counterpart relevant to the judiciary. In fact, nowhere in article III of the Constitution is the judicial branch given any tangible restraint which it is able to apply against the operations of the president or the Congress. Therefore, it is only through the general exercise of the judicial power that the courts perform a checking function. These general judicial powers, however, have been quite sufficient to restrain excessive power-seeking by the legislature and the executive.

The power of judicial review, of course, is the most important check the courts can apply. In the case of legislative or executive abuse of authority, the victims of governmental excesses may petition the courts to strike down the unconstitutional actions. The threat of receiving a judicial declaration that they have exceeded the bounds imposed by the Constitution has generally encouraged the occupants of legislative and executive posts to remain within constitutionally acceptable limits. Therefore, the exercise of the power of judicial review as well as the potential use of that power has worked as a practical check on the actions of the political branches of the government.

The courts, of course, have the power to interpret the law. In the final analysis it is the judiciary to whom we entrust the responsibility to tell us what the law is. No matter what Congress may intend by a specific piece of legislation, and no matter what policy goals the president may have in administering the law, the courts act as the final arbiter in determining the meaning of an existing statute or administrative order. Therefore, a judiciary that supports the actions of the legislature or the executive branch may be instrumental in the implementation of governmental policy by favorably interpreting and applying the law. Conversely, if the judiciary provides roadblocks through unfavorable interpretations and applications of the law, the political departments of the federal government may have great difficulty imposing their policy preferences. This lesson, of course, was learned well by Franklin Roosevelt, who met stiff Court opposition to his New Deal economic regulation programs prior to 1937.

The judiciary, however, may be the most vulnerable of the three branches in the scheme of the separation of powers doctrine. After all, the judiciary is the only branch whose very selection of officials is dependent upon the other two branches of government. Congress and the president are elected by the people. They have an independent base of political power. Not so the judges, who must obtain their positions through the discretion of the executive and legislative branches. The very courts themselves are created by Congress. Only the Supreme Court has a constitutional basis for its existence. The inferior courts were created by Congress and may be eliminated by Congress. The jurisdiction of the courts is also largely determined by Congress. The Supreme Court may be stripped of most of its appellate jurisdiction with the stroke of a single legislative action. If the judiciary interprets a law in a manner not to the liking of the legislature, Congress may simply alter the law. An exercise of the power of judicial review can be overturned with the proposal for constitutional amendment. It is clear that the court system could not survive repeated, serious political battles with the legislature and the executive branch without having the judicial institution badly damaged. Perhaps the constitutional vulnerability of the judicial branch is as it should be, for no other nation gives its judiciary the immense power and influence over governmental and societal affairs as does the United States.

Summary

The existence of a relatively free society in the United States for two centuries has been at least partially due to the maintenance of a well-functioning, effective judicial branch. The nation has employed a vigilant court system to help insure that governmental abuses are checked before irreparable damage to the political system occurs. The courts are the political agency to which citizens may take their disputes with the governmental system for an impartial hearing. The courts function as protectors of civil rights and liberties. Without the judiciary operating as an independent, coequal branch of the government, these goals and objectives of a free society would be much more difficult to realize.

The American judiciary is created in article III of the Constitution. The short constitutional description of the court system leaves a great deal of discretion to the Congress for the establishment of inferior courts and the development of federal court jurisdiction. The Constitution grants the federal courts the authority to exercise the traditional powers of a judiciary. In addition, the courts have assumed the power of judicial review, which allows the members of the bench to review challenged statutes and other governmental actions for constitutional defects. The power of judicial review is an effective mechanism to restrain excessive actions by Congress and the president. The selection of generally well qualified judges by the president has to a large measure contributed to the overall success of the judicial branch throughout the nation's history. The power of the judicial system has normally been exercised in a reasonable, prudent, and politically acceptable manner. Each of these factors has been significant in America's ability to retain a strong and independent judiciary even in times of national crisis and emergency. By so doing we have received the benefits that accrue to a political system with a firm commitment to the rule of law.

Notes

1. 4 Wallace 2 (1866).
2. See, however, J. W. Paltason, *Fifty-Eight Lonely Men* (Urbana: University of Illinois Press, 1971).
3. See Robert Scigliano, *The Supreme Court and the Presidency* (New York: Free Press, 1971); Henry J. Abraham, *Justices and Presidents* (New York: Oxford University Press, 1974).

Further Reading

Abraham, Henry J. *Justices and Presidents.* New York: Oxford University Press, 1974.

Bickel, Alexander M. *The Least Dangerous Branch.* Indianapolis: Bobbs-Merrill, 1963.

Chase, Harold W. *Federal Judges: The Appointing Process.* Minneapolis: University of Minnesota Press, 1973.

Dean, H. *Judicial Review and Democracy.* New York: Random House, 1966.

Ernst, Morris L. *The Great Reversals.* New York: Weybright and Talley, 1973.

Fleming, M. *The Price of Perfect Justice.* New York: Basic Books, 1974.

Goldman, Sheldon, and Thomas P. Jahnige. *The Federal Courts as a Political System.* New York: Harper and Row, 2nd ed., 1976.

Jacob, Herbert. *Justice in America.* Boston: Little, Brown, 1972.

Mendelson, Wallace (ed.). *The Supreme Court: Law and Discretion.* Indianapolis: Bobbs-Merrill, 1967.

Murphy, Walter F. *Elements of Judicial Strategy.* Chicago: University of Chicago Press, 1964.

Richardson, Richard J., and Kenneth N. Vines. *The Politics of Federal Courts.* Boston: Little, Brown, 1970.

Wasby, Stephen L. *The Impact of the United States Supreme Court.* Homewood, Ill.: Dorsey Press, 1970.

The Constitution and American Politics: Continuity and Change

On January 20, 1977, former Georgia governor Jimmy Carter placed his hand on a Bible and took the oath of office administered by Chief Justice Warren Burger to become the president of the United States. The torch of power had been passed to a new executive administration. Carter had defeated incumbent Gerald Ford for the presidency, and his victorious Democratic party had gained control of the White House, which had been under Republican party domination for the previous eight years.

To most Americans Inauguration Day of 1977 was notable, but not a particularly outstanding event. After all, the designation of a new chief executive had occurred to some thirty-eight persons before Carter took the oath of office. Each newly elected president assumed the position by following the same inaugural ritual and articulating the same oath of office. However, what was a relatively common event in the experiences of American citizens must have been perceived as highly unusual by the residents of many nations.

In the first place, Jimmy Carter had gained power through election procedures tightly regulated by law. The accession to the presidency was a peaceful one. There had been no violence, no covert seizure of control, no military intervention. There was even an absence of major charges of voting fraud and election irregularities. The campaign had taken place with both candidates and their respective party organizations free to express ideas, proposals, and criticisms without major restraints. The news media was relatively unrestricted in engaging in critical analysis of campaign events while disseminating election information to the American public. And perhaps most significant, the nation's electorate had been able to go to the polls to express their preferences for the presidency and hundreds of other elective

196

offices. Each citizen was able to cast a single vote, regardless of race, religion, ethnic affiliation, sex, or economic status. The integrity of the election process remained largely intact, just as it had many times previously.

Second, it must have appeared strange to many in other sections of the world to observe both Jimmy Carter and Gerald Ford on the same inaugural platform. The two major rival candidates were able to meet in a peaceful, cordial fashion after having competed for what most consider the prime leadership position of the world's most powerful nation. The two represented different political philosophies, approaches to government, and political parties. President Ford had been removed from office and replaced by Jimmy Carter, certainly a very difficult and strenuous experience, and yet the former president graced the installation of his opponent with his personal presence. Carter, having competed in a fiercely contested election campaign against Mr. Ford, devoted the first words of his inaugural address to the former president, stating: "For myself and our nation, I want to thank my predecessor for all he has done to heal our land."

Finally, the response of the American people to the 1977 transfer of power must have puzzled many. There were no massive demonstrations, no organized resistance, no acts of violence. The Ford supporters accepted the defeat of their candidate honorably and for the most part wished the new president a successful administration. Americans, regardless of their political persuasions, were convinced that the decision on national leadership had been made in a legitimate fashion, and all accepted the outcome.

The events surrounding the Carter inauguration would appear unusual to many non-Americans because such a free and peaceful transfer of power rarely occurs in a number of other countries. The leadership of a majority of nation-states is not decided by free and open elections; nor is there a total absence of violence in struggles for power. The fact that the military had virtually no role in the election would be unheard of in many nations, and a two-party competitive system is foreign to most societies. In many countries an incumbent executive would not step down from power so gracefully, but might well resort to extra-legal tactics to remain in control. In a different political culture, Gerald Ford, having lost the battle for the presidency, might have been the victim of disgrace, exile, or worse.

The peace and stability of the transfer of power, however, is expected by the American citizenry. Since the first inauguration of George Washington, the country's political leaders, party organizers, and voting public have lived up to these expectations, conducting election campaigns according to relatively high standards of ethics and integrity. To those who have violated this tradition, the nation has reserved harsh treatment. No better example can be given than that of Richard Nixon, elected to the nation's highest post in 1972 by a historically large margin, only to be hounded out of office in disgrace because his selection was tainted by illegal election campaign activities and his unsuccessful attempts to cover up the wrongdoing.

America's success at providing stable, responsible government has largely been due to its national commitment to the Constitution and to the rule of law. Elections and the execution of governmental powers take place within the bounds and prescriptions contained in the document drafted at the Philadelphia Convention of 1787. To violate that basic framework is more than just a transgression of law; it constitutes a violation of the nation's political culture and heritage.

The Constitution of the United States dictates the contours of American political activity. The American populace has internalized the values contained in the Constitution to the extent that obviously unconstitutional programs or policies are seriously proposed only on rare occasions. Similarly, a governmental action attacked as violating the Constitution may have an uphill battle to gain acceptance regardless of the merits of the specific program.

A nation that has as firm a commitment to its Constitution as does the American republic necessarily confers a large degree of power upon the individual or institution responsible for interpreting that document. In the United States the people have entrusted the judiciary with the responsibility of deciding upon the proper meaning of the Constitution. Armed with the power of judicial review, the courts not only interpret the document, but are capable of striking down executive and legislative actions that the judges perceive as repugnant to the Constitution. These extensive powers make the American judiciary unique among governmental institutions in the western world. We live under a Constitution, but as Chief Justice Hughes noted: "The Constitution is what the judges say it is."

As we have seen in previous chapters, the Constitution as interpreted by the courts to a large extent controls the American political process. The Constitution establishes the basic principles for the political system, including the republican form of government, the rule of law, the separation of powers, and the federal union. The Constitution controls the basic civil liberties enjoyed by the American people, including the right of the citizenry to express political views, organize for political ends, and exercise the privilege of the franchise. Furthermore, the nation's governmental institutions are fashioned by the Constitution, including the processes by which governmental officials are selected, under what conditions they serve, and what powers the basic agencies of the government exercise.

In American society, as Justice Felix Frankfurter observed: "Law touches every concern of man. Nothing that is human is alien to it." Certainly the Constitution and laws of the United States have had an important influence on the American political process. Relatively few major political events have not concerned the judiciary. Since the end of the Second World War the judicial system has been especially active in the sphere of politics. Hardly a major governmental program or alteration in societal standards has occurred during the last three decades without active court participation. Many of the changes in American life during this time have been initiated by the judiciary and its interpretation of the Constitution. A brief review of some of the major political events and trends in recent history will illustrate the dramatically important role played by the courts in American political and social life.

Perhaps the most obvious change between the postwar era and the present has been in the area of race relations. Following the cessation of hostilities, racial segregation and discrimination were common conditions within American society. In several states schools, public facilities, business establishments, and other public accommodations were separated on the basis of race. Blacks and other minorities were often practically eliminated from public service positions, political office, and even jury duty. Universal voting rights were largely confined to white citizens. Employment opportunities, advanced educational possibilities, and business and professional pursuits were commonly closed to black Americans. The reduction in these and other racially discriminatory policies began in 1954 with the Supreme Court's *Brown* decision. For almost an entire decade the judiciary alone advanced the reality of a color-blind Constitution. Little assistance was provided by the executive or legislative branches. It was not until 1964 and 1965 that Congress began passing meaningful civil rights legislation. The race relations revolution was initiated through the judiciary's interpretation of the Fourteenth Amendment to the United States Constitution. Today the courts remain active in this controversy. Contemporary disputes over school busing, affirmative action, and public housing have been and continue to be reactions to judicial interpretations of law and constitutional rights.

Similar advances have occurred in the area of freedom of expression. Court rulings have made American society a much more open system than existed three decades ago. Responsible political controversy and discussion can now take place without fear of repression or costly libel suits. Material having sexual themes or references may now be distributed with relative freedom. Artistic expression may occur with fewer restrictions and a general absence of censorship. Public demonstrations, even with massive participation, have been given constitutional protection. The liberty to organize with others for political purposes, even if a group's objectives are unpopular, has received constitutional approval. Again, it has been the judiciary, often acting in a manner inconsistent with the prevailing will of the Congress and the presidency, which has been responsible for initiating and pursuing these changes in American liberties.

In the field of criminal due process, the courts have affected a revolution of no lesser magnitude. Three decades ago law-enforcement officials were given much wider latitude than they are today. Coerced confessions, illegal searches and seizures, "third-degree" interrogations, and a lack of respect for procedural regularities were commonplace. The judiciary sharply reduced these abuses of official power, often extending rulings beyond the limits of public approval. Formerly, unequal treatment of criminal defendants on the basis of economic status was universal. The courts extended the right to counsel to indigent suspects and removed many of the economically based inequities in the criminal justice system. These changes occurred as a direct result of judicial interpretations of the Bill of Rights.

During the 1960s, the judiciary's interpretation of the Constitution gave birth to a new liberty—the right to privacy. This recent creation has already had a substantial impact on American society, particularly in the area of marital and sexual behavior. No longer can there be laws banning the distribution of contraceptive devices, nor can birth control information and methods be denied to unmarried individuals. The government is much more restricted in its inquiries into a person's marital and sexual activities. The right to privacy has made impermissible certain governmental intrusions into the home and marital lives of Americans. And perhaps most significant, the right to privacy has been extended by the courts to protect the right of a woman to terminate a pregnancy without governmental interference. The modifications in American societal standards of conduct that have resulted from this judicial action have been substantial.

The courts have also become heavily involved in areas of discrimination other than race. The intention of those persons who drafted the Due Process Clause and the Equal Protection Clause of the Fourteenth Amendment was to protect Negro Americans from discriminatory governmental actions. Judicial construction of these provisions in recent years, however, has extended Fourteenth Amendment protections to ban many forms of official discrimination based upon sex, age, economic, and political characteristics.

While the foregoing judicially inspired advances in civil rights and liberties have received the bulk of the nation's attention with respect to the role of the courts in American society, similarly important changes have been prompted in the political process itself. The Supreme Court's decisions on reapportionment in the 1960s radically changed the constitutional basis for representation, and these principles have been applied to Congress, state legislatures, and local governmental units. Decisions such as *Buckley* v. *Valeo* have given a constitutional stamp of approval to reforms of the electoral process without allowing Congress to transgress constitutionally imposed limitations.

During the past three decades, the courts have umpired several significant disputes regarding the nature and scope of governmental power. Increased authority to regulate the economy has been permitted, including broad delegations of power to the president to impose measures designed to promote economic stability. The courts have disallowed the exercise of excessive amounts of power by the president in situations such as Truman's seizure of the steel mills and Nixon's impoundment of congressionally appropriated funds. Such foreign policy actions as the war in Vietnam could not have been maintained had not the Supreme Court consistently upheld the power of the government to conscript military personnel and had it not refused to entertain arguments that the war effort was unconstitutional because of its undeclared origins. In addition, the Supreme Court's denial of President Nixon's argument for executive privilege in *Nixon* v. *United States* not only had an all important impact on politics in the 1970s, but also defined presidential power for future generations.

In almost every important public issue over the past several years—war, poverty, civil rights, politics, governmental power, the economy, foreign relations—the role of the Constitution and the judicial branch has been significant. Many policies, programs, and movements have been fully instigated by the courts; others have achieved success because of judicial support; and still others have quickly died because of judicial disapproval. The activity of the judicial branch in the United States is substantially more significant than in the political life of any other nation. Undoubtedly the political role of the courts will remain vital in future decades.

The purpose of this short volume has been to explore the relationship between American politics and the Constitution. The Constitution was born as a political as well as a legal document. It continues to make significant contributions along both dimensions. The Constitution structures and shapes American government and political activity. Through politically inspired tradition, practice, interpretation, and modification the Constitution evolves. The judicial branch is entrusted with the responsibility of interpreting and applying the Constitution. Therefore, the courts assume both a political and a legal character. The American judiciary gives the Constitution its flexibility, allowing an eighteenth-century document to be current without substantially breaching its ties to the past. American politics cannot be understood without a proper comprehension of the United States Constitution; nor can the Constitution be understood without an adequate knowledge of American politics. The two continuously interact.

The most significant characteristic of the American system of government is that it is workable. Although the government has not solved all of society's problems, it has enjoyed relative stability and success. To a large measure this success is attributable to the framework upon which the political system is built. The Constitution and the judicial branch to which it is entrusted provide a unique combination of law and politics, of tradition and change, of established principles and practical flexibility. The nation has committed itself to the Constitution and the Constitution has served the nation well.

The Constitution of
The United States of America

Appendix

We the People of the United States, in Order to form a more perfect Union, establish Justice, insure domestic Tranquility, provide for the common defense, promote the general Welfare, and secure the Blessings of Liberty to ourselves and our Posterity, do ordain and establish this Constitution for the United States of America.

Article I

Section 1. All legislative Powers herein granted shall be vested in a Congress of the United States, which shall consist of a Senate and House of Representatives.

Section 2. The House of Representatives shall be composed of Members chosen every second Year by the People of the several States, and the Electors in each State shall have the Qualifications requisite for Electors of the most numerous Branch of the State Legislature.

No Person shall be a Representative who shall not have attained to the age of twenty five Years, and been seven Years a Citizen of the United States, and who shall not, when elected, be an Inhabitant of that State in which he shall be chosen.

Representatives and direct Taxes shall be apportioned among the several States which may be included within this Union, according to their respective Numbers, *which shall be determined by adding to the whole Number of free Persons, including those bound to Service for a Term of Years,* and excluding Indians not taxed, *three fifths of all other persons.*[1] The actual Enumeration shall be made within three Years after the first Meeting of the Congress of the United States, and within every subsequent Term of ten Years, in such Manner as they shall by Law direct. The Number of Representatives shall not

---

[1] Superseded by the 14th Amendment. Throughout, italics are used to indicate passages altered by subsequent amendments.

203

exceed one for every thirty Thousand, but each State shall have at Least one Representative; and until such enumeration shall be made, the State of New Hampshire shall be entitled to chuse three, Massachusetts eight, Rhode-Island and Providence Plantations one, Connecticut five, New-York six, New Jersey four, Pennsylvania eight, Delaware one, Maryland six, Virginia ten, North Carolina five, South Carolina five, and Georgia three.

When vacancies happen in the Representation from any State, the Executive Authority thereof shall issue Writs of Election to fill such Vacancies.

The House of Representatives shall chuse their Speaker and other Officers; and shall have the sole Power of Impeachment.

Section 3.   The Senate of the United States shall be composed of two Senators from each State, chosen by the *Legislature thereof,*[2] for six Years; and each Senator shall have one Vote.

Immediately after they shall be assembled in Consequence of the first Election, they shall be divided as equally as may be into three Classes. The Seats of the Senators of the first Class shall be vacated at the Expiration of the second Year, of the second Class at the Expiration of the fourth Year, and of the third Class at the Expiration of the sixth Year, so that one third may be chosen every second Year; *and if Vacancies happen by Resignation, or otherwise, during the Recess of the Legislature of any State, the Executive thereof may make temporary Appointments until the next Meeting of the Legislature, which shall then fill such Vacancies.*[3]

No Person shall be a Senator who shall not have attained to the Age of thirty Years, and been nine Years a Citizen of the United States, and who shall not, when elected, be an Inhabitant of the State for which he shall be chosen.

The Vice President of the United States shall be President of the Senate, but shall have no Vote, unless they be equally divided.

The Senate shall chuse their other Officers, and also a President pro tempore, in the Absence of the Vice President, or when he shall exercise the Office of President of the United States.

The Senate shall have the sole Power to try all Impeachments. When sitting for that Purpose, they shall be on Oath or Affirmation. When the President of the United States is tried, the Chief Justice shall preside: And no Person shall be convicted without the Concurrence of two thirds of the Members present.

Judgment in Cases of Impeachment shall not extend further than to removal from Office, and disqualification to hold and enjoy any Office of Honor, Trust or Profit under the United States: but the Party convicted shall nevertheless be liable and subject to Indictment, Trial, Judgment and Punishment, according to Law.

Section 4.   The Times, Places and Manner of holding Elections for Senators and Representatives, shall be prescribed in each State by the Legislature thereof; but the Congress may at any time by Law make or alter such Regulations, except as to the Places of chusing Senators.

The Congress shall assemble at least once in every Year, and such Meeting shall be on the first Monday in December, unless they shall by Law appoint a different Day.[4]

---

[2] See 17th Amendment.
[3] See 17th Amendment.
[4] See 20th Amendment.

Section 5.   Each House shall be the Judge of the Elections, Returns and Qualifications of its own Members, and a Majority of each shall constitute a Quorum to do Business; but a smaller Number may adjourn from day to day, and may be authorized to compel the Attendance of absent Members, in such Manner, and under such Penalties as each House may provide.

Each House may determine the Rules of its Proceedings, punish its Members for disorderly Behaviour, and, with the Concurrence of two thirds, expel a Member.

Each House shall keep a Journal of its Proceedings, and from time to time publish the same, excepting such Parts as may in their Judgment require Secrecy; and the Yeas and Nays of the Members of either House on any question shall, at the Desire of one fifth of those Present, be entered on the Journal.

Neither House, during the Session of Congress, shall, without the Consent of the other, adjourn for more than three days, nor to any other Place than that in which the two Houses shall be sitting.

Section 6.   The Senators and Representatives shall receive a Compensation for their Services, to be ascertained by Law, and paid out of the Treasury of the United States. They shall in all Cases, except Treason, Felony and Breach of the Peace, be privileged from Arrest during their Attendance at the Session of their respective Houses, and in going to and returning from the same; and for any Speech or Debate in either House, they shall not be questioned in any other Place.

No Senator or Representative shall, during the Time for which he was elected, be appointed to any civil Office under the Authority of the United States, which shall have been created, or the Emoluments whereof shall have been encreased during such time; and no Person holding any Office under the United States, shall be a Member of either House during his Continuance in Office.

Section 7.   All Bills for raising Revenue shall originate in the House of Representatives; but the Senate may propose or concur with Amendments as on other Bills.

Every Bill which shall have passed the House of Representatives and the Senate, shall, before it become a Law, be presented to the President of the United States; If he approve he shall sign it, but if not he shall return it, with his Objections to that House in which it shall have originated, who shall enter the Objections at large on their Journal, and proceed to reconsider it. If after such Reconsideration two thirds of that House shall agree to pass the Bill, it shall be sent, together with the Objections, to the other House, by which it shall likewise be reconsidered, and if approved by two thirds of that House, it shall become a Law. But in all such Cases the Votes of both Houses shall be determined by Yeas and Nays, and the Names of the Persons voting for and against the Bill shall be entered on the Journal of each House respectively. If any Bill shall not be returned by the President within ten Days (Sundays excepted) after it shall have been presented to him, the Same shall be a Law, in like Manner as if he had signed it, unless the Congress by their Adjournment prevent its Return, in which Case it shall not be a Law.

Every Order, Resolution, or Vote to which the Concurrence of the Senate and House of Representatives may be necessary (except on a question of Adjournment) shall be presented to the President of the United States; and before the Same shall take Effect, shall be approved by him, or being disapproved by him, shall be repassed by two thirds of the Senate and House of Representatives, according to the Rules and Limitations prescribed in the Case of a Bill.

Section 8.   The Congress shall have Power To lay and collect Taxes, Duties, Imposts and Excises, to pay the Debts and provide for the common Defence and general Welfare of the United States; but all Duties, Imposts and Excises shall be uniform throughout the United States;

To borrow Money on the credit of the United States;

To regulate Commerce with foreign Nations, and among the several States, and with the Indian Tribes;

To establish an uniform Rule of Naturalization, and uniform Laws on the subject of Bankruptcies throughout the United States;

To coin Money, regulate the Value thereof, and of foreign Coin, and fix the Standard of Weights and Measures;

To provide for the Punishment of counterfeiting the Securities and current Coin of the United States;

To establish Post Offices and post Roads;

To promote the Progress of Science and useful Arts, by securing for limited Times to Authors and Inventors the exclusive Right to their respective Writings and Discoveries;

To constitute Tribunals inferior to the Supreme Court;

To define and punish Piracies and Felonies committed on the high Seas, and Offences against the Law of Nations;

To declare War, grant Letters of Marque and Reprisal, and make Rules concerning Captures on Land and Water;

To raise and support Armies, but no Appropriation of Money to that Use shall be for a longer Term than two Years;

To provide and maintain a Navy;

To make Rules for the Government and Regulation of the land and naval Forces;

To provide for calling forth the Militia to execute the Laws of the Union, suppress Insurrections and repel Invasions;

To provide for organizing, arming, and disciplining, the Militia, and for governing such Part of them as may be employed in the Service of the United States, reserving to the States respectively, the Appointment of the Officers, and the Authority of training the Militia according to the discipline prescribed by Congress;

To exercise exclusive Legislation in all Cases whatsoever, over such District (not exceeding ten Miles square) as may, by Cession of particular States, and the Acceptance of Congress, become the Seat of the Government of the United States, and to exercise like Authority over all Places purchased by the Consent of the Legislature of the State in which the Same shall be, for the Erection of Forts, Magazines, Arsenals, dock-Yards, and other needful Buildings;—And

To make all Laws which shall be necessary and proper for carrying into Execution the foregoing Powers, and all other Powers vested by this Constitution in the Government of the United States, or in any Department or Officer thereof.

Section 9.   The Migration or Importation of such Persons as any of the States now existing shall think proper to admit, shall not be prohibited by the Congress prior to the Year one thousand eight hundred and eight, but a Tax or duty may be imposed on such Importation, not exceeding ten dollars for each Person.

The Privilege of the Writ of Habeas Corpus shall not be suspended, unless when in Cases of Rebellion or Invasion the public Safety may require it.

No Bill of Attainder or ex post facto Law shall be passed.

No Capitation, or other direct, Tax shall be laid, unless in Proportion to the Census or Enumeration herein before directed to be taken.

No Tax or Duty shall be laid on Articles exported from any State.

No Preference shall be given by any Regulation of Commerce or Revenue to the Ports of one State over those of another: nor shall Vessels bound to, or from, one State, be obliged to enter, clear, or pay Duties in another.

No Money shall be drawn from the Treasury, but in Consequence of Appropriations made by Law; and a regular Statement and Account of the Receipts and Expenditures of all public Money shall be published from time to time.

No Title of Nobility shall be granted by the United States: And no Person holding any Office of Profit or Trust under them, shall, without the Consent of the Congress, accept of any present, Emolument, Office, or Title, of any kind whatever, from any King, Prince, or foreign State.

Section 10.   No State shall enter into any Treaty, Alliance, or Confederation; grant Letters of Marque and Reprisal; coin Money; emit Bills of Credit; make any Thing but gold and silver Coin a Tender in Payment of Debts; pass any Bill of Attainder, ex post facto Law, or Law impairing the Obligation of Contracts, or grant any Title of Nobility.

No State shall, without the Consent of the Congress, lay any Imposts or Duties on Imports or Exports, except what may be absolutely necessary for executing its inspection Laws: and the net Produce of all Duties and Imposts, laid by any State on Imports or Exports, shall be for the Use of the Treasury of the United States; and all such Laws shall be subject to the Revision and Controul of the Congress.

No State shall, without the Consent of Congress, lay any Duty of Tonnage, keep Troops, or Ships of War in time of Peace, enter into any Agreement or Compact with another State, or with a foreign Power, or engage in War, unless actually invaded, or in such imminent Danger as will not admit of delay.

Article II

Section 1.   The executive Power shall be vested in a President of the United States of America. He shall hold his Office during the Term of four Years, and, together with the Vice President, chosen for the same Term, be elected, as follows:

Each State shall appoint, in such Manner as the Legislature thereof may direct, a Number of Electors, equal to the whole Number of Senators and Representatives to which the State may be entitled in the Congress: but no Senator or Representative, or Person holding an Office of Trust or Profit under the United States, shall be appointed an Elector.

The Electors shall meet in their respective States, and vote by Ballot for two Persons, of whom one at least shall not be an Inhabitant of the same State with themselves. And they shall make a List of all the Persons voted for, and of the Number of Votes for each; which List they shall sign and certify, and transmit sealed to the Seat of the Government of the United States, directed to the President of the Senate. The President of the Senate shall, in the Presence of the Senate and House of Representatives, open all the Certificates, and the Votes shall then be counted. The Person having the greatest Number of Votes shall be the President, if such Number be a Majority of the whole Number of Electors appointed; and if there be more than one who have such Majority, and have an equal Number of

Votes, then the House of Representatives shall immediately chuse by Ballot one of them for President; and if no Person have a Majority, then from the five highest on the List the said House shall in like Manner chuse the President. But in chusing the President, the Votes shall be taken by States, the Representation from each State having one Vote: A quorum for this Purpose shall consist of a Member or Members from two thirds of the States, and a Majority of all the States shall be necessary to a Choice. In every Case, after the Choice of the President, the Person having the greatest Number of Votes of the Electors shall be the Vice President. But if there should remain two or more who have equal Votes, the Senate shall chuse from them by Ballot the Vice President.[5]

The Congress may determine the Time of chusing the Electors, and the Day on which they shall give their Votes; which Day shall be the same throughout the United States.

No Person except a natural born Citizen, or a Citizen of the United States, at the time of the Adoption of this Constitution, shall be eligible to the Office of President; neither shall any Person be eligible to that Office who shall not have attained to the Age of thirty five Years, and been fourteen Years a Resident within the United States.

In Case of the Removal of the President from Office, or of his Death, Resignation, or Inability to discharge the Powers and Duties of the said Office, the Same shall devolve on the Vice President, and the Congress may by Law provide for the Case of Removal, Death, Resignation or Inability, both of the President and Vice President, declaring what Officer shall then act as President, and such Officer shall act accordingly, until the Disability be removed, or a President shall be elected.[6]

The President shall, at stated Times, receive for his Services, a Compensation which shall neither be encreased nor diminished during the Period for which he shall have been elected, and he shall not receive within that Period any other Emolument from the United States, or any of them.

Before he enter on the Execution of his Office, he shall take the following Oath or Affirmation:—"I do solemnly swear (or affirm) that I will faithfully execute the Office of President of the United States, and will to the best of my Ability, preserve, protect and defend the Constitution of the United States."

Section 2.   The President shall be Commander in Chief of the Army and Navy of the United States, and of the Militia of the several States, when called into the actual Service of the United States; he may require the Opinion, in writing, of the principal Officer in each of the executive Departments, upon any Subject relating to the Duties of their respective Offices, and he shall have Power to grant Reprieves and Pardons for Offences against the United States, except in Cases of Impeachment.

He shall have Power, by and with the Advice and Consent of the Senate, to make Treaties, provided two thirds of the Senators present concur; and he shall nominate, and by and with the Advice and Consent of the Senate, shall appoint Ambassadors, other public Ministers and Consuls, Judges of the supreme Court, and all other Officers of the United States, whose Appointments are not herein otherwise provided for, and which shall be established by Law: but the Congress may by Law vest the Appointment of such inferior officers, as they think proper, in the President alone, in the Courts of Law, or in the Heads of Departments.

---

[5] Superseded by the 12th Amendment.
[6] See 25th Amendment.

The President shall have Power to fill up all Vacancies that may happen during the Recess of the Senate, by granting Commissions which shall expire at the End of their next Session.

Section 3. He shall from time to time give to the Congress Information of the State of the Union, and recommend to their Consideration such Measures as he shall judge necessary and expedient; he may, on extraordinary Occasions, convene both Houses, or either of them, and in Case of Disagreement between them, with Respect to the Time of Adjournment, he may adjourn them to such Time as he shall think proper; he shall receive Ambassadors and other public Ministers; he shall take Care that the Laws be faithfully executed, and shall Commission all the Officers of the United States.

Section 4. The President, Vice President, and all civil Officers of the United States, shall be removed from Office on Impeachment for, and Conviction of, Treason, Bribery, or other high Crimes and Misdemeanors.

Article III

Section 1. The judicial Power of the United States, shall be vested in one supreme Court and in such inferior Courts as the Congress may from time to time ordain and establish. The Judges, both of the supreme and inferior Courts, shall hold their Offices during good Behaviour, and shall, at stated Times, receive for their Services, a Compensation, which shall not be diminished during their Continuance in Office.

Section 2. The judicial Power shall extend to all Cases, in Law and Equity, arising under this Constitution, the Laws of the United States, and Treaties made, or which shall be made, under their Authority;—to all Cases affecting Ambassadors, other public Ministers and Consuls;—to all Cases of admiralty and maritime Jurisdiction;—to Controversies to which the United States shall be a Party—to Controversies between two or more States;—*between a State and Citizens of another State* [7];—between Citizens of different States;—between Citizens of the same State claiming Lands under Grants of different States, *and between a State or the Citizens thereof, and foreign States, Citizens, or Subjects.* [8]

In all Cases affecting Ambassadors, other public Ministers and Consuls, and those in which a State shall be Party, the supreme Court shall have original Jurisdiction. In all the other Cases before mentioned, the supreme Court shall have appellate Jurisdiction, both as to Law and Fact, with such Exceptions, and under such Regulations as the Congress shall make.

The Trial of all Crimes, except in Cases of Impeachment, shall be by Jury; and such Trial shall be held in the State where the said Crimes shall have been committed; but when not committed within any State, the Trial shall be at such Place or Places as the Congress may by Law have directed.

Section 3. Treason against the United States, shall consist only in levying War against them, or in adhering to their Enemies, giving them Aid and Comfort. No Person shall be convicted of Treason unless on the Testimony of two Witnesses to the same overt Act, or on Confession in open Court.

---

[7] See 11th Amendment.
[8] See 11th Amendment.

The Congress shall have Power to declare the Punishment of Treason, but no Attainder of Treason shall work Corruption of Blood, or Forfeiture except during the Life of the Person attainted.

Article IV

Section 1. Full Faith and Credit shall be given in each State to the public Acts, Records, and judicial Proceedings of every other State. And the Congress may by general Laws prescribe the Manner in which such Acts, Records, and Proceedings shall be proved, and the Effect thereof.

Section 2. The Citizens of each State shall be entitled to all Privileges and Immunities of Citizens in the several States.

A Person charged in any State with Treason, Felony, or other Crime, who shall flee from Justice, and be found in another State, shall on Demand of the executive Authority of the State from which he fled, be delivered up, to be removed to the State having Jurisdiction of the Crime.

No Person held to Service or Labour in one State, under the Laws thereof, escaping into another, shall, in Consequence of any Law or Regulation therein, be discharged from such Service or Labour, but shall be delivered up on Claim of the Party to whom such Service or Labour may be due.[9]

Section 3. New States may be admitted by the Congress into this Union; but no new State shall be formed or erected within the Jurisdiction of any other State; nor any State be formed by the Junction of two or more States, or Parts of States, without the Consent of the Legislatures of the States concerned as well as of the Congress.

The Congress shall have Power to dispose of and make all needful Rules and Regulations respecting the Territory or other Property belonging to the United States; and nothing in this Constitution shall be so construed as to Prejudice any claims of the United States, or of any particular State.

Section 4. The United States shall guarantee to every State in this Union a Republican Form of Government, and shall protect each of them against Invasion; and on Application of the Legislature, or of the Executive (when the Legislature cannot be convened) against domestic Violence.

Article V

The Congress, whenever two thirds of both Houses shall deem it necessary, shall propose Amendments to this Constitution, or, on the Application of the Legislatures of two thirds of the several States, shall call a Convention for proposing Amendments, which, in either Case, shall be valid to all Intents and Purposes, as Part of this Constitution, when ratified by the Legislatures of three fourths of the several States, or by Conventions in three fourths thereof, as the one or the other Mode of Ratification may be proposed by the Congress; Provided that no Amendment which may be made prior to the Year One thousand eight hundred and eight shall in any Manner affect the first and fourth Clauses in the Ninth

[9] See 13th Amendment.

Section of the first Article; and that no State, without its Consent, shall be deprived of its equal Suffrage in the Senate.

Article VI

All Debts contracted and Engagements entered into, before the Adoption of this Constitution, shall be as valid against the United States under this Constitution, as under the Confederation.

This Constitution, and the Laws of the United States which shall be made in Pursuance thereof; and all Treaties made, or which shall be made, under the Authority of the United States, shall be the supreme Law of the Land; and the Judges in every State shall be bound thereby, any Thing in the Constitution or Laws of any State to the Contrary notwithstanding.

The Senators and Representatives before mentioned, and the Members of the several State Legislatures, and all executive and judicial Officers, both of the United States and of the several States, shall be bound by Oath or Affirmation, to support this Constitution; but no religious Test shall ever be required as a Qualification to any Office or public Trust under the United States.

Article VII

The Ratification of the Conventions of nine States, shall be sufficient for the Establishment of this Constitution between the States so ratifying the Same.

Done in Convention by the Unanimous Consent of the States present the Seventeenth Day of September in the Year of our Lord one thousand seven hundred and eighty seven and of the Independence of the United States of America the Twelfth. In witness whereof We have hereunto subscribed our Names.

ARTICLES IN ADDITION TO, AND AMENDMENT OF, THE CONSTITUTION OF THE UNITED STATES OF AMERICA, PROPOSED BY CONGRESS, AND RATIFIED BY THE SEVERAL STATES, PURSUANT TO THE FIFTH ARTICLE OF THE ORIGINAL CONSTITUTION:

Amendment I

(Ratification of the first ten amendments was completed December 15, 1791.)
Congress shall make no law respecting an establishment of religion, or prohibiting the free exercise thereof; or abridging the freedom of speech, or of the press; or the right of the people peaceably to assemble, and to petition the Government for a redress of grievances.

Amendment II

A well regulated Militia, being necessary to the security of a free State, the right of the people to keep and bear Arms, shall not be infringed.

Amendment III

No Soldier shall, in time of peace be quartered in any house, without the consent of the Owner, nor in time of war, but in a manner to be prescribed by law.

Amendment IV

The right of the people to be secure in their persons, houses, papers, and effects, against unreasonable searches and seizures, shall not be violated, and no Warrants shall issue, but upon probable cause, supported by Oath or affirmation, and particularly describing the place to be searched, and the persons or things to be seized.

Amendment V

No person shall be held to answer for a capital, or otherwise infamous crime, unless on a presentment or indictment of a Grand Jury, except in cases arising in the land or naval forces, or in the Militia, when in actual service in time of War or public danger; nor shall any person be subject for the same offence to be twice put in jeopardy of life or limb; nor shall be compelled in any criminal case to be a witness against himself, nor be deprived of life, liberty, or property, without due process of law; nor shall private property be taken for public use, without just compensation.

Amendment VI

In all criminal prosecutions, the accused shall enjoy the right to a speedy and public trial, by an impartial jury of the State and district wherein the crime shall have been committed, which district shall have been previously ascertained by law, and to be informed of the nature and cause of the accusation; to be confronted with the witness against him; to have compulsory process for obtaining witnesses in his favor, and to have the Assistance of Counsel for his defence.

Amendment VII

In Suits at common law, where the value in controversy shall exceed twenty dollars, the right of trial by jury shall be preserved, and no fact tried by a jury, shall be otherwise reexamined in any Court of the United States, than according to the rules of the common law.

Amendment VIII

Excessive bail shall not be required, nor excessive fines imposed, nor cruel and unusual punishments inflicted.

Amendment IX

The enumeration in the Constitution, of certain rights, shall not be construed to deny or disparage others retained by the people.

Amendment X

The powers not delegated to the United States by the Constitution, nor prohibited by it to the States, are reserved to the States respectively, or to the people.

Amendment XI (1798)

The Judicial power of the United States shall not be construed to extend to any suit in law or equity, commenced or prosecuted against one of the United States by Citizens of another State, or by Citizens or Subjects of any Foreign States.

Amendment XII (1804)

The Electors shall meet in their respective states and vote by ballot for President and Vice-President, one of whom, at least, shall not be an inhabitant of the same state with themselves; they shall name in their ballots the person voted for as President, and in distinct ballots the person voted for as Vice-President, and they shall make distinct lists of all persons voted for as President, and of all persons voted for as Vice-President, and of the number of votes for each, which lists they shall sign and certify, and transmit sealed to the seat of the government of the United States, directed to the President of the Senate;— The President of the Senate shall, in the presence of Senate and House of Representatives, open all the certificates and the votes shall then be counted;—The person having the greatest number of votes for President, shall be the President, if such number be a majority of the whole number of Electors appointed; and if no person have such majority, then from the persons having the highest numbers not exceeding three on the list of those voted for as President, the House of Representatives shall choose immediately, by ballot, the President. But in choosing the President, the votes shall be taken by states, the representation from each state having one vote; a quorum for this purpose shall consist of a member or members from two-thirds of the states, and a majority of all the states shall be necessary to a choice. And if the House of Representatives shall not choose a President whenever the right of choice shall devolve upon them, *before the fourth day of March next following,*[10] then the Vice-President shall act as President, as in the case of the death or other constitutional disability of the President.—The person having the greatest number of votes as Vice-President shall be the Vice-President, if such number be a majority of the whole number of Electors appointed, and if no person have a majority, then from the two highest numbers on the list, the Senate shall choose the Vice-President; a quorum for the purpose shall consist of two-thirds of the whole number of Senators, and a majority of the whole number shall be necessary to a choice. But no person constitutionally ineligible to the office of President shall be eligible to that of Vice-President of the United States.

Amendment XIII (1865)

Section 1. Neither slavery nor involuntary servitude, except as a punishment for crime whereof the party shall have been duly convicted, shall exist within the United States, or any place subject to their jurisdiction.

---

[10] Altered by the 20th Amendment.

Section 2. Congress shall have the power to enforce this article by appropriate legislation.

Amendment XIV (1868)

Section 1. All persons born or naturalized in the United States, and subject to the jurisdiction thereof, are citizens of the United States and of the State wherein they reside. No State shall make or enforce any law which shall abridge the privileges or immunities of citizens of the United States; nor shall any State deprive any person of life, liberty, or property, without due process of law; nor deny to any person within its jurisdiction the equal protection of the laws.

Section 2. Representatives shall be apportioned among the several States according to their respective numbers, counting the whole number of persons in each State, excluding Indians not taxed. But when the right to vote at any election for the choice of electors for President and Vice President of the United States, Representatives in Congress, the Executive and Judicial officers of a State, or the members of the Legislature thereof, is denied to any of the male inhabitants of such State, being twenty-one years of age, and citizens of the United States, or in any way abridged, except for participation in rebellion, or other crime, the basis of representation therein shall be reduced in the proportion which the number of such male citizens shall bear to the whole number of male citizens twenty-one years of age in such State.

Section 3. No person shall be a Senator or Representative in Congress, or elector of President and Vice President, or hold any office, civil or military, under the United States, or under any State, who, having previously taken an oath, as a member of Congress, or as an officer of the United States, or as a member of any State legislature, or as an executive or judicial officer of any State, to support the Constitution of the United States, shall have engaged in insurrection or rebellion against the same, or given aid or comfort to the enemies thereof. But Congress may by a vote of two-thirds of each House, remove such disability.

Section 4. The validity of the public debt of the United States, authorized by law, including debts incurred for payment of pensions and bounties for services in suppressing insurrection or rebellion, shall not be questioned. But neither the United States nor any State shall assume or pay any debt or obligation incurred in aid of insurrection or rebellion against the United States, or any claim for the loss or emancipation of any slave; but all such debts, obligations, and claims shall be held illegal and void.

Section 5. The Congress shall have power to enforce, by appropriate legislation, the provisions of this article.

Amendment XV (1870)

Section 1. The right of citizens of the United States to vote shall not be denied or abridged by the United States or by any State on account of race, color, or previous condition of servitude.

Section 2. The Congress shall have power to enforce this article by appropriate legislation.

Amendment XVI (1913)

The Congress shall have power to lay and collect taxes on incomes, from whatever source derived, without apportionment among the several States, and without regard to any census or enumeration.

Amendment XVII (1913)

The Senate of the United States shall be composed of two Senators from each State, elected by the people thereof, for six years; and each Senator shall have one vote. The electors in each State shall have the qualifications requisite for electors of the most numerous branch of the State legislatures.

When vacancies happen in the representation of any State in the Senate, the executive authority of such State shall issue writs of election to fill such vacancies: *Provided*, That the legislature of any State may empower the executive thereof to make temporary appointments until the people fill the vacancies by election as the legislature may direct.

This amendment shall not be so construed as to affect the election or term of any Senator chosen before it becomes valid as part of the Constitution.

Amendment XVIII (1919)

Section 1. After one year from the ratification of this article the manufacture, sale, or transportation of intoxicating liquors within, the importation thereof into, or the exportation thereof from the United States and all territory subject to the jurisdiction thereof for beverage purposes is hereby prohibited.

Section 2. The Congress and the several States shall have concurrent power to enforce this article by appropriate legislation.

Section 3. This article shall be inoperative unless it shall have been ratified as an amendment to the Constitution by the legislatures of the several States, as provided in the Constitution, within seven years from the date of the submission hereof to the States by the Congress.[11]

Amendment XIX (1920)

The right of citizens of the United States to vote shall not be denied or abridged by the United States or by any State on account of sex.

Congress shall have power to enforce this article by appropriate legislation.

Amendment XX (1933)

Section 1. The terms of the President and Vice President shall end at noon on the 20th day of January, and the terms of Senators and Representatives at noon on the 3rd

---

[11] Repealed by the 21st Amendment.

day of January, of the years in which such terms would have ended if this article had not been ratified; and the terms of their successors shall then begin.

Section 2.   The Congress shall assemble at least once in every year, and such meeting shall begin at noon on the 3rd day of January, unless they shall by law appoint a different day.

Section 3.   If, at the time fixed for the beginning of the term of the President, the President elect shall have died, the Vice President elect shall become President. If a President shall not have been chosen before the time fixed for the beginning of his term, or if the President elect shall have failed to qualify, then the Vice President elect shall act as President until a President shall have qualified; and the Congress may by law provide for the case wherein neither a President elect nor a Vice President elect shall have qualified, declaring who shall then act as President, or the manner in which one who is to act shall be selected, and such person shall act accordingly until a President or Vice President shall have qualified.

Section 4.   The Congress may by law provide for the case of the death of any of the persons from whom the House of Representatives may choose a President whenever the right of choice shall have devolved upon them, and for the case of the death of any of the persons from whom the Senate may choose a Vice President whenever the right of choice shall have devolved upon them.

Section 5.   Sections 1 and 2 shall take effect on the 15th day of October following the ratification of this article.

Section 6.   This article shall be inoperative unless it shall have been ratified as an amendment to the Constitution by the legislatures of three-fourths of the several States within seven years from the date of its submission.

Amendment XXI (1933)

Section 1.   The eighteenth article of amendment to the Constitution of the United States is hereby repealed.

Section 2.   The transportation or importation into any State, Territory, or possession of the United States for delivery or use therein of intoxicating liquors, in violation of the laws thereof, is hereby prohibited.

Section 3.   This article shall be inoperative unless it shall have been ratified as an amendment to the Constitution by conventions in the several States, as provided in the Constitution, within seven years from the date of the submission hereof to the States by the Congress.

Amendment XXII (1951)

Section 1.   No person shall be elected to the office of the President more than twice, and no person who has held the office of President, or acted as President for more than two years of a term to which some other person was elected President shall be elected to the office of President more than once. But this Article shall not apply to any person holding the office of President when this Article was proposed by the Congress, and shall not prevent any person who may be holding the office of President, or acting as President, during the term within which this Article becomes operative from holding the office of President or acting as President during the remainder of such term.

Section 2. This article shall be inoperative unless it shall have been ratified as an amendment to the Constitution by the legislatures of three-fourths of the several States within seven years from the date of its submission to the States by the Congress.

Amendment XXIII (1961)

Section 1. The District constituting the seat of Government of the United States shall appoint in such manner as the Congress may direct:

A number of electors of President and Vice President equal to the whole number of Senators and Representatives in Congress to which the District would be entitled if it were a State, but in no event more than the least populous State; they shall be in addition to those appointed by the States, but they shall be considered, for the purposes of the election of President and Vice President, to be electors appointd by a State; and they shall meet in the District and perform such duties as provided by the twelfth article of amendment.

Section 2. The Congress shall have power to enforce this article by appropriate legislation.

Amendment XXIV (1964)

Section 1. The right of citizens of the United States to vote in any primary or other election for President or Vice President, for electors for President or Vice President, or for Senator or Representative in Congress, shall not be denied or abridged by the United States or any state by reason of failure to pay any poll tax or other tax.

Section 2. The Congress shall have the power to enforce this article by appropriate legislation.

Amendment XXV (1967)

Section 1. In case of the removal of the President from office or of his death or resignation, the Vice President shall become President.

Section 2. Whenever there is a vacancy in the office of the Vice President, the President shall nominate a Vice President who shall take office upon confirmation by a majority vote of both Houses of Congress.

Section 3. Whenever the President transmits to the President pro tempore of the Senate and the Speaker of the House of Representatives his written declaration that he is unable to discharge the powers and duties of his office, and until he transmits to them a written declaration to the contrary, such powers and duties shall be discharged by the Vice President as Acting President.

Section 4. Whenever the Vice President and a majority of either the principal officers of the executive departments or of such other body as Congress may by law provide, transmit to the President pro tempore of the Senate and the Speaker of the House of Representatives their written declaration that the President is unable to discharge the powers and duties of his office, the Vice President shall immediately assume the powers and duties of the office as Acting President.

Thereafter, when the President transmits to the President pro tempore of the Senate and the Speaker of the House of Representatives his written declaration that no inability exists, he shall resume the powers and duties of his office unless the Vice President and a majority of either the principal officers of the executive departments or of such other body as Congress may by law provide, transmit within four days to the President pro tempore of the Senate and the Speaker of the House of Representatives their written declaration that the President is unable to discharge the powers and duties of his office. Thereupon Congress shall decide the issue, assembling within forty-eight hours for that purpose if not in session. If the Congress, within twenty-one days after receipt of the latter written declaration, or, if Congress is not in session, within twenty-one days after Congress is required to assemble, determines by two-thirds vote of both Houses that the President is unable to discharge the powers and duties of his office, the Vice President shall continue to discharge the same as Acting President; otherwise, the President shall resume the powers and duties of his office.

Amendment XXVI (1971)

Section 1. The right of citizens of the United States, who are 18 years of age or older, to vote shall not be denied or abridged by the United States or any state on account of age.

Section 2. The Congress shall have the power to enforce this article by appropriate legislation.

Index